PUBLIC POLICY AND COLLECTIVE BARGAINING

INDUSTRIAL RELATIONS RESEARCH
ASSOCIATION

———

PUBLICATION NO. 27

———

PUBLIC POLICY
AND
COLLECTIVE BARGAINING

EDITORS

JOSEPH SHISTER
Chairman, Department of Industrial Relations
University of Buffalo

BENJAMIN AARON
Professor of Law
Director, Institute of Industrial Relations
University of California, Los Angeles

CLYDE W. SUMMERS
Professor of Law
Yale University

GREENWOOD PRESS, PUBLISHERS
WESTPORT, CONNECTICUT

Library of Congress Cataloging in Publication Data
Main entry under title:

Public policy and collective bargaining.

Reprint. Originally published: 1st ed. New York :
Harper & Row, 1962. (Publication / Industrial Relations
Research Association ; no. 27)
Includes bibliographical references and index.
Contents: Historical evolution / Douglass V. Brown
and Charles A. Myers -- Employer free speech / Benjamin
Aaron -- The obligation to bargain in good faith /
Robben W. Fleming -- [etc.]
1. Collective labor agreements--United States--Ad-
dresses, essays, lectures. 2. Labor laws and legisla-
tion--United States--Addresses, essays, lectures.
3. Industrial relations--United States--Addresses,
essays, lectures. I. Shister, Joseph. II. Aaron,
Benjamin. III. Summers, Clyde W. IV. Series: Publication (Industrial Relations Research Association) ; no. 27.
KF3408.A5P8 1982   344.73'0189   81-20181
ISBN 0-313-23455-8 (lib. bdg.) 347.304189   AACR2

Reprinted with the permission of Harper and Row
Publishers, Inc.

Reprinted in 1982 by Greenwood Press,
A division of Congressional Information Service, Inc.
88 Post Road West, Westport, Connecticut 06881

Printed in the United States of America

10 9 8 7 6 5 4 3 2 1

CONTENTS

PREFACE

To say that the legal framework in the United States has had a profound impact on American collective bargaining is to spell out the obvious. Far from obvious, however, is the full meaning of this impact—the "how" and "why," if you will. The purpose of this volume, therefore, is to come to grips with this "how" and "why." Given the complexity of the legal framework in collective bargaining—federal and state jurisdictions; legislative, executive, administrative, and judicial levels; numerous substantive areas—it goes without saying that no single volume can provide definitive answers to all the questions involved. Nor, for that matter, should one realistically expect final answers even for the limited number of queries raised by our authors, if only because of space limitations. But at the least, the contributors have made an impressive start.

The topics we have selected for analysis seem to us important.* Other observers of the labor scene, with equally good credentials, might have selected different subjects in terms of relative importance. But no one would deny that the material in this volume focuses on some significant matters of public policy and collective bargaining.

While the book may prove of interest to the labor law specialist, it is not designed primarily for him. Rather, it addresses itself dominantly to the informed observer who has a general knowledge of the field but is not necessarily a specialist in the areas covered. But by the same token, the reader who has little or no understanding of

---

* This book contains no material on emergency disputes, since the Industrial Relations Research Association has already issued an entire volume dealing with that topic (*Emergency Disputes and National Policy*, New York: Harper & Brothers, 1955).

the legal framework in collective bargaining will probably find himself beyond his depth.

An editorial board like ours is of course confronted with the perennial problem of how much leeway the contributors should have in fashioning the form and content of their essays. Our own solution was in favor of maximum freedom. More specifically, we merely suggested a broad and flexible framework into which each author was then free to pour what he thought best—subject only to the unavoidable maximum length limitation. Not only did we feel secure in so proceeding because of the authors' qualifications; we also believed that this approach would greatly stimulate original thought.

JOSEPH SHISTER
BENJAMIN AARON
CLYDE W. SUMMERS

1

HISTORICAL EVOLUTION

DOUGLASS V. BROWN
Professor of Industrial Management,
Massachusetts Institute of Technology

CHARLES A. MYERS
Professor of Industrial Relations,
Massachusetts Institute of Technology

The story of the development of public policy in this country with respect to labor-management relations has been told many times, by many authors, in many different veins, and at many levels of generality or specificity.[1] It is not the purpose of this introductory chapter to retrace this voluminous material or even to summarize it in a systematic fashion.

It is rather our hope that the present chapter may serve as a useful backdrop to the chapters that follow. Toward this more limited purpose, it should be possible to confine our presentation of the "factual" development of public policy to brief, and undoubtedly oversimplified, reminders of policies as they appear to have evolved and of some of the landmarks by which they are symbolized. This task is attempted in the first three sections. In later sections, comments will be made upon such matters as the factors underlying the choice of policy, the process of policy formation, the relative activity of the federal government and of the states, and the respective roles of the legislatures, the courts, and the administrative agencies.

I

Until roughly 1890, public policy on labor relations was expressed through common law decisions in state courts, without benefit of statutory guidance. *Philadelphia Cordwainers* in 1806 was such; so was *Commonwealth* vs. *Hunt* in Massachusetts in 1842. Put in the simplest terms, the former case held that a combination of workmen to raise wages was *per se* illegal; the latter case identified illegality not with the fact of combination but with the existence of a criminal or unlawful purpose (not including that of attempting to raise wages) or the use of criminal or unlawful means. Neither case seems to have been followed slavishly but, as Millis and Montgomery put it, "After *Commonwealth* vs. *Hunt,* the history of American labor law was a steady accumulation of instances in which the line was drawn between purposes and acts permitted and those forbidden."[2] It is not surprising that the courts in different states and at different times did not always draw the line in the same way.

At this point it is well to remind ourselves that, in spite of the present federal preemption of many matters formerly residing with the states, and in spite of the more recent statutory enactments at both the state and the federal level, state common law still has a role to play in the area of labor relations. Many things still rest with the states, and many states have little or no legislation in this area. The 1959 amendments to the Taft-Hartley Act, ceding to the states cases in which the National Labor Relations Board declines to take jurisdiction, lend added significance to this point.

The passage of the Sherman Act in 1890 is important in at least two respects. In the first place, it initiated a *statutory* approach to labor relations. In the second place, it marked the entry of the *federal* government into the area of industrial disputes. Whether or not the act was intended by Congress to apply to labor organizations is a matter of some debate.[3] For our purposes, the important point is that it was so applied, and that its thrust was in the direction of curtailing self-help activities on the part of unions.

The Clayton Act, passed in 1914, did not alter the situation. The story of labor's satisfaction at the time the Act was passed and of its subsequent disillusionment is a familiar one and need not be repeated here. Suffice it to recall that the Supreme Court, in interpreting the Clayton Act, concluded that the 1914 legislation had not changed the concepts of lawful and unlawful acts as they had existed prior to its passage. Again, in such cases as *Duplex Printing*[4] and *Bedford Cut Stone*,[5] the unions found themselves in violation of the statute.

To round out the picture of the nineteenth and earlier twentieth centuries, it is necessary to backtrack and to mention four other developments.

The first of these is, of course, the use of the injunction in labor disputes.[6] Apparently, the earliest use of this equity weapon by state courts in labor cases was made in the 1880's. In the next decade, the labor injunction made its appearance in the federal courts. From that time on, through roughly the 1920's, the injunction became, to labor and perhaps to management as well, the primary symbol of government's power and willingness to curb the activities of unions. As a practical matter, the effects of the use of the injunction in preventing violence or strikes or in affecting the outcome of strikes may have been exaggerated;[7] nonetheless, the emotional aura of the injunction persists today. Some of the reactions to the (watered-down) re-institution of the labor injunction in Taft-Hartley can be understood only in the light of history.

The second topic concerns the suit for damages against unions and union members. This weapon seems clearly to have been of less importance than the injunction, partly because of the inadequacy of funds against which damages could be assessed. In the context of the period under discussion, however, it is worthy of mention because, in general, barriers to the effective use of the weapon tended to become less formidable. At the state level a number of laws were passed relaxing the necessity of bringing suit against union members as individuals. At the federal level the Court, in *Danbury Hatters*,[8] ruled that the assets of individual union members were subject to assessment and, in *Coronado*, that a union, though unincorporated, was a legal entity, its funds subject to suit.[9]

The third topic, the yellow-dog contract, impinges directly upon an area that was to be a major concern of later legislation—the protection of the right to organize. In its simplest form, the yellow-dog contract was an undertaking on the part of an employee that, as a condition of employment, he would not join a labor organization. In a number of states and, at the federal level, in the Erdman Act of 1898, there were enactments that would have made illegal the requirement by employers of such undertakings. Legislation of this sort was invalidated both by state courts and by the United States Supreme Court.[10] Going further, in the *Hitchman* case[11] the Supreme Court ruled that injunctions could be issued against attempts to induce a breach of the yellow-dog contract. Taken together, this series of decisions erected barriers to the "right to organize" in two senses: the right of the individual to join an organization, and the right of the organization to exert efforts to enlist him.

The fourth aspect of this earlier period that should be mentioned is of a more general nature. It has to do with the view of the Constitution as seen by, or as utilized by, the courts. The point can be expressed in various ways, none of which may be wholly true, but each of which perhaps conveys something of the flavor of the contrast with later interpretations. One formulation might run in terms of the courts' preoccupation with freedom of contract, to the relative neglect of the factual question as to the existence of freedom *to* contract.[12] Another might be phrased in terms of the hackneyed, but perhaps still meaningful, question of the relative importance attached to "property" rights, on the one hand, and to "human" rights, on the other. Still another might involve positions with respect to the degree of "give" to be permitted legislative bodies in areas where questions of constitutionality are debatable. For whatever reasons, constitutional issues tended to be resolved in ways which contributed to restraints on the organization and activities of unions.

The picture of the period prior to 1930 would not be complete, however, without mention of three other developments which foreshadowed policies of the later period. The first of these was the passage of the Lloyd-LaFollette Act in 1912.[13] This act protected the right of postal employees to organize into unions, subject to the condition that the unions not be affiliated with outside organizations imposing an obligation to strike against the government. According to Braun, "In the absence of legislation guaranteeing freedom of association of government employees outside the postal service, the Lloyd-LaFollette Act has been widely regarded as containing the principles guiding general public policy in this respect, at least in the *federal* public service."[14]

The second development centers upon events of World War I.[15] On the recommendation of a conference of representatives of labor and industry, the National War Labor Board was established in 1918. One of the principles recommended by the conference and adopted by the Board read in part as follows: "The right of workers to organize in trade unions and to bargain collectively through chosen representatives is recognized and affirmed. The right should not be denied, abridged, or interfered with by the employers in any manner whatsoever. . . . Employers should not discharge workers for membership in trade unions, nor for legitimate trade union activities." The policy statement was not an empty gesture; it was implemented on several occasions. In a more limited area, that of the railroads under federal operation, there was also adopted a policy of "no discrimination" with respect to union membership. These policies were, of course, war-time phenomena, and they lapsed thereafter.

The third important and atypical development of the period prior to 1930 was the Railway Labor Act of 1926.[16] The dispute settlement provisions of the act need not concern us here. Two points, however, deserve emphasis. The first is the fact that the act was supported both by the railroads and by the railroad unions. The second is the declaration of policy with respect to the right to organize. The declaration was expressed in vigorous terms, as the following excerpts indicate.

> Representatives, for the purposes of this Act, shall be designated by the respective parties without interference, influence, or coercion by either party over the designation of representatives by the other; and neither party shall in any way interfere with, influence, or coerce the other in its choice of representatives.

> Employees shall have the right to organize and bargain collectively through representatives of their own choosing. . . . it shall be unlawful for any carrier to interfere in any way with the organization of its employees . . . or to influence or coerce employees in an effort to induce them to join or remain or not to join or remain members of any labor organization. . . .

These provisions of the law were upheld and enforced by the Supreme Court in 1930.[17]

There is little evidence that the policies thus enunciated had a direct causal effect through simple extensions into other areas on the shape of things to come. There is no question, however, that the policies were more compatible with the climate of the 1930's than they were with that of the period in which they were adopted.

Cox has stated[18] that, in the light of its economic orientation, "the American labor movement made two principal demands upon the law. One was for the right to form, join, and assist labor organizations and, through them, to bargain collectively with employers. The second was for the maximum freedom to use economic weapons—strikes, boycotts, picketing, and other concerted activities—to spread unionization and wring concessions from employers."

In the framework of these two "demands," the situation of about 1930 may be set forth in summary fashion.

With respect to the first, the right to organize, the situation was reasonably clear. Unions as such were not illegal, and employees had the privilege of organizing, if they could. But employers could discriminate against union members,[19] and yellow-dog contracts were enforceable and protected against efforts to organize employees covered by them. Conversely, organizing efforts on the part of unions were often limited by restraints placed upon organizing tactics.

With respect to the second demand of the labor movement, the freedom to use economic weapons, the situation was not uniform, because of diversity of jurisdiction. In the federal courts, and in such state courts as those of Massachusetts, unions were likely to find their use of economic weapons stringently circumscribed. In other states, such as New York or California, the courts took a much more tolerant view. Witte, writing in 1932, summed up the picture as follows:

> The restrictions upon union activity in this country are very real. While labor unions are recognized as lawful, many of the methods they employ in advancement of their purposes are in many jurisdictions unlawful and, almost everywhere, subject to doubt and legal attack. With the exception of the New York and Ohio courts, moreover, the tendency seems to be toward increasing restrictions.[20]

In short, the general climate of public policy in 1930 may be described as one in which unions were tolerated as institutions, but as institutions whose existence was not actively encouraged and whose activities were subjected to varying but substantial degrees of restraint.

II

During roughly the 1930's the two basic demands which Cox ascribes to the labor movement were abundantly met. In the area of the right to organize, the primary vehicles were Section 7(a) of the National Industrial Recovery Act of 1933 and the National Labor Relations (Wagner) Act of 1935. In the area of the use of the economic weapons, both for organizing and for other purposes, restrictions by the wholesale were swept away by the Norris-LaGuardia Act of 1932 and by court decisions in cases arising under the Sherman and Clayton Acts and, notably in *Thornhill*,[21] in cases involving picketing. The adoption in a number of states of "baby" Wagner and Norris-LaGuardia acts furthered the process.

These various enactments and decisions need not be discussed in detail, particularly since many of the aspects will be dealt with in later chapters in this volume. A few comments, however, may be in order.

Section 7(a) set forth the right to organize and bargain collectively, in language not too dissimilar to that of the Railway Labor Act. Its importance lay more in its symbolic or psychological effects than in its direct legal effects. Unwillingness of employers to accept the policy plus the lack of effective enforcement machinery combined to produce many situations in which the law was nugatory. But the notion that "the President wants you to join a union" was a powerful stimulus to organization. During the period of NIRA, union membership increased by approximately one-third.

The provisions of the Wagner Act with respect to free choice of representatives and proscription of unfair labor practices by employers are well known, and need not be elaborated here. A few comments may be made, however. In the first place, the act [unlike Section 7(a)] established an administrative agency to police its provisions and gave to the agency the right to seek enforcement in the courts. As subsequent events were to demonstrate, the agency proved to be not only a locus of enforcement but an additional forum for hair-splitting litigation.[22] In the second place, the policy of an exclusive bargaining agent freely selected by the majority of employees in an appropriate unit ran counter to the traditional policy of the labor movement—exclusive jurisdiction. The spurt of industrial unionism in the 1930's magnified, but did not solely account for, the resulting problems. In the third place, it was soon apparent that the policies of the Wagner and of the Norris-LaGuardia Acts were not coincident at all points. For example, an employer might be told by Wagner that he must bargain with, and only with, the union selected freely by his employees, while he was denied by Norris-LaGuardia the protection he needed from efforts by a rival union to force him to act illegally.[23] Finally, the absence of strictures on unions in the Wagner Act was a basis for the charge of "one-sidedness" that was to form part of the appeal of Taft-Hartley.

Norris-LaGuardia affected the right to organize in two ways. One was by making yellow-dog contracts unenforceable in the federal courts. The second was the curbing of the injunctive remedy against the use of economic weapons by unions in labor disputes, the latter defined to include controversies "regardless of whether or not the disputants stand in the proximate relation of employer and employee." The greater freedom in the use of economic weapons was not confined to organizing situations.[24] Nor was the impact of Norris-LaGuardia unrelated to developments in other areas of policy.

One of these areas was that of anti-trust. Since this is the subject of a later chapter, only brief reference need be made here. Roughly speaking, it may be said that in the relatively brief period of time from *Bedford Cut Stone* in 1927 to *Hutcheson*[25] in 1941, the Supreme Court had swung from a position in which a union's use of economic weapons in situations affecting interstate commerce was suspect or tabu to one in which such activities were immune under anti-trust legislation unless they were carried out in collusion with employers. Norris-LaGuardia was the bridge used by the Court to span the gap between the two positions.

To conclude our survey of the period ending about 1940, we may mention the *Thornhill* case. In essence, in this case the Supreme Court equated peaceful picketing to speech, and extended to it the constitutional protection of freedom of speech. Our concern here is not with the technicalities of this or similar cases. The relevant point is that, in this case, the Court went further than it had previously gone (and further than it was to go subsequently) in extending protection to the use of this particular weapon of unions. The decision is, in short, another illustration of the extent to which public policy, reflected both in legislation and in court interpretations, had shifted.

III

In retrospect, it seems clear that 1940 represented not a way station on the ascent, nor the attainment of a plateau, but rather the pinnacle in labor's achievement of its two demands. From that point on, changes in policy have almost consistently been in the direction of erecting barriers to the unions' use of economic weapons and, to the extent that these weapons are important in their organizing activities, to their "freedom to organize."

Within the space of only a couple of years, the Supreme Court retreated from the position it had taken in *Thornhill*.[26] Henceforth, picketing was to be judged in the light of the circumstances in which it took place, and legislative restrictions were not ruled out.

There were other evidences that the courts were not entirely at ease with the general positions that had been arrived at. In at least two of the states, courts cut their way through the impasse of the policy conflict between baby Wagner and Norris-LaGuardia acts[27] and provided injunctive relief. At both the federal and the state level, courts have been unwilling to go all the way with the doctrine of the union's immunity from anti-trust action in the absence of collusion with employers.[28] The escape hatch—the finding that no labor dispute was involved—may indeed seem rather far-fetched in these particular cases. Again, however, we are not concerned with the technical aspects of the cases; it is the change in the flavor of policy that is significant.

At the legislative level, both the states and the Congress have been active in the past two decades, and, with relatively minor exceptions, the policies adopted have been in the direction of a re-imposition of controls upon the activities of unions. Beginning in 1939, a number of states either repealed legislation similar to the Wagner Act and replaced it with legislation curtailing union activities, or enacted new laws containing similar restrictive measures. In more than a third of the states, "right to work" policies have been established, through legislation or through constitutional amendment.

At the federal level, the year 1943 saw the passage of the War Labor Disputes Act. As one of its provisions, this act required as a pre-condition to a strike a secret ballot poll of union members "on the question whether they will permit such interruption of war production." This provision stemmed largely from the widely-held but largely-unfounded belief, which was to play a prominent role four years later in the formulation of Taft-Hartley provisions, that the union leaders did not reflect the wishes of their members.

The two major legislative landmarks of the period following World War II are, of course, Taft-Hartley and Landrum-Griffin. The specific provisions of these enactments provide the focal point for much of the discussion in the remainder of this volume. Accordingly, only a few comments will be made at this point.

At the time Taft-Hartley was passed, it was fashionable in union circles to refer to it as a "slave labor act." Obviously, it was not that. From the vantage point of Wagner and Norris-LaGuardia, it was indeed an act imposing restrictions upon unions and their activities. But if the pre-1930 period were to be used as the benchmark, and if those portions of Wagner and Norris-LaGuardia which were not altered by Taft-Hartley were taken into account, the 1947 act would have to be reckoned, from the point of view of the unions, as a step forward. Many of the "unfair labor practices of unions" as formalized by Taft-Hartley had been held to be just that in the earlier period; the "unfair labor practices of employers" had been added. The use of injunctions was partially re-introduced, but the initiation of proceedings was limited to a governmental agency, and the activities which might be enjoined were specifically restricted.

In the context of 1947, however, Taft-Hartley could properly be viewed as a restrictive, and in some respects, as a retributive, act. The wave of strikes in 1946 undoubtedly contributed both to the timing and to parts of the substance of the act. The inclusion of the national emergency provisions may well be an example; certainly the fiat that boards of inquiry make no recommendations was a Congressional reaction to events immediately preceding the passage of the act.

It would be a mistake, however, to attach too much weight to the influence of contemporary events. As we have suggested earlier, the idea of "balancing" the Wagner Act had enjoyed a considerable amount of support from 1935 onward. There was a long history of antipathy to the secondary boycott and the jurisdictional strike. The closed shop had been a rallying point for emotions decade after decade. In the outcome, the proscriptions on featherbedding and excessive initiation fees proved to be tilting at windmills, but the windmills were not of recent construction. In short, Taft-Hartley must be considered not merely as a reaction to the unsettled period immediately following the war, but also as a reflection of a more deep-seated feeling that unions could not be left to their own devices.

Another comment with respect to Taft-Hartley, already alluded to, should be made. This has to do with the belief that there was a gap, or that there were conflicting desires, between the union leaders and the union membership. That this belief shaped many of the provisions of Taft-Hartley can hardly be doubted. The requirement of union-shop authorization elections, the financial reporting provisions, the vote on the employer's last offer in national emergency disputes—all of these aspects of the act, as well as others, rest in large part upon this belief. Much of the resentment felt by union leaders can be accounted for in terms of their recognition of this strand in the motivation that contributed to the passage of the act.

Still another group of provisions in Taft-Hartley stemmed, in whole or in part, from Congressional dissatisfaction with interpretations given to the Wagner Act by the NLRB or the courts. As examples of this group, there may be mentioned the "free speech" provision [Section 8(c)], the exclusion of supervisors from the protection of the act, and the restrictions on the Board's freedom in establishing the appropriate bargaining unit [e.g., Sections 9(b) and 9(c)(5)].

Taft-Hartley also marked the entry of the federal government into the area of the regulation of the internal affairs of unions. To be sure, the intrusion was of a limited nature, involving as it did only the denial of the use of facilities of the Board to those unions who failed to file financial and other information with the Secretary of Labor or to furnish their members with financial information, or whose officers failed to file non-Communist affidavits. But these provisions were important, both as setting a precedent for federal action and, in retrospect, as foreshadowing the much more extensive regulations of Landrum-Griffin twelve years later.

Whatever may have been the effect of some of the interpretations of the Wagner Act, neither the text of that act nor the apparent intentions of its sponsors seemed to call for specific regulation of either the process of bargaining or the content of bargained agreements. In the oft-quoted words of Senator Walsh, after the representatives of the employees had been escorted to the employer's door, "What happens behind those doors is not inquired into, and the bill does not seek to inquire into it." Taft-Hartley, on the other hand, got down to specifics in both areas. Section 8(d) set forth a number of procedural requirements to be met if the charge of "refusal to bargain collectively" were to be avoided. In the area of content, the act barred closed shop clauses and granted to the states the right to bar other forms of union security clauses as well.

One final comment may be made before we leave Taft-Hartley. The Wagner Act had spawned a large amount of litigation, even though some 90 per cent of charges filed were settled at lower levels without the need for formal action by the Board or the courts. At the time the Taft-Hartley Act was passed, it was facetiously referred to in many quarters as "The Full Employment Act for Lawyers." While statistical evidence to demonstrate the truth or falsity of this characterization is lacking, the fact remains that the act set in motion a stream of litigation that continues, apparently unabated, to the present day.

The Landrum-Griffin Act of 1959 was primarily concerned with the regulation of internal union matters. Since this topic is the subject of Chapter 7, we shall not comment on these aspects of the legislation except to note the importance of the McClellan Committee investigations as a factor in determining both the timing of the act and much of its substantive content.

But Landrum-Griffin also contained amendments to the Taft-Hartley Act, and a few comments on these are in order here. The general tenor of these amendments was to strengthen or add to the restrictions placed upon the activities of unions. Into this category fall such provisions as those tightening secondary boycott limitations, restricting recognition and organizational picketing, and banning most "hot cargo" clauses. Again, as in Taft-Hartley vis-à-vis Wagner, the desire to "correct" some of the interpretations of Taft-Hartley seems to have contributed to the amendments in the 1959 act. The amendments are interesting, also, in that they introduced "special treatment" for particular groups. Thus, "prehire" agreements are legalized in the construction industries, and the ban on hot cargo clauses is relaxed in the cases of construction activities at the site and of sub-contracting in the clothing industry.[29]

We may conclude this review of some of the aspects of the development of public policy with a few summary comments. Exactly one hundred and fifty years have elapsed since *Philadelphia Cordwainers*. If we compare merely the two terminal years of the period, it is clear that public policy is now more solicitous of the right to organize and more tolerant of the activities of unions. But movement has not consistently been in the same direction, and recent years, in particular, have witnessed the re-imposition of a number of barriers. Over the period, the once-exclusive jurisdiction of the states has been invaded, nay, even overrun, by the federal government. So, too, the role of the courts has been diluted by a proliferation of statutes and decisions of administrative agencies, established by statute at both the federal and the state levels. We have, indeed, come a long way from the *Cordwainers*.

IV

What are some of the factors that seem to have lain behind the choice of policies in the area of labor-management relations in this country?

A look at countries that today are pushing hard along the road of industrialization may suggest important clues to one of these factors. Restrictions on the right to organize, or at least upon the activities of labor organizations, are familiar phenomena in many of these countries. Rapid capital formation is regarded as essential to the process of industrialization, and unions may be viewed as impediments.[30]

Something like this sort of view seems to have played a part in shaping policy toward labor organization in this country in the nineteenth, and even into the twentieth, century. "What's good for business is good for the country" undoubtedly evoked fewer cynical responses then than it does today. The unions, let alone other groups in the population, did not tend to portray themselves as agents of industrial development. Rather they presented themselves as defenders of the interests of those down-trodden by the employers—the same employers who, in their capacity as entrepreneurs, were viewed by many as spear-heading the progress toward making the United States the leading industrial nation in the world.[31]

Another factor making for a negative view toward labor organizations was, of course, the strong tradition of individualism, particularly as it was associated with the belief that the individual was responsible for his own destiny. The tradition was reflected not only in policy toward organization, but in attitudes toward legislation on such matters as social security, limitation of hours of work, and even factory legislation.

Interwoven with these attitudes were two others: the belief in the free market, and the protection of the rights of private property. Whether or not the market was, in fact, free was a question that seems to have been raised only infrequently and only when the departures seemed so glaring that they could not be ignored, e.g., the trusts. The Fifth and Fourteenth Amendments of the Constitution provided ample leverage to implement the prevailing attitudes toward private property. Unionism tended to run counter to "virtue" on both counts, as modifiers of the free market and as threats to property rights.

Labor leaders, and others, have often placed much of the onus for obstructions to unionism upon the courts, upon judge-made law. While it may be that the legal training of the judges, with its emphasis upon precedent, as well as their social background, contributed to their dragging their heels, it is not unlikely that, for at least the greater part of the period prior to 1930, on the whole they reflected prevailing attitudes.[32] It is arguable that interpretations of the Clayton Act were at variance with the intent of Congress when the act was passed, but it is not at all clear that the decisions handed down during the 1920's were a distorted reflection of the then-prevailing climate. As in earlier periods, the important determinants of policy may well have been the pervasive views with respect to property rights, on the one hand, and unionism, on the other.

In any explanation of policies toward unions in the late nineteenth and early twentieth centuries, two other points cannot be neglected. The first has to do with the importance of agriculture and of the farm states in the formulation of policy, both at the state and at the federal level. Typically, those states in which agriculture predominated tended to take a less "liberal" view toward unions and their activities than did many of the more industrialized states. And because of the structure of our governmental arrangements, the farm states had, and continue to have, a disproportionate voice in formulating federal policy, even though their relative economic importance has steadily declined.

The second point has to do with the immigration which we experienced in large quantities during most of the period from the middle of the nineteenth century until the onset of World War I. This immigration we viewed in two ways. It was, at one and the same time, both a source of strength and a resource for our development, and a scapegoat for our deficiencies. In the latter sense, it was easy, if not wholly or even mainly correct, for immigrants to be associated with unionism, and for the labor movement to be tagged with the label of un-Americanism. The truth or falsity of this association is of no importance for present purposes. The significant points are that those who were already inclined to discredit unions found an additional reason and an appealing slogan, and that others were made uneasy by the specter of the "foreign agitator."

The impact of the depression of the 1930's, in retrospect, must be classed as shattering. Large-scale immigration had ceased almost a generation earlier, and in any event the times demanded a less transparent scapegoat. Agriculture was too busy licking its (now real) wounds to be interested in launching a frontal attack on a traditional enemy. The image of business as the motivating force toward Utopia was badly tarnished. The concept of individual responsibility for adversity was impossible to maintain. Things had sunk so low that even the free market showed signs of having clay feet. The day was ripe to try almost anything, including the encouragement of unionism and the removal of restrictions on its activities.

In our judgment, nobody who looks back upon the development of labor policy in the United States could fail to emphasize the importance of the depression of the 1930's and the alterations that it produced in the climate of public opinion. It is possible, however, to assess this importance in either of two ways. Quite possibly, both of these assessments have germs of truth.

The first, and probably the more orthodox, assessment is that the depression marked a definitive turning point in attitudes and policy, in the sense that things would never be the same again. This view is not inconsistent with a modified "pendulum" view of the process of policy formation in a democracy such as ours. Consistency is attained if we hold (1) that the pre-1930 climate was so intolerable that change was inevitable, (2) that, in typical American fashion, the change went too far, and (3) that the revisions that have occurred since, say, 1940 have served merely to damp down the exuberances or excesses that characterized the period of the 1930's. Under this view, the equilibrium that would be reached, if equilibrium could ever be reached in an economy such as ours, would still be far to the left of that which was characteristic of the earlier period.

Under the second evaluation, the period of the 1930's would be viewed not as a watershed but as an aberration. The encouragement of unionism and the removal of the wraps on its activities, it might be said, were a product of desperation, or even of panic. Once the crisis situation was over, it would be only natural to expect that things would revert to normal, here defined as what had prevailed in the past. Developments since 1940 could be cited as evidence that we are on our way back to normal. By implication, we still have some distance to go before we reach a point of rest.

It would be a bold man who would place his money unqualifiedly on one or the other of these hypotheses. As we have suggested, both of them probably contain important elements of truth. Indeed, they are inconsistent only insofar as they project differences in the ultimate locus of policy or, perhaps more accurately, in the ultimate locus of the central point of the pendulum.

Since, as we have said, the more orthodox view is that we moved into new territory following 1930, it may be incumbent upon us to indicate somewhat more specifically our reasons for believing that the alternative assessment cannot be summarily rejected. Basically, we are impressed by what seems to have been before 1930, and what seems to exist to-day, a feeling of "unease" in the presence of unions on the part of large segments of the population. We would appear to be on firm ground if we stated that unions have not been "accepted" in this country to the extent that they have been accepted elsewhere, notably in Britain, Germany, Scandinavia, Australia, and New Zealand.[33] We would obviously be on less firm ground if we ventured predictions into the future. The present-day reaction to what, in any book, are excesses on the part of some unions is easily understandable. But the reactions, and the emotional content thereof, both on the part of employers and of other groups in the population, to many activities of unions which in other countries would pass almost without notice can only be explained, we believe, on the basis of an underlying discomfort in the contemplation of unions.

At this writing, the only supportable conclusion must be a negative one. We are not convinced that the policy of the 1930's, even as it has been modified in the intervening years, is necessarily the forecast for the future. On the other hand, neither are we convinced that we are about to enter an era in which *Danbury Hatters* or *Adair* or *Duplex*, let alone the *Cordwainers*, will again be the appropriate landmarks. We merely record our doubts that the developments of the 1930's necessarily typify the future course of events.

V

From speculations with respect to the fundamental *factors* underlying the choice of public policies in the area of labor-management relations, we turn now to a few comments having to do with the *process* of policy formation. We shall confine ourselves to comments on two aspects and to certain corollaries of these characteristics.

The first characteristic of the process of policy formulation has been stressed by John Dunlop.[34] As he quite properly points out, one of the distinguishing features of the American scene is the lack of consensus as to the direction that public policy should take in this area, and the consequent fumbling and accommodation to pressure groups. We would not quarrel with his analysis of the process, nor with his evaluation of the results of the process. We would disagree with him, if at all, only with respect to his implication that consensus is possible. Our own evaluation of the present climate of opinion would lay great stress upon the incompatibilities between the aspirations of employers and of unions and would lead us to the conclusion that consensus on public labor policy is not likely to be achieved in the years immediately ahead.

The second aspect of the process of policy formation is closely related to the first. In the absence of consensus, policy formation has tended to be inordinately influenced by current events. A few examples may serve to demonstrate this point. The exigencies of World War I led to a sympathetic attitude toward unions that, it is fair to say, was unprecedented. The general return to "normalcy" in the 1920's was accompanied by a return to "normalcy" in labor-management policy. The depression of the 1930's saw an almost complete *volte-face* in the attitude of government, and probably of the country as a whole. The strikes of 1946 provided ammunition, if not a *casus belli*, for Taft-Hartley in 1947. The McClellan investigations clearly triggered off Landrum-Griffin. The record suggests that contemporary events did indeed play an important role in the formalization of policy.

Without detracting from the part played by current events, it is still possible to remark that the events pointing in one direction— a world war[35] and a great depression—were of a quite different order of magnitude from those that led to the re-imposition of restraints on unions. This observation is consistent with, but does not prove, our earlier speculation that unions have not been fully accepted at most points of time in our history.

The combination of the lack of consensus on the fundamentals of public policy and the attendant influence of contemporary events shows up clearly when we look at two corollary manifestations. Neither is surprising.

The first is perhaps best described as volatility. The proverbial man from Mars would undoubtedly be amazed to witness the transition from the National War Labor Board (World War I variety) to *Duplex* and *Bedford Cut Stone*. He would be no less amazed at the transition from *Thornhill* to *Ritter*. If he managed to regain his equilibrium, the contrasting spirit of Wagner and Taft-Hartley would at least force him to pause for serious reflection. He could hardly be blamed if he concluded that these Earth people had great difficulties in making up their minds.

The second corollary stems also from what might be termed the impulsiveness in our process of policy formation. The consequence takes the form of policies that are less than wholly consistent internally. Basic conflicts between the Wagner Act and Norris-LaGuardia have already been mentioned. Taft-Hartley, with its blessing upon the union shop in Section 8(a)(3) and its conferral upon the states, in Section 14(b), of the right to remove this blessing, exhibits what might be charitably called a measure of ambivalence. The special treatment accorded to the construction and clothing industries in Landrum-Griffin may or may not represent a wise application of policy; the question may properly be raised as to why similar treatment was not accorded to other situations in which conditions are essentially similar.

To ask this question—and others like it—in the context of our process of policy formation is to answer it. Where there is a void, in the sense of a lack of consensus on fundamentals, the way is open for solutions based upon expediency. In this connection, it should be noted that expediency is not synonymous with compromise. The latter process, carried out in a framework in which there is agreement on broad issues, can produce results that are at least acceptable to all concerned and that provide a reasonably stable base. Solutions stemming from expediency run a two-fold danger: they may be distasteful to most, or even all, of the parties concerned, and they form an uncertain and unstable base from which to project future developments.

This last consideration supplies an important part of the explanation for the volatility that has characterized policy formation in recent times. Paradoxically, also, it may account for the fact that there has not been even more volatility. Why, for example, have major pieces of legislation come at intervals of twelve years instead of, say, every two years? The answer may be that the guidelines are so indistinct that, in the absence of such events as a great depression, a wave of strikes, or a dramatic exposé, the risks are so great as to deter *everybody* from opening Pandora's box. Thus, in a quaint sort of way, we manage to achieve a certain measure of pseudo-stability on the legislative front.

That even this measure of apparent stability lacks substance is attested to in many ways. The pronouncements of the AFL-CIO, the NAM, and the United States Chamber of Commerce leave little doubt of their dissatisfaction with the *status quo*. Nor is there any greater consensus within the ranks of politicians, of newspaper editors, or of "respected" citizens of the community. Few issues are calculated to raise more emotional and more diverse responses than those associated with unions and union-management relations. A cynic, noting the divergent views and the seemingly unlimited amount of litigation that goes on during periods of legislative inactivity, might be tempted to conclude that the legislation was designed, not to set forth policy, but to avoid setting it forth. As Dunlop has observed: "Formal compromises in words assure unending litigation."[36]

For whatever reasons, the legislatures and the courts, as well as administrative agencies, have been busy in the area of labor relations. In the next section of this chapter, we discuss some aspects of the roles played by these various groups, and of the trends that have appeared.

VI

One of the most striking trends has to do with the shift in the relative importance of state and of federal agencies over the last century and a half. As we have suggested earlier, "labor relations law" during most of the nineteenth century was to be ascertained from the decisions of the state courts. As we have also suggested, the states did not all proceed in the same directions. In the area with which we are concerned, "states' rights" were hardly an issue, since the supremacy of the states was not called into question.

Today, federal policy applies to labor-management relations in establishments in which most of the working force of the country is employed. To be sure, the different states still set different policies on matters that are conceded to be within their jurisdiction, and the federal government has permitted them to act in still other areas in which federal supremacy, but for the indulgence, is now reasonably settled. No discussion of labor policy in the United States would be complete if it overlooked the activities of the states. It is even more true, however, that no discussion of American labor policy would be meaningful unless the focus were at the federal level.

In retrospect, it seems inevitable that this shift should have occurred. From the point of view of economics, the states have increasingly become artificial entities. Markets, companies, and unions transcend state boundaries. Congress, the courts, and the public, albeit with a certain amount of reluctance, have been forced to face up to these particular facts of economic life.

The shift in the center of gravity from the states to the federal government has been marked by three interrelated lines of development. The first was the assertion by Congress of its concern with the area of labor-management relations. With respect to the railroads, the evidence of this concern dates back to the Arbitration Act of 1888, followed by the Erdman Act in 1898, the Newlands Act in 1913, and, of course, the Railway Labor Act in 1926. For industry generally, the concern was evidenced, perhaps inadvertently in the Sherman Act, but certainly consciously in the Clayton Act and in Norris-LaGuardia, Wagner, Taft-Hartley, and Landrum-Griffin. The second line of development was the expansion of the concept of interstate commerce and, accordingly, the broadening of the base to which federal legislation could apply. The third was the ruling by the Supreme Court that, in the substantive areas covered by federal legislation, the federal law was paramount and the states could not exercise concurrent jurisdiction,[37] provided the parties fell within the (expanded) concept of interstate commerce.

The present situation of federal supremacy was not achieved

without a struggle. Immediately after the passage of the Wagner Act, there was a widespread belief that the act was unconstitutional since the Supreme Court had held that Congress' power to regulate did not, under the commerce clause, extend to manufacturing and mining. The Court's decision upholding the constitutionality of the act was by the narrowest of margins, five to four.[38] And the extent and limitations of federal preemption are still not crystal-clear. The broad implications of the *Garner* case[39] have been somewhat narrowed in later cases.[40] Undoubtedly the last word has not yet been spoken on this question.

Quite apart from the legal questions involved, the issue of states' rights in regulating labor relations is not dead. Section 14(b) of Taft-Hartley (permitting state right-to-work laws to take precedence over general federal policy) is one witness to this fact. So also is the Landrum-Griffin approach to the disposition of the problem of the "no man's land." This problem came into focus as the result of (1) the NLRB's declining to exercise jurisdiction over certain cases that fell within its purview, and (2) the Supreme Court's ruling that federal preemption of the substantive area precluded the states from taking jurisdiction in these cases.[41] Three possible solutions were available. First, the NLRB could be instructed, and provided with the necessary funds, to process all such cases. Second, the states could be permitted to process these cases, applying federal principles. Third, the states could be allowed to process the cases, applying their own principles. The last was the solution adopted.

In the labor area, the proponents of states' rights are motivated by more than a general resistance to federal "encroachment." It seems clear that, for the most part, state policy is likely to be more restrictive of union activities than is federal policy.[42] Recognition of this point is essential to an understanding of the persistent warfare between those who espouse the cause of federal supremacy and those who advocate a broader role for the states. Once more we see a reflection of the lack of consensus on major lines of policy.

Up to now, the battle-tides have tended to sweep federal agencies in the direction of victory. But it is by no means certain that the struggle is over. To put it perhaps more accurately, it is not certain that the "feds" will win if they continue to maneuver behind the same flags.

VII

Just as the states have had to accept a diminution in their policy-determining role in the field of labor-management relations over the last century and a half, so also have the courts found that they have had to share their virtual monopoly of the field with other institutions. There are now statutes, and there are administrative agencies. There are, moreover, even private agencies, in the form of arbitration and mediation tribunals, which participate in policy formation. Earlier, these private agencies were accorded what, at best, could be described as grudging acknowledgment. For the moment, at least, they are the recipients of accolades by the Supreme Court.[43]

It would be wrong to assert that the existence of statutes, of administrative agencies, and even of private procedures has not altered the role of the courts in the area of labor relations. But it would be equally wrong to jump to the conclusion that the courts have been relegated to a subordinate position.

We have seen that the Supreme Court abandoned a narrow interpretation of the commerce clause in the Constitution, in part as an aftermath of the passage of the Wagner Act. We have seen, too, that the combined impact of the Clayton and Norris-LaGuardia Acts produced a shift in the Court's views in the area of antitrust. But we have also seen that the Court resisted the words of the Clayton Act for a considerable period of time, and that more than one court has found refuge from what was felt to be an intolerable restraint on the issuance of injunctions by finding that no labor dispute was involved.

In spite, therefore, of efforts to curtail or to complement the activities of the courts, they continue to play an impressive role. In part, this role is required of them under our system of government, with its emphasis upon the separation of powers. In part, the role has been thrust upon them by the proclivities of legislatures to avoid coming to firm grips with policy issues. "We won't know what this clause means until the courts get through interpreting it" is more than a statement of fact; it is also a commentary on the legislative process. To the extent that legislators abdicate the function of policy-making, the courts will inevitably have to act as surrogates.

The device of the administrative agency was, and is, probably a necessary one in the light of the complexities of life in this century. A strong *a priori* case can be made for the creation of bodies whose function it is to provide the expertise that the courts, ranging over a wide area, cannot be expected to possess. Regretfully, we are forced to conclude that the NLRB and the corresponding state agencies have not fully measured up to expectations in this respect. Perhaps any agency, once enmeshed in the governmental process, is bound to progress in the direction of increasing attention to technicalities and diminished attention to reality. Perhaps the denial, by Congress, of funds that would have permitted the NLRB to assess the results of its activities has contributed to the same end. Perhaps the apparently growing belief that only lawyers are competent to be members of the Board has fortified the trend, or perhaps it merely reflects the trend. In any event, the aura is more and more that of a "little court" rather than that of an expert body.[44]

These comments are not intended as a condemnation of the NLRB. Nor are they intended to imply that the NLRB has differed from other administrative agencies in tending toward legalism. Indeed, similar tendencies are apparent even in the private institution of arbitration. It may well be that the trend is an inevitable concomitant of the increasing complexity of the world in which we live.

The important point is that, despite the multiplication of statutes, of administrative agencies, and of private institutions, the courts still occupy an extremely important role in policy matters, a much less diminished role than might have been expected in advance. Unquestionably, "public policy" is different today from what it would have been in the absence of statutory enactments. Perhaps, however, the differences are not so great as those we might assume.

VIII

Fortunately, our task does not include projections into the future. We may conclude, however, by quoting some observations expressed more than a hundred years ago. These comments were clearly relevant to our past, and may be so to the years ahead.

If, then, there is a subject upon which a democratic people is peculiarly liable to abandon itself, blindly and extravagantly, to general ideas, the best corrective that can be used will be to make that subject a part of their daily practical occupation. They will then be compelled to enter into details, and the details will teach them the weak points of the theory. This remedy may frequently be a painful one, but its effect is certain.[45]

NOTES

1. For a few of the more general treatments, see: Alpheus T. Mason, *Organized Labor and the Law*, Durham, N. C.: Duke University Press, 1925; Edwin E. Witte, *The Government and Labor Disputes*, New York: McGraw-Hill Book Co., Inc., 1932; Harry A. Millis and Royal E. Montgomery, *Organized Labor*, New York: McGraw-Hill Book Company, Inc., 1945; Chapters XI and XII; Archibald Cox, *Law and the National Labor Policy*, Los Angeles: Institute of Industrial Relations, University of California, 1960; and Charles O. Gregory, *Labor and the Law*, New York: W. W. Norton and Co., 1958.

2. Millis and Montgomery, *op. cit.*, p. 504.

3. On this point, see Mason, *op. cit.*, Part III, and Edward Berman, *Labor and the Sherman Act*, New York: Harper & Brothers, 1930, Part I.

4. 254 U.S. 443 (1921).

5. 274 U.S. 37 (1927).

6. Needless to say, the monumental work in this area is Felix Frankfurter and Nathan Greene, *The Labor Injunction*, New York: The Macmillan Co., 1930.

7. Cf. Witte, *op cit.*, Chapter 6.

8. *Loewe* vs. *Lawlor*, 208 U.S. 274 (1908) and *Lawlor* vs. *Loewe*, 235 U.S. 522 (1915).

9. *United Mine Workers* vs. *Coronado Coal Co.*, 259 U.S. 344 (1922).

10. Notably in *Adair* vs. *U.S.*, 208 U.S. 161 (1908) and *Coppage* vs. *Kansas*, 236 U.S. 1 (1915).

11. *Hitchman Coal and Coke Co.*, vs. *Mitchell*, 245 U.S. 229 (1917).

12. Cf. Roscoe Pound, "Liberty of Contract," *Yale Law Journal*, Vol. XVIII (1909), pp. 454-487.

13. 37 Stat. 555. The act, and its implications, are discussed in Kurt Braun, *The Right to Organize and Its Limits*, New York: The Brookings Institution, 1950, pp. 110-111.

14. *Ibid.*, p. 110.

15. For a concise account, see Fred Witney, *Government and Collective Bargaining*, New York: J. B. Lippincott Co., 1951, pp. 189-191. See also, Witte, *op. cit.*, pp. 246-251.

16. 44 Stat. 577.

17. *Texas and New Orleans Railway Co. et al.* vs. *Brotherhood of Railway and Steamship Clerks et al.*, 281 U.S. 548.

18. Cox, *op. cit.*, p. 2.

19. Some 25 states had laws against blacklisting, but these were almost completely ineffectual. Cf. Witte, *op. cit.*, pp. 213 ff.

20. *Ibid.*, p. 45.

21. *Thornhill* vs. *Alabama*, 310 U.S. 88 (1940).

22. The issue of "refusal to bargain" is illuminating in this respect.

23. See, for example, *NLRB* vs. *Star Publishing Co.*, 97 F. 2d 465 (CCA 9, 1938).

24. On the meaning and effects of Norris-LaGuardia, see, for example, Gregory, *op. cit.*, particularly pp. 185 ff., and Witney, *op. cit.*, Chapter 5.

25. *United States* vs. *Hutcheson*, 312 U.S. 219.

26. *Milk Wagon Drivers' Union* vs. *Meadowmoor Dairies, Inc.*, 312 U.S. 287 (1941); *Carpenters' and Joiners' Union* vs. *Ritter's Cafe*, 315 U.S. 722 (1942). For a general discussion of the picketing cases, see Gregory, *op cit.*, Chapter XI. It is interesting to note that this chapter is entitled "The Rise and Decline of the *Thornhill* Doctrine."

27. In Massachusetts, *R. H. White* vs. *Murphy*, 38 N.E. 2d 685 (1942); in New York, *Florsheim Shoe Store* vs. *Retail Shoe Salesmen's Union*, 42 N.E. 2d 480 (1942).

28. See, for example, *Columbia River Packers' Association* vs. *Hinton*, 315 U.S. 143 (1942); *Hawaiian Tuna Packers* vs. *International Longshoremen's and Warehousemen's Union*, 72 F Supp. 562 (1947); and *Commonwealth of Massachusetts* vs. *McHugh*, 93 N.E. (2d) 751 (1950).

29. Sections 8(f) and 8(e) of the (as amended) Taft-Hartley Act.

30. At least, "free unions" may be so regarded. Other forms of organization may be fostered and their activities "controlled" in the right directions. Cf. Clark Kerr, et al., *Industrialism and Industrial Man*, Cambridge: Harvard University Press, 1960, Chapter 8.

31. The self-picture of unions as promotors of economic development (e.g., as the stimulant of increased purchasing power or as the vehicles for bringing about constructive governmental action) emerged primarily in the period after 1930.

32. Cf. Pound, *loc. cit.*

33. Cf. Douglass V. Brown and Charles A. Myers, "The Changing Industrial Relations Philosophy of American Management," *Proceedings of Ninth Annual Meeting of Industrial Relations Research Association* (1956) pp. 84 ff.

34. John T. Dunlop, "Consensus and National Labor Policy," *Proceedings of Thirteenth Annual Meeting of Industrial Relations Research Association* (1960), pp. 2 ff.

35. It is at least arguable that World War II, and its requirements, delayed a reaction that would have been forthcoming in the absence of emergency conditions.

36. *Op. cit.*, p. 6.

37. On federal preemption and related matters, see Archibald Cox, "Federalism in the Law of Labor Relations," 67 *Harvard Law Review* (1954), 1297 and Bernard D. Meltzer, "The Supreme Court, Congress and State Jurisdiction over Labor Relations," 59 *Columbia Law Review* (1959), 6 and 269. See also Gregory, *op. cit.*, pp. 530 ff.

38. *NLRB* vs. *Jones and Laughlin Steel Corporation*, 301 U.S. 1, and other cases decided at the same time.

39. *Garner* vs. *Teamsters' Union*, 346 U.S. 485 (1953).

40. See, for example, *United Construction Workers* vs. *Laburnum Construction Corporation*, 347 U.S. 656 (1954) and *United Auto Workers, CIO* vs. *WERB*, 351 U.S. 266 (1956).

41. *Guss* vs. *Utah LRB*, 353 U.S. 1 (1957).

42. Cox (*Law and the National Labor Policy*, pp. 17-18), speaking of federal preemption, says: "The rule protects labor activities wherever the Taft-Hartley restrictions upon strikes, boycotts, and picketing are less severe than those which would be imposed through state court injunctions, a condition which prevails in most states."

43. See *Steelworkers* vs. *Warrior and Gulf Navigation Co.*, 363 U.S. 574 (1960), and companion cases decided on the same day, in which recourse to arbitration was directed.

44. We are not unmindful of the high proportion of charges filed that are settled at the regional level without formal proceedings. Matters of "policy," however, seem to gravitate to higher levels.

45. Alexis de Tocqueville, *Democracy in America*, New York: Vintage Books, 1959, p. 20.

2

EMPLOYER FREE SPEECH:

THE SEARCH FOR A POLICY

BENJAMIN AARON

*Professor of Law and Director, Institute of Industrial Relations,
University of California, Los Angeles*

The so-called "free-speech" issue in labor-management relations is, in a sense, misnamed; it is more accurately described as one aspect of the larger problem of what constitutes illegal interference, restraint, or coercion.[1] Thus it is generally conceded that both unions and employers should have considerable latitude in publicly expressing opinions about each other, however uncomplimentary or unfounded in fact those views may be. Many such expressions, particularly those made in the heat of an organizing campaign or a labor dispute, are undoubtedly libelous or slanderous, yet they seldom result in the filing of legal actions for damages or even in demands for formal retraction. Both the organizations and the persons involved are concerned with bigger game—a representation election, a strike, or a boycott.

The crucial problem involving free speech, therefore, is the development of standards by which to determine when it extends beyond the limits of permissibility and becomes a verbal or written act of interference or intimidation forbidden by the National Labor Relations Act. The most difficult questions arise when speech is considered in the context of other activities which are themselves unfair labor practices. On the union side, we have seen how the legal status of picketing has fluctuated over the years, at one time being equated with free speech, and at other times being viewed as a form of intimidation.[2] Indeed, union free speech is an inextricable element in the general subject of picketing and boycotting, which is dealt with separately in this volume.[3] Accordingly, this chapter will be limited primarily to a discussion of employer free speech in the industrial relations context. The literature on even this limited aspect of the general problem is substantial.[4] Any analysis of the shifting winds of doctrine that have been let loose to play upon the subject of employer free speech since the enactment of the Wagner Act in 1935 must inevitably cover much that is now familiar. Some recapitulation is necessary, however, since current issues cannot be fully understood if they are considered apart from their historical development.

EMPLOYER FREE SPEECH UNDER THE WAGNER ACT

Enforced Neutrality Through Silence

For approximately the first six years under the Wagner Act (1935-1941), the NLRB tended to find that any statement by an employer against unionism was coercive *per se*. Mere expressions of opinion and simple factual statements were held to violate the Act.[5] The crusading spirit with which the Board at first attempted to protect employees' rights guaranteed by the Act is reflected in the following excerpt from its First Annual Report:

> Apart from discrimination against union members and leaders, and threats of discrimination, the most common form of interference with self-organization engaged in by employers is to spread propaganda against unions and thus not only poison the minds of workers against them but also indicate that the employers are antagonistic to unions and are prepared to make this antagonism effective. In the final analysis, most of this propaganda, *even when it contains no direct or even indirect threat*, is aimed at the worker's fear of loss of his job.[6]

To anyone unfamiliar with the climate of labor relations in the thirties, it must come as something of a shock to be reminded that the Board once regarded as "patently intimidatory or coercive" such statements as "We don't want no outside union to come in and run our business for us," or "the union principles are fine, but we don't want no union in our plant."[7] These expressions of opinion were considered in themselves to violate the Act; the following were also held to be unlawful when examined in the context of surrounding circumstances:

> statements to employees describing union organizers as "racketeers," "parasites," or as persons interested solely in their own monetary advancement; statements asserting that union dues are used by organizers to buy clothes, get drunk, or to purchase big black cigars; statements depicting unions as "rotten" or "corrupt," and the employees who join them as "thugs and highwaymen," "cutthroats," and "reds." In one case the union was termed a "dark cloud" or "stranger" which would destroy the "happy family" relationship between the company and its employees.[8]

Of course, the "surrounding circumstances" often included threats to move the plant if the workers organized, discharges of employees who "talked union," or even physical violence. These facts help to explain, if not completely to justify, the Board's early tendency to "press the policies of the . . . Act to extremes at the expense of competing considerations of equal or greater importance,"[9] including the employer's right of free speech.

Moreover, the Board's insistence upon a policy of employer neutrality through silence received a considerable amount of judicial support. One court, in upholding the Board's findings and remedial order against the employer, stated in part:

> . . . the position of the employer is a most delicate one. Surely, he has the right to his views. And, the right to entertain views is rather valueless if it be not accompanied by the right to express them. . . . And yet, the voice of authority may, by tone inflection, as well as by the substance of the words uttered, provoke fear and awe quite as readily as it may bespeak fatherly advice. The position of the employer . . . [under some circumstances] carries such weight and influence that his words may be coercive when they would not be so if the relation of master and servant did not exist.[10]

When more than one union sought to represent a group of employees, the employer was denied the opportunity to express even a preference as between the rival organizations. "Slight suggestions as to the employer's choice between unions," said the Supreme Court, "may have telling effect among men who know the consequences of incurring that employer's strong displeasure."[11] Considering that the Court had earlier that same year said, by way of dictum in a picketing case, that "the dissemination of information concerning facts of a labor dispute must be regarded as within the area of free discussion that is guaranteed by the Constitution,"[12] it is scarcely surprising that employers began to feel that a double standard of permissible speech was being applied to them and to unions.

Yet even in the comparatively early days of the Act there was some tendency on the part of reviewing courts to curb the Board's excessive zeal in suppressing employers' opinions. In *Ford Motor Co.*,[13] against a background of violent anti-union activity by the employer, the Board sought to prohibit the future dissemination of Henry Ford's "Fordisms" ("Figure it out for yourself. If you go into a union they have GOT YOU—but what have YOU got?") directly to his employees. The court of appeals refused to enforce that portion of the Board's order, saying: "The right to form opinion is of little value if such opinion may not be expressed, and the right to express it is of little value if it may not be communicated to those immediately concerned."[14]

Continuance of the Board's policy toward employers' expression of views resulted in an increasing number of appeals by employers to the courts, and during the period 1940-1941, the various circuit courts of appeal divided on the question of how much latitude should be permitted.[15] Finally, in 1941, the Supreme Court decided a case squarely presenting this issue. The Board had found that a bulletin posted by the Virginia Electric & Power Co. and two speeches made by company spokesmen interfered with, restrained, and coerced the employees in the exercise of the rights guaranteed them by the Act. In deciding the case on appeal the Supreme Court ruled that the NLRA did not prohibit employers from expressing their views about labor unions; but the Court added:

> . . . conduct, though evidenced in part by speech, may amount, in connection with other circumstances, to coercion within the meaning of the Act. . . . And in determining whether a course of conduct amounts to restraint or coercion, pressure exerted vocally by the employer may no more be disregarded than pressure exerted in other ways.[16]

The case was remanded for redetermination in the light of the whole course of the company's conduct. The Board subsequently found that the speech, not alone but in the context of other coercive conduct, amounted to an unfair labor practice,[17] and this finding was upheld.[18]

The Development of the "Captive Audience" Doctrine

Although in the *Virginia Electric & Power* case the employees had been directed to send representatives to the meetings addressed by the employer's spokesmen, that issue was ignored by both the Board and the Court. In *American Tube Bending Co.*,[19] however, the Board turned its attention to the "captive audience" feature. The day before an election virtually all work had been stopped in the plant and the employees were directed by supervision to assemble at a designated place, where they were addressed by the company's president. They were subsequently paid for the time spent at the meeting. The Board took the position that the act of addressing a forced audience on company property was in itself an unfair labor practice. It characterized such addresses as "tactical advantages which the unions could not possibly match, and the utilization of which brought heavily into play the economic dependence of the employees upon the respondent for their livelihood."[20]

On appeal to the Second Circuit, however, the Board's decision was reversed and the case dismissed. The court did not refer to the captive audience feature, but simply declared that the case was indistinguishable from the *Virginia Electric & Power* case, since it found nothing in the record but the speech, "an argument temperate in form, that a union would be against the employees' interests as well as the employer's, and that the continued prosperity of the company depended on going on as they had been."[21] Other circuits, now emphasizing the right of employers under the First Amendment to express views hostile to unions, so long as they refrained from making threats, refused to enforce Board orders based on the theory that employer speeches and written communications were coercive.[22] The Supreme Court, although declining to review any of these cases, nevertheless indirectly provided the Board with some further guidance as to the degree of restraint it could impose on employers' statements.

The Court's views were set forth in *Thomas* vs. *Collins*,[23] a case involving the constitutionality of a Texas law requiring the registration of union organizers as a prerequisite to the solicitation of union membership within the state. As applied to the facts of that case, the requirement was held, by a vote of five to four, to be an unconstitutional limitation on the rights of free speech and assembly. The obvious parallel with employer free speech, however, could not be ignored.

In a separate concurrence, Mr. Justice Jackson conceded that the Court had in fact established a double standard for determining the legality of restrictions on union and employer free speech, and had applied to unions "a rule the benefit of which in all its breadth and vigor this Court denies to employers in National Labor Relations Board cases." He thought, however, that "the remedy is not to allow Texas improperly to deny the right of free speech but to apply the same rule and spirit to free speech cases whoever the speaker."[24]

Mr. Justice Douglas, joined by Justices Black and Murphy, took issue with Mr. Justice Jackson's "intimation that the principle announced in this case serves labor alone and not an employer." The NLRB cases, he said, would be relevant only if the Court were dealing with legislation which regulated the relation between unions and their members.

> No one [he continued] may be required to obtain a license in order to speak. But once he uses the economic power he has over other men and their jobs to influence their action, he is doing more than exercising the freedom of speech protected by the First Amendment. That is true whether he be an employer or an employee. But as long as he does no more than speak he has the same unfettered right, no matter what side of an issue he espouses.[25]

It is, perhaps, unfair to characterize the conflicting dicta in *Thomas* vs. *Collins* as "guidance" to the NLRB. The lack of a definitive judicial policy regarding permissible limitations on employer free speech under the Act may have accounted for the conflicting opinions with respect to compulsory audiences handed down by the Board during this period. In two cases involving, respectively, employee assemblies called once or twice a month over an extended period,[26] and speeches delivered the day before an election,[27] the Board held, invoking the *American Tube Bending* doctrine, that the speeches were constitutionally protected in the absence of actual threats or promises. On the other hand, the Board reached the opposite conclusion in *Thompson Products, Inc.*[28] There, employees were assembled during working hours on six different occasions to hear anti-union speeches. They had been instructed by supervision to attend and were paid for the time so spent. With little reference to what was actually said at these meetings, the Board held that they constituted unlawful restraint and interference, saying:

> While we recognize an employer's right of free speech even where a Board election is involved, in this case [the companies] took advantage of an avenue of communication to bring to bear upon the employees the weight of [their] economic power in a manner not available to the unions. . . . In view of the economic dependence of the listeners upon the [companies], a factor which rendered the employees unduly responsive to the slightest suggestions of the speakers, and in view of the compulsion upon the listeners to give heed, the adjurations of the speakers passed from the realm of the free competition of ideas envisaged by the First Amendment into that of coercion.[29]

The case most commonly associated with the "captive audience" doctrine, however, is *Clark Bros. Co.*[30] Employees had been assembled during working hours to listen to speeches by company officials one hour before the polls opened in a run-off election between a CIO union and a company association. The Board, in a split decision, held that compelling employees to listen to speeches under these circumstances independently constituted interference and coercion, "wholly apart from the fact that the speech itself may be privileged under the Constitution."[31] Although the Board majority expressly refused to adopt the trial examiner's statement that the employees had a "constitutional right of non-assembly," it achieved the same result, according to the dissenting member, "by propounding the idea that the exercise of constitutional rights on time paid for by another is an unconditional one."[32]

On appeal to the Second Circuit, the Board's order was enforced,[33] but on different grounds from those relied upon by the NLRB. The court declared that the facts in the *Clark Bros.* case did not justify a rule that the right of employees to be free to determine whether or not to receive aid, advice, and information concerning their self-organization for collective bargaining was violated "whenever the employer utilizes his power to compel them to assemble and listen to speeches relative to matters of organization."[34] In place of so broad a proscription the court substituted the following:

> An employer has an interest in presenting his views on labor relations to his employees. We should hesitate to hold that he may not do this on company time and pay, *provided a similar opportunity to address them were accorded representatives of the union.*[35]

The court also concluded, however, that in this case the speech was coercive and an interference with the employees' collective bargaining rights when considered in the context of the employer's other unfair practices.

This was the situation at about the time the NLRA amendments incorporated in the Labor Management Relations (Taft-Hartley) Act, 1947, went into effect. In the preceding twelve years the Board, prodded by the courts, had developed a policy concerning employer free speech which had gone through three distinct phases. The first was characterized by the requirement that the employer maintain strict neutrality by remaining silent; the second, by the concession that the employer could express his anti-union views, so long as they were not accompanied by threats or promises, and so long as employees were not required to listen; and the third, by the refinement that the employer could make non-coercive anti-union speeches to compulsory audiences of his employees, provided that similar opportunities were afforded union representatives to express their views.

Employer Free Speech Under the Taft-Hartley Act
Demise of the "Captive Audience" Doctrine

As amended by the Taft-Hartley Act, the NLRA now includes a provision, Section 8(c), which states:

> The expressing of any views, argument, or opinion, or the dissemination thereof, whether in written, printed, graphic, or visual form, shall not constitute or be evidence of an unfair labor practice under any of the provisions of this Act, if such expression contains no threat of reprisal or force or promise of benefit.

Both in the Senate hearings[36] and in the majority report on the Taft bill (S.1126), which eventually passed the Senate, the Board's decisions on employer free speech were criticized. On this point the majority report on S.1126 commented:

> The Supreme Court in *Thomas* vs. *Collins* . . . held, contrary to some earlier decisions of the Labor Board, that the Constitution guarantees freedom of speech on either side in labor controversies and approved the doctrine of the American Tube Bending case. . . . The Board has placed a limited construction upon these decisions by holding such speeches by employers to be coercive if the employer was found guilty of some other unfair labor practice, even though severable or unrelated . . . or if the speech was made in the plant on working time (*Clark Brothers* . . .). The committee believes these decisions to be too restrictive. . . .[37]

In *Babcock & Wilcox Co.*,[38] the first case squarely raising the "captive audience" issue to come before the Board after the NLRA was amended, the Board formally capitulated to the will of Congress. It conceded that

> . . . the language of Section 8(c) of the amended Act, and its legislative history, make it clear that the doctrine of the *Clark Bros.* case no longer exists as a basis for finding unfair labor practices in [these] circumstances. . . .[39]

For the next few years, although NLRB regional directors and trial examiners continued to apply the "captive audience" doctrine as modified by the Second Circuit, the Board just as regularly overruled them, or based its conclusions on other grounds.[40] The extent of the Board's shift is evident from its decision in *S & S Corrugated Paper Machinery Co.*[41] There the president of the company made several pre-election speeches to compulsory audiences of employees, and ignored the union's request to address the same group. The regional director found this to be an interference with the employees' rights, but the Board overruled that finding on the ground that the speeches were protected by Section 8(c) and the company's denial of equal opportunity to use its facilities was therefore not illegal.

Rebirth of the Phoenix: The Bonwit Teller Doctrine

The *Babcock & Wilcox* and *S & S Corrugated Paper* cases had seemed to destroy the last vestiges of the "captive audience" doctrine; yet, in little more than a year following the latter decision a new version of that doctrine emerged from the ashes of the old. In *Bonwit Teller, Inc.*,[42] a week before a representation election, the employer shut its department store one-half hour before closing time, and its president then delivered an anti-union speech to the employees assembled on the main selling floor. Prior to that speech, the employer had enforced a valid rule prohibiting solicitation of membership by union organizers on the selling floor at all times.[43] A few days after the speech, the union requested permission to address the employees under similar circumstances, but the employer ignored the request. After losing the election, the union filed an unfair labor practice charge.

Purporting to rely upon the Second Circuit's decision in the *Clark Bros.* case, and overruling *S & S Corrugated Paper*, the Board, one member dissenting, held that the denial of the union's request to reply constituted illegal interference with the employees' rights of self-organization and grounds for setting aside the election. To the dissenting member's charge that "hinging an employer's right to speak upon his readiness to make available the means by which his arguments, views, and opinions can be nullified, effectively emasculates Section 8(c) as it applies to the right of an employer to address his employees,"[44] the majority replied that it had not proscribed either what the employer said or the manner in which the audience was assembled. It was concerned, rather, with what the employer had refused to do. Denial of the union's "reasonable request" to address the same audience under similar circumstances, said the majority, was tantamount to a discriminatory enforcement of the no-solicitation rule, in that it prevented the employees from hearing both sides of the union representation issue.

The Board's decision in the *Bonwit Teller* case fairly bristled with qualifications which suggested that it would have only limited application to other situations. Thus, the majority opinion, after enunciating the principle that Section 7 of the Act "necessarily encompasses the right to hear both sides of the story under circumstances which reasonably approximate equality," added the following caveat:

That is not to say that the employer is proscribed from addressing his employees and urging that they reject a union unless he invites a union representative to come into his plant and make an appeal for support of the union. Nor does it mean that under any and all circumstances an employer is under an obligation to accede to a union's request that it be granted an opportunity to address the employees on the employer's premises.[45]

What seemed to emerge, therefore, was the rather narrow rule that the employer could not lawfully deny a union's request to address his employees "where the circumstances are such that only by granting such request will the employees have a reasonable opportunity to hear both sides."[46] Moreover, these "circumstances," in the *Bonwit Teller* case, included not only a broad no-solicitation rule, but also the proximity of the employer's speech to the election, which limited the union's time for effective rebuttal by other means.

The decision of the Second Circuit on the appeal[47] seemed to support this interpretation. It held that neither Section 8(c) nor the issue of employer free speech was involved in *Bonwit Teller;* the issue, rather, was the discriminatory application of a no-solicitation rule. Normally, the court pointed out, the employer could not forbid union solicitation on company property during non-working time even where there was no showing that solicitation away from the plant would be ineffective.[48] But the Board had allowed retail department stores the special privilege of prohibiting all solicitation within the selling areas of the store during both working and non-working hours.[49] Therefore, Bonwit Teller, having availed itself of that privilege, was "required to abstain from campaigning against the Union on the same premises to which the Union was denied access; if it should be otherwise, the practical advantage to the employer . . . would constitute serious interference with the right of his employees to organize."[50]

Even so, the court held that the Board's remedial order was too broad. The violation of the Act consisted in the discriminatory application of the no-solicitation rule; if the rule were abandoned, however, the company would no longer be required to accord the union a similar opportunity every time the company's president made an anti-union speech. "Nothing in the Act nor in reason," the majority concluded, "compels such 'an eye for an eye, a tooth for a tooth' result so long as the avenues of communication are kept open to both sides."[51]

Despite all these initial indications to the contrary, the Board began almost immediately to ignore the distinctions made by both its own and the Second Circuit's opinions in the *Bonwit Teller* case. In subsequent cases it dismissed as irrelevant such circumstances as the absence of a broad no-solicitation rule and the availability to the union of alternate means of communication with the employees.[52]

The shift in the Board's emphasis following congressional rejection of the "captive audience" doctrine thus became clear: in the *Clark Bros.* case the Board stressed the right of employees not to receive information they did not want to hear; in the *Bonwit Teller* and succeeding cases it insisted on the employees' right to receive *all* available information.[53]

It is also clear, however, that the latter approach had no firmer judicial support than the former. In a later case[54] in which the employer, a factory owner, delivered an anti-union speech to a compulsory audience on company time and premises, while maintaining a rule against solicitation of union membership on company time or property, the Second Circuit upheld the Board's finding of an unfair labor practice solely on the ground that the no-solicitation rule was invalid. It went on to say, however, that if the Board's order had depended upon the employer's refusal or failure to allow the union representative to address the employees on the property during working hours, "it could not stand." The same court's opinion in the *Bonwit Teller* case, it reiterated, had been based "wholly upon" the breadth of the no-solicitation rule there involved.[55]

Nevertheless, it seems likely that the Board would probably have persisted in its view unless specifically overruled by a majority of the circuit courts or by the Supreme Court. There is more than one way to change a policy, however, and what Congress and the judiciary had failed to do was accomplished with comparative ease by a change in administration.

New Men and New Rules

Shortly after the Republican Administration took office in 1953, the chairman and one member of the NLRB were replaced by appointees of the new President. In less than six months the reconstituted Board repudiated the *Bonwit Teller* case, its ancestors, and its progeny, and established the doctrine presently in effect. This result was brought about by decisions handed down the same day by a divided Board in *Peerless Plywood Co.*[56] and *Livingston Shirt Corp.*[57] The former was a representation case in which the issue was whether an election should be set aside; the latter was an unfair labor practice case involving both the validity of an election and the question whether the employer had violated Section 8(a)(1) of the Act. The common elements in both cases were the employer's speeches to compulsory audiences on company time and property and its refusal to afford the union an opportunity to address the same audience under similar circumstances. Both cases merit detailed consideration.

In the *Livingston Shirt* case there were two elections. Approximately 25 hours before the first was scheduled to begin, and during working hours, the company president made a non-coercive anti-union speech to the assembled employees. Subsequently, he refused requests by union representatives for a similar opportunity to address the employees. The union lost the election, but the NLRB regional director, relying upon the *Bonwit Teller* case, set it aside. Shortly before the second election, the company president again delivered a non-coercive anti-union speech to assembled employees on company premises during working hours. The union's request for a similar opportunity was again refused, the election was lost, and the regional director again set it aside. This time the union followed up its defeat by filing charges of unfair labor practices with the Board.

A majority of the Board, though for different reasons, found that the employer did not commit an unfair labor practice by denying the union the use of its time and property to reply to the employer's speech. Two of the four members who participated, Chairman Farmer and Member Rodgers, based their decision squarely on Section 8(c) of the Act. Noting that this provision specifically prohibits a finding that "an uncoercive speech, whenever delivered by the employer, constitutes an unfair labor practice," they argued that "any attempt to rationalize a proscription against an employer who makes a privileged speech must necessarily be rested on the theory that the employer's vice is not in making a speech but in denying the union an opportunity to reply on company premises." But such a theory is an "untenable basis" for a finding of unfair labor practices, since it grafts upon the privilege of free speech "conditions which are tantamount to negation."[58]

Farmer and Rodgers were unable to find anything in the statute "which even hints at any Congressional intent to restrict an employer in the use of his own premises for the purpose of airing his views." Those premises, they thought, are his "natural forum," just as the union's hall is its "inviolable forum." It seemed unlikely to them that the employer's refusal to open up his premises for group meetings would unduly hinder unions in their organizing activities, "since this is the area from which they have traditionally been excluded, and there remains open to them all the customary means for communicating with employees."[59] They saw no real distinction between giving the union the statutory right to make campaign speeches to assembled employees on the employer's premises and at his expense and according a similar right to the employer to make anti-union speeches to union members assembled in the union hall.

The *Bonwit Teller* doctrine, the two Board members continued, was not only bad law but bad policy. It did not provide for an orderly debate of the issues; rather, it "visualized that first one party and then the other should address the employees, and so on *seriatim* and *ad infinitum,* thus compelling a game of wits and endless jockeying for position, the winner's prize being the treasured back-fence advantage of having the last word."[60]

The opinion concluded with the following statement of the new rule:

> . . . absent special circumstances as hereinafter indicated, there is nothing improper in an employer refusing to grant to the union a right equal to his own in his plant. We rule therefore that, in the absence of either an unlawful broad no-solicitation rule (prohibiting union access to company premises on other than working time) or a privileged no-solicitation rule (broad, but not unlawful because of the character of the business),[61] an employer does not commit an unfair labor practice if he makes a pre-election speech on company time and premises to his employees and denies the union's request for an opportunity to reply.[62]

Member Peterson, who concurred in the decision, did so on the theory that neither Section 8(c) nor the issue of employer free speech was involved. His holding was based solely on the principle that, "as the union had access to the employer's premises, it was not an unfair labor practice for him to deny the use of his time as well as his property to reply to the employer's speech."[63]

In the *Peerless Plywood* case the union lost an election conducted on the morning of May 26, 1953. On May 20 the union had written to the employer requesting equal time and facilities in the event that the employer made a speech to the employees on company time and property. The employer denied this request on May 22, pointing out that it did not have a no-solicitation rule. On the afternoon of May 25, less than 24 hours before the election, the employer assembled the employees on company property to hear a non-coercive speech about the election delivered by an officer of the company. After the speech was read, mimeographed copies were delivered to those employees present. On the night of May 25 the union held a meeting of employees at its hall to discuss the election.

In this case Chairman Farmer and Members Rodgers and Peterson were fully in agreement that the election should be set aside, though for different reasons than those relied upon by the regional director. Referring to the decision in the *Livingston Shirt* case, the majority pointed out that although they had abandoned the *Bonwit Teller* doctrine in complaint cases, this did not dispose of the problem as it affected the conduct of elections. As to the latter the majority stated:

> It is our considered view . . . that last-minute speeches by either employers or unions delivered to massed assemblies of employees on company time have an unwholesome and unsettling effect and tend to interfere with that sober and thoughtful choice which a free election is designed to reflect. . . . Such [speeches], because of [their] timing, [tend] to create a mass psychology which overrides arguments made through other campaign media and gives an unfair advantage to the party . . . who in this manner obtains the last most telling word.[64]

On the foregoing premise the majority enunciated a new rule: employers and unions alike would be prohibited from making election speeches on company time to massed assemblies of employees within 24 hours before the scheduled times for elections. Violations of this rule would result in the election being set aside whenever valid objections were filed.

In further explication of the rule the majority indicated that two elements bringing it into play were "(1) the use of Company time for pre-election speeches and (2) the delivery of such speeches on the eve of the election [which tends] to destroy freedom of choice and establish an atmosphere in which a free election cannot be held." On the other hand, non-coercive speeches made prior to the proscribed period would not justify invocation of the rule, since there would still be "time for their effect to be neutralized by the impact of other media of employee persuasion."[65]

Similarly, the rule would not interfere with the rights of unions or employers "to circulate campaign literature on or off the premises at any time prior to the election," nor would it prohibit the use of "any other legitimate campaign propaganda or media."[66] Coercive speeches at any time would still be outlawed, but prior to the 24-hour period, an employer would be free to make non-coercive anti-union speeches on company time without giving the union an opportunity to reply. Finally, the rule would not prohibit employers or unions from making campaign speeches on or off company premises during the 24-hour period if employee attendance were voluntary and on the employees' own time.

The New Rules in Action.

Although the rules enunciated in the *Livingston Shirt* and *Peerless Plywood* cases are scarcely invulnerable to attack,[67] they appeared at first blush to have a certain Procrustean simplicity; yet almost immediately the sharp outlines of the new policy began to blur into ambiguity. The first intimation of this development was the *Woolworth* case.[68] There, the company had a broad, but privileged, no-solicitation rule. A company officer delivered two non-coercive anti-union speeches to assembled employees on company time and property before a scheduled election; on each occasion the union requested and was refused the opportunity to reply under similar circumstances. The Board, as it had previously indicated in the *Livingston Shirt* case,[69] found that the company had applied its no-solicitation rule in a discriminatory fashion, thereby violating Section 8(a)(1) of the Act.

The Sixth Circuit, however, refused to enforce the Board's

order,[70] and the three separate opinions accompanying its decision cannot be said to have clarified the status of the *Livingston Shirt* rule. The author of the court's opinion based his ruling squarely on the First Amendment and on Section 8(c); any attempt to interpret a no-solicitation rule as depriving the employer of the right to "confer" with his employees about such important matters as unionization violated both the Constitution and the statutory provision. The employer's economic power was irrelevant: "Freedom of speech is guaranteed under the Constitution alike to the weak and the powerful."[71] A second judge concurred on the ground that the only portion of the employer's broad no-solicitation rule involved in the case was that which prohibited solicitation during working hours; the portion relating to non-working time was not involved and not enforced. He concluded that the discriminatory application of a valid rule against solicitation during working hours was not an unfair labor practice. A third judge dissented on the ground that the rule against solicitation on company property during non-working hours *was* enforced and thereby tainted the company's entire no-solicitation policy.

The *Woolworth* case was followed by two others that eventually reached the Supreme Court. In *Nutone, Inc.*[72] the issue presented was "whether an employer commits an unfair labor practice if during a pre-election period, it enforces an otherwise valid rule against employee distribution of literature in the plant, while, during the same period, itself distributing non-coercive anti-union literature within the plant in a context of other unfair labor practices, committed prior to the election period and thereafter."[73]

Finding that the employer's other unfair labor practices were unrelated to this particular issue, the Board concluded:

> Valid plant rules against solicitation and other forms of union activity do not control an employer's actions. Management prerogative certainly extends far enough so as to permit an employer to make rules that do not bind himself.[74]

This reasoning did not persuade the District of Columbia Circuit, which reversed the Board. Conceding that Section 8(c) "wipes out the taint of discrimination"[75] from a non-coercive anti-union speech, the court nevertheless considered that the employer's no-distribution rule must have a valid reason to be enforced (e.g., to preserve cleanliness, order, production, or discipline in the plant).[76] By itself distributing literature, the employer had nullified the basis for its rule. Thus, the court expressly rejected the theory enunciated in the *Woolworth* case that the rights guaranteed by Section 8(c) are absolute and cannot be diminished by a no-solicitation (and by inference, a no-distribution) rule.

Avondale Mills[77] involved similar facts, but there the Board felt that the employer's coercive anti-union campaign rendered its enforcement of a no-solicitation rule discriminatory and illegal. The Fifth Circuit disagreed and denied enforcement of that portion of the Board's order.[78]

The Supreme Court granted *certiorari* in both the *Nutone* and *Avondale Mills* cases and disposed of them in a single opinion, holding that under principles equally applicable to both, the employer's conduct was not illegal under the specific circumstances involved.[79] Speaking for the Court, Mr. Justice Frankfurter pronounced the issue to be "very narrow and almost abstract," deriving from the claim that "when the employer himself engages in anti-union solicitation that if engaged in by employees would constitute a violation of the rule . . . his enforcement of an otherwise valid no-solicitation rule against the employees is itself an unfair labor practice." Declining to lay down a rule of law that "the coincidence of these circumstances necessarily violates the Act, regardless of the way in which the particular controversy arose or whether the employer's conduct to any considerable degree created an imbalance in the opportunities for organizational communication," he declared that to do so "would show indifference to the responsibilities imposed by the Act primarily on the Board to appraise carefully the interest of both sides . . . in the diverse circumstances of particular cases and in the light of the Board's special understanding of these industrial situations." [80]

Among the considerations which the Court thought relevant were whether the unions had asked the employers "to make an exception to the [no-solicitation] rules for pro-union solicitation" (they had not), and whether the no-solicitation rules "truly diminished the ability of the labor organizations involved to carry their messages to the employees" (no such showing had been made). With respect to the latter, the Court observed that the Act "does not command that labor organizations, as a matter of abstract law, under all circumstances, be protected in the use of every possible means of reaching the minds of individual workers, nor that they are entitled to use a medium of communication simply because the employer is using it."[81] If the union's opportunities for effectively reaching the employees with a pro-union message, in spite of a no-solicitation rule, are "at least as great" as the employer's ability to promote his non-coercive anti-union views, there is no basis for invalidating the rule.

What, then, are the present limitations on the employer's methods of exercising his freedom of speech? Clearly, the privilege granted by Section 8(c) is not absolute, as suggested in the *Woolworth* case. It is doubtful, however, that the presence of either a broad but privileged no-solicitation rule or an unlawful broad no-solicitation rule will automatically convert the otherwise privileged exercise of free speech into an unfair labor practice. Thus, the Board will be required to determine in each case, not only the validity of a no-solicitation rule, but also whether the union has the ability, "at least as great" as that of the employer, "effectively" to reach the employees with its message by other means than in-plant solicitation.[82] Past experience suggests that the Board will find these principles sufficiently flexible to permit it to reach the same conclusions it arrived at in the *Nutone* and *Avondale Mills* cases.[83]

Meanwhile, the Board has continued to apply the 24-hour election rule enunciated in the *Peerless Plywood* case, with numerous refinements.[84] To the limited extent that these decisions have been reviewed by the courts, they have been upheld.[85]

The Substance of Employer Speech

The legislative history of Section 8(c)[86] indicates that the wording finally adopted was a compromise between the Hartley and Taft bills. The former would have overruled the Board's "totality of conduct" doctrine by prohibiting the use of an argument or expression of opinion as evidence of an unfair labor practice "if it does not by its own terms threaten force or economic reprisal."[87] The latter would have proscribed a finding of an unfair labor practice based on an argument or opinion "if such statement contains *under all the circumstances* no threat, express or implied, of reprisal or force, or offer, express or implied, of benefit."[88] Section 8(c), as finally adopted, aroused immediate criticism, because, literally construed, it precludes a consideration of the employer's state of mind. In the words of Archibald Cox:

> here, as often in the law, the privilege to engage in conduct crossing the interest of others depends on the purpose for which the conduct is undertaken. In such cases expressions of desire or opinion will often indicate the motive of otherwise ambiguous acts, and normal rules of evidence permit proof of the actor's declarations to show his state of mind.[89]

In its first annual report following passage of the Taft-Hartley Act, the NLRB commented that Section 8(c) "appears to enlarge somewhat the protection previously accorded by the original statute and to grant immunity beyond that contemplated by the free speech guarantees of the Constitution." Conceding that a noncoercive speech could no longer be held to violate the Act simply because "at other times, and on other occasions," the employer had committed unfair labor practices, the Board insisted, nevertheless, that "words and conduct may be so intertwined as to be considered a single coercive act."[90] The issue has thus become whether the protected words and the anti-union conduct are sufficiently "intertwined" to justify a finding of an unfair labor practice. In general, the courts have sustained the Board's findings.[91]

When employer statements are considered apart from other behavior, it appears that "section 8(c) privileges a wide range of anti-union speech."[92] Illustrative cases cited by Professor Koretz hold that "employers may urge their employees to reject or repudiate unionization or to vote for a particular union, recount existing benefits and suggest that a union could obtain no more, and disparage the union and its representatives and question their motives in seeking representative status."[93]

The Board and the NLRB general counsel have also been reluctant to regard as unfair labor practices or as grounds for setting aside elections overt appeals by employers to racial or religious prejudices.[94] Thus, the Board held it was not an unfair labor practice for a supervisor to state to an employee, "don't you know if you all get the Union up here, you'll be sitting up here by niggers?"[95] In another case it refused to set aside an election because a Negro vice president of the employer, in order to induce Negroes not to vote for the union, told them that "some of the employees didn't want to be represented by me because of my race," and that the "white employees were jealous of my position with the Company."[96] "While we do not condone appeals to race prejudice," said the Board, "we do not find that the injection of the issue, or the context in which it [arose], sufficient ground for invalidation of the results."[97]

The NLRB policy appears to be the same when the appeal to racial or religious prejudice is made by the union. When a Puerto Rican union issued a statement to the employees, "If you want to avoid that the Jew Sandler continue to mistreat you, vote for UTM," the Board overruled the employer's objection to the election, on the ground that "mere mention of a racial or religious issue is not grounds for setting aside an election."[98]

In one case that has aroused considerable criticism the general counsel refused to include in a complaint against the employer charges based on the latter's pre-election conduct, which included posting throughout its plant reproductions of an inflammatory Mississippi newspaper article featuring a picture of the union's president dancing with a Negro "lady friend" (actually the wife of a Nigerian official), and holding a compulsory meeting on company time and property at which the employer's president accused the union of being "nigger lovers." Noting that the general counsel had given no reason for his refusal to include in his complaint charges based on this conduct, the court of appeals said: "Whatever his reason, no party to this record has defended his action on the ground that the employer's conduct, if proved, would not constitute a violation of the Act."[99]

NLRB critics reserve for their special chamber of horrors, however, those cases in which the Board has sought to distinguish between illegal "threats" or "promises," on the one hand, and privileged "predictions," "prophecies," or "expressions of legal position" on the other.[100] A few examples will suffice.[101]

Statements by employer spokesmen that "if the union won, they would be forced to move the plant," and that "they would move the plant if they so desired," were held by the Board to be insufficient grounds for setting aside an election, for the following reasons:

> We view these statements, under the circumstances, as nothing more than predictions of the possible impact of wage demands upon the Employer's business. A prophecy that unionization might ultimately lead to a loss of employment is not coercive where there is no threat that the Employer will use its economic power to make its prophecy come true.[102]

A pre-election statement by the employer admonishing employees to "remember that a vote on May 17th in favor of the Union will be your invitation to further unemployment" was held by the Board not to be, "in the context in which it was made, a threat of economic reprisal." The "context" was the statement itself, in which the employer also said, "By voting for the union you are voting for more strikes not only at this Company, but you also may be called upon to perform picket duty at other places." Thus, the Board concluded that the statement, as a whole, should be considered only as a "prediction of unemployment."[103]

It is probably impossible to evaluate fairly any of the foregoing statements apart from the record of the case as a whole; but even after making allowances, some of the distinctions drawn by the Board approach the metaphysical.[104]

Interrogation by Employers

It has been customary to include in discussions of employer free speech references to the employer interrogation cases arising under the NLRA. As others have pointed out, however, "although interrogation involves speech, it is not primarily a means of expressing an opinion; it is rather a process of gathering information. Accordingly, the policy reasons for permitting an employer to freely state his views, arguments, and opinions do not apply to interrogation. . . ."[105] Since the Board does not apply Section 8(c) to interrogation, cases involving that practice are not discussed in this chapter.[106]

SOME REFLECTIONS

A review of the crowded and often confusing historical record of the search for fair and workable rules governing freedom of speech under the National Labor Relations Act leads to the conviction that those rules have continuously been made subservient to other policy considerations. More specifically, they have been tailored to conform to fluctuating evaluations of the relative importance of organizing employees for collective bargaining, as compared with such competing considerations as protecting the right of employers to speak out against unions.

In the early Wagner Act period whenever these two objectives seemed to conflict, the Board almost uniformly elected to advance the former at the expense of the latter. Certainly, the constitutional right of employers to express their views and opinions was violated in many instances. On the other hand, it is arguable whether the great organizational gains of unions during the thirties could have been accomplished if the scales of governmental authority had not been tipped in their favor. Those who argue that a beneficent result never justifies the use of improper means to achieve it are likely to conclude that the Board went too far in the early days in imposing a neutrality-by-silence on employers. Others, not troubled by the philosophical question, may yet wonder either whether the end achieved was wholly beneficent, or whether it would not have been achieved even in the face of the employers' outspoken opposition.

The Taft-Hartley Act represented, among other things, a massive shift in public opinion away from an emphasis on the social utility of collective bargaining and toward an emphasis on individual rights of both employers and employees. It was inevitable, therefore, even without the pressure from the courts, that the reconstituted Board would expand the scope of permissible employer speech on collective bargaining matters.

In 1954 a highly respected authority in this field advanced the thesis that following the national election of 1952, a "political" factor entered into decisions of the reconstituted Board, and that the new majority wrought its changes in the policy governing employer communication "less in the fashion of judges bringing new vision into the law of the land than in that of ward politicians sweeping out everything the other scoundrels left behind."[107] He went on to point out that the Board seemed to be attaching new significance to broad "principles" of general jurisprudence and less to the purposes of this particular statute, and also that the complexity of the rules of the game seemed to be growing as their individual importance diminished.

There is undoubtedly considerable disagreement over the fairness of the first observation, but the accuracy of the other two is indisputable. Let us consider, first, the circumstances under which an employer may now communicate his views on collective bargaining matters to his employees. Subject to the qualifications set forth in the *Livingston Shirt* decision, and prior to 24 hours before an election, he may compel them to listen to an anti-union speech on his premises during working time. He need not afford the union a similar opportunity because the plant is his "natural forum," just as the union's hall is its "inviolable forum." Here we have enunciated the broad "principle" of equality of access: both the employer and the union have approximately the same opportunity to make their respective appeals to the employees; therefore, neither has the right to be heard on the other's time or property.

But surely, despite the symmetry of this formulation, the "principle" is no more than a disingenuous rationalization of a policy permitting employers to exploit economic power under the guise of exercising their right of free speech. The point is not that the union and the employer have the same right to deny each other permission to address employees assembled in their respective "forums"; rather, it is that the employer has the power, derived from the employment relation, to compel employees to listen, and that the union has not. It cannot make employees come to the union hall to hear a pre-election exhortation, even assuming the unlikely fact that there is often such a meeting place conveniently at hand.

The rule of the *Peerless Plywood* case, banning speeches by either employers or unions to massed assemblies of employees on company time less than 24 hours before an election, is also based on a "principle" which is offensive to the spirit of freedom that it purports to serve. The Board's opinion in that case is the authentic voice of Big Brother, dispassionate, paternal, and arbitrary. Employees must be protected from "unwholesome and unsettling" effects which interfere with a "sober and thoughtful choice." The assumption that appeals which are "unwholesome and unsettling"

if made 23 hours prior to an election somehow are shorn of their
baneful influence if made 25 hours in advance is arrant nonsense;
the suggestion that the Board is responsible for insuring that the
election represents a "sober and thoughtful choice," if taken seriously, has chilling implications. Given this responsibility, the Board
must develop standards for measuring sobriety and thoughtfulness
of choice, and logically, it should then be given the power to set
aside elections in which it concludes that the employees, because
of a "mass psychology which overrides arguments made through
other campaign media," have exercised their voting rights freely
but foolishly.

Contrary to the statements in the *Peerless Plywood* majority
opinion, the rule therein enunciated is more than merely "an extension of" its established prohibition against "prohibiting elec-
tioneering at or near the polling place";[108] nor is it similar to the
ban on the use of sound trucks to project propaganda into the
polling place from outside the plant area,[109] or to the decision to
set aside an election because an "atmosphere of terror" was created
by individual employees whose conduct was not attributable to
either the union or the employer.[110] The *Peerless Plywood* rule,
if its expressed rationale is to be taken literally, represents a difference of kind, rather than of degree, from other rules designed to
insure the integrity of the election process.

It is doubtful that the Board ever intended that its decision in
the *Peerless Plywood* case should be construed as establishing
anything but a mechanical rule prohibiting election speeches by
employers or unions to compulsory audiences of employees on
company time and property within 24 hours of an election. Had
the Board frankly conceded that it wished to adopt such a rule
as a matter of administrative convenience, there would be far less
cause for criticism. The real vice of the case is not in the rule for
which it stands; rather it is in the rationale of the rule, which suggests an omniscience that the Board obviously lacks and a reserve
power that exceeds the outmost limits of permissible discretion.

It is easier to find flaws in the rules laid down in the *Livingston
Shirt* and *Peerless Plywood* cases, however, than to propose others
that are demonstrably more equitable and workable. An ideal
arrangement, perhaps, but one impossible to attain, would insure

that the union and the employer have exactly the same access to all employees through exactly the same communication media. Alternatively, it seems better to move in the opposite direction and to emancipate the captive audience altogether by returning to the principle enunciated by the Board in the *Clark Bros.* case. This would preserve against both employer and union the individual employee's right not to listen and would separate the employer's exercise of free speech from his economic power to compel his employees to listen. It would also increase the odds that the union's opportunities for effectively reaching employees with a pro-union message will be "at least as great" as those of the employer.

The task of working out an appropriate standard by which to determine what constitutes an illegal threat or promise, as distinguished from a permissible expression of opinion or advice, is infinitely more troublesome. The continued popularity of extremist approaches to the problem may be explained in part by the relative ease of their application, whereas any concept of balancing interests can be applied only with great difficulty and uncertainty and, inevitably, with a certain amount of unfairness. At one extreme are those who still argue that neither the employees' decision to organize nor their choice of bargaining agents is of any legitimate concern to the employer; accordingly, they would deny the employer any voice whatever in those decisions. At the other extreme are those who would exalt the right of free speech above all else, and who argue that employers and unions should be given the widest latitude in expressing their views, even though these may sometimes be reasonably interpreted as threats. Thus, proponents of this approach assert that if it is permissible for an employer to go out of business after his plant has been organized, he should be permitted to warn his employees before the election of the possibility that he may do so if the union wins.

The short answer to both of these proposals is that they run contrary to cherished notions of fair play and are politically impossible. The former policy would also raise serious questions of constitutionality, while the latter would drastically reduce the rights guaranteed by Section 7 of the Act; for the threat to exercise a legal right, if made insincerely, and simply for the purpose of discouraging and interfering with the organization of employees, is indistinguishable in character from the threat to discharge for union activity.

The middle ground, uncertain though it may be, offers the best hope of approaching the unattainable ideal of absolute equality under the law. The path is a familiar one; even the pitfalls are well known. The structure of our economic system gives the employer an advantage over individual employees; hence the policy to encourage collective bargaining and to prohibit attempts by the employer, by means of threats and promises, to frustrate the efforts of employees to organize. The employer has the right to communicate his opinions and his advice, whether or not they are solicited, but not in such a way as to suggest, however subtly, that his employees will be penalized if they do not give heed to his views.

Thus, it becomes clear that to interpret the employer's words solely in terms of their dictionary meaning makes a mockery of the legal sanction. As Judge Learned Hand has said:

> Words are not pebbles in alien juxtaposition; they have only a communal existence; and not only does the meaning of each interpenetrate the other, but all in their aggregate take their purport from the setting in which they are used, of which the relation between the speaker and the hearer is perhaps the most important. What to an outsider will be no more than the vigorous presentation of a conviction, to an employee may be the manifestation of a determination which it is not safe to thwart.[111]

The determination of what the speaker intends and what the listener understands, in the light of all the surrounding circumstances, is a function that requires intimate familiarity with the varied facts of industrial life, a balanced judgment, and a certain amount of empathic perception. Only someone who is endowed with these qualities can appreciate that "words which may only antagonize a hard-bitten truck driver in Detroit may seriously intimidate a rural textile hand in a company village where the mill owners dominate every aspect of life."[112] Moreover, as Archibald Cox has also pointed out, this function cannot be performed by "review attorneys sitting in Washington"; it must be vested in the trial examiners "who absorb the atmosphere by visiting the community and observing the parties and witnesses."[113]

Adherence to this approach would undoubtedly result in occasional injustice; it would also lead to varying adjustments between the rights of employers and unions, depending upon differences in the relative strength of the parties, community attitudes, and other relevant factors. Despite its weaknesses, however, it offers considerable hope of improvement over the present system, which emphasizes the form of speech rather than its substance and gives too little weight to the psychological factors in labor-management relations. The recently proposed reorganization plan for the NLRB,[114] which would permit the Board to delegate its functions to trial examiners or to its own employees, affords an opportunity to put some of the foregoing ideas into practice, but it is too early to tell whether the newly reconstituted Board will do so.

Whatever policy is adopted by the Board, the question of how to treat the exploitation by employers or unions of racial or religious prejudices is sure to cause grave concern. A recent study supports the Board's refusal to invalidate elections because of the injection of racial issues on the ground that "toleration of noncoercive discussion of such issues appears to be required by free speech considerations."[115] It also concludes, however, that

> in determining whether such statements are coercive or otherwise impair a free election, it is appropriate to recognize that the impact of particular statements on particular groups will be significantly affected by the group experience with discrimination in hiring and in other relationships.[116]

This approach is consistent with the one recommended above. It does not deal with the whole problem, which obviously involves much more than simply the labor-management relationship and must be attacked in a variety of different ways.

If the foregoing review and analysis of the search for a policy governing employer free speech proves anything, it is that the ideal solution, if indeed there is one, is not likely to be attained. But surely the goal is worthy of pursuit.

NOTES

1. Section 8(a)(1) of the National Labor Relations Act, as amended, makes it an unfair labor practice for an employer to "interfere with, restrain, or coerce" employees in the exercise of their rights to organize, bargain collectively, and engage in other concerted activities, which are guaranteed in § 7.

This provision is the same as § 8(1) of the original Wagner Act. Section 8(b)(1), added by the Taft-Hartley amendments, makes it an unfair labor practice for a union to "restrain or coerce" employees in the exercise of rights guaranteed in § 7.

2. Compare *Thornhill* vs. *Alabama*, 310 U.S. 88 (1940), with *Atchison, T. & S. F. Ry.* vs. *Gee*, 139 Fed. 582 (C.C.S.D. Iowa 1905) and *Hughes* vs. *Superior Court*, 339 U.S. 460 (1950).

3. See Chapter 5.

4. The following is a partial list of articles and notes devoted exclusively to this subject: Bloom, "Freedom of Communication Under the Labor Relations Act," *N.Y.U. Eighth Annual Conference on Labor* (1955), 219; Burke, "Employer Free Speech," 26 *Fordham L. Rev.* (1957), 266; Koretz, "Employer Interference with Union Organization Versus Employer Free Speech," 29 *Geo. Wash. L. Rev.* (1960), 399; Mittenthal, "Employer Speech—A Life Cycle," 5 *Lab. L.J.* (1954), 101; Sinsheimer, "Employer Free Speech—A Comparative Analysis," 14 *U. Chi. L. Rev.* (1947), 617; Sinsheimer, "What May Properly Be Done by Employers and Unions in Relation to Elections Before the National Labor Relations Board," 12 *U. Fla. L. Rev.* (1959), 423; Stochaj, "Free Speech Policies," 8 *Lab. L. J.* (1957), 531; Wirtz, "The New National Labor Relations Board; Herein of 'Employer Persuasion,'" 49 *Nw. U. L. Rev.* (1954), 594; Wollett and Rowen, "Employer Speech and Related Issues," 16 *Ohio St. L. J.* (1955), 380; Wyle and Englander, "'Free Speech' or Lawful Coercion?," 5 *Lab. L. J.* (1954), 270; Note, "The Coercive Character of Employer Speech: Context and Setting," 43 *Geo. L. J.* (1955), 405; Note, "Limitations upon an Employer's Right of Noncoercive Free Speech," 38 *Va. L. Rev.* (1952), 1037; 14 *U. Chi. L. Rev.* (1946), 104.

5. E.g., *Union Pacific Stages, Inc.*, 2 NLRB 471 (1936), enforcement denied, 99 F. 2d 153 (9th Cir. 1938).

6. 1 NLRB Ann. Rep. 73 (1936) (italics added).

7. 3 NLRB Ann. Rep. 59 (1939).

8. *Ibid.*, at 59-60.

9. Cox, "Some Aspects of the Labor Management Relations Act, 1947," pt. 1, 61 *Harv. L. Rev.* (1947), 1, 15.

10. *NLRB* vs. *Falk Corp.*, 102 F. 2d 383, 389 (7th Cir. 1939).

11. *International Ass'n of Machinists* vs. *NLRB*, 311 U.S. 72, 78 (1940).

12. *Thornhill* vs. *Alabama*, 310 U.S. 88, 102 (1940).

13. 14 NLRB 346 (1939).

14. *Ford Motor Co.* vs. *NLRB*, 114 F. 2d 905, 913 (6th Cir. 1940), cert. denied, 312 U.S. 689 (1941).

15. Note, 38 *Va. L. Rev.* (1952), 1037, 1039-40, and cases there cited.

16. *NLRB* vs. *Virginia Electric & Power Co.*, 314 U.S. 469, 477 (1941).

17. 44 NLRB 404 (1942).

18. 132 F. 2d 390 (4th Cir. 1942), aff'd, 319 U.S. 533 (1943).

19. 44 NLRB 121 (1942).

20. *Ibid.*, at 133.

21. 134 F. 2d 993 (2d Cir.), cert. denied, 320 U.S. 768 (1943).

22. Note, 38 *Va. L. Rev.* (1952), 1037, 1042-43, and cases there cited.

23. 323 U.S. 516 (1945).

24. *Ibid.*, at 548.

25. *Ibid.*, at 543-44.

26. *Republic Drill & Tool Co.*, 66 NLRB 955 (1946).

27. *Oval Wood Disk Co.*, 62 NLRB 1129 (1945).
28. 60 NLRB 1381 (1945).
29. *Ibid.*, at 1385-86.
30. 70 NLRB 802 (1946).
31. *Ibid.*, at 805.
32. *Ibid.*, at 812.
33. *NLRB* vs. *Clark Bros. Co.*, 163 F. 2d 373 (2d Cir. 1947).
34. *Ibid.*, at 376.
35. *Ibid.*, (italics added).
36. Hearings before Committee on Labor and Public Welfare, 80th Cong., 1st Sess. 302, 304 (1947).
37. S. Rep. No. 105, 80th Cong., 1st Sess. 23-24 (1947).
38. 77 NLRB 577 (1948).
39. *Ibid.*, at 578.
40. Note, 38 *Va. L. Rev.* (1952), 1037, 1050.
41. 89 NLRB 1363 (1950).
42. 96 NLRB 608 (1951).
43. See *May Department Stores*, 59 NLRB 976 (1944), enforced as modified, 154 F. 2d 533 (8th Cir. 1946), cert. denied, 329 U.S. 725 (1946).
44. *Bonwit Teller, Inc.*, 96 NLRB 608, 617 (1951).
45. *Ibid.*, at 612.
46. *Ibid.*
47. *Bonwit Teller, Inc.* vs. *NLRB*, 197 F. 2d 640 (2d Cir. 1952), cert. denied, 345 U.S. 905 (1953).
48. The United States Supreme Court had so decided in *Republic Aviation Corp.* vs. *NLRB*, 324 U.S. 793 (1945).
49. May Department Stores, *supra*, note 43.
50. *Bonwit Teller, Inc.* vs. *NLRB*, 197 F. 2d 640, 645 (2d Cir. 1952).
51. *Ibid.*, at 646.
52. E.g., *Metropolitan Auto Parts, Inc.*, 99 NLRB 401 (1952); *Onondago Pottery Co.*, 100 NLRB 1143 (1952); *Wilson & Co.*, 100 NLRB 1512 (1952); *National Screw & Mfg. Co. of California*, 101 NLRB 1360 (1952).
53. 102 NLRB 1634 (1953).
54. Mittenthal, *supra*, note 4, at 105.
55. *NLRB* vs. *American Tube Bending Co.*, 205 F. 2d 45, 46 (2d Cir. 1953).
56. 107 NLRB 427 (1953).
57. 107 NLRB 400 (1953).
58. *Ibid.*, at 405-06.
59. *Ibid.*, at 406.
60. *Ibid.*, at 407.
61. See *May Department Stores*, *supra*, note 43; *Marshall Field & Co.*, 98 NLRB 88, enforced as modified, 200 F. 2d 375 (7th Cir. 1952).
62. *Livingston Shirt Corp.*, 107 NLRB 400, 408-09 (1953).
63. *Ibid.*, at 410.
64. *Peerless Plywood Co.*, 107 NLRB 427, 429 (1953).
65. *Ibid.*, at 430.
66. *Ibid.*
67. See, for example, the dissenting opinions of Member Murdock in both cases. 107 NLRB at 410-27, 431-35. See also the discussion herein on pp. 51-52.

68. 102 NLRB 581 (1953).
69. See note 61, *supra.*
70. *NLRB* vs. *F. W. Woolworth Co.,* 214 F. 2d 78 (6th Cir. 1954).
71. *Ibid.,* at 82.
72. 112 NLRB 1153 (1955).
73. *United Steelworkers of America* vs. *NLRB,* 243 F. 2d 593, 596 (D.C. Cir. 1956).
74. *Supra,* note 72, at 1154.
75. *Supra,* note 73, at 600.
76. See *Republic Aviation Corp.* vs. *NLRB,* 324 U.S. 793 (1945); *NLRB* vs. *Babcock & Wilcox Co.,* 351 U.S. 105 (1956).
77. 115 NLRB 840 (1956).
78. *NLRB* vs. *Avondale Mills,* 242 F. 2d 669 (5th Cir. 1957).
79. *NLRB* vs. *United Steelworkers of America,* 357 U.S. 357 (1958). Justices Black and Douglas dissented in both cases. The Chief Justice dissented in *Avondale Mills.*
80. *Ibid.,* at 362-63.
81. *Ibid.,* at 363-64.
82. Koretz, *supra,* note 4, at 408-09.
83. Cox, "The Labor Decisions of the Supreme Court at the October Term 1957," in *1958 Proceedings Section of Labor Relations Law,* American Bar Association 12, 29.
84. See Koretz, *supra,* note 4, at 409-10.
85. E.g., *NLRB* vs. *Shirlington Supermarket,* 224 F. 2d 649 (4th Cir. 1955), cert. denied, 350 U.S. 914 (1955).
86. See p. 36.
87. H.R. 3020, 80th Cong., 1st Sess. § 8(d) (1947).
88. S. 1126, 80th Cong., 1st Sess. § 8(c) (1947) (italics added).
89. Cox, *supra,* note 9, at 19.
90. 13 NLRB Ann. Rep. 49 (1948).
91. Koretz, *supra,* note 4, at 411-12.
92. *Ibid.,* at 412.
93. *Ibid.,* at 412-13.
94. See Funke, "Board Regulation of Pre-Election Conduct," 36 *Texas L. Rev.* (1958), 893, 899-900; 1959 *Report of the Committee on Development of the Law under National Labor Relations Act,* Section of Labor Relations Law, American Bar Association 28-31.
95. *Happ Bros. Co.,* 90 NLRB 1513, 1533 (1950).
96. *Chock Full O' Nuts* 120 NLRB 1296, 1298 (1958).
97. *Ibid.,* at 1299.
98. *Paula Shoe Co.,* 121 NLRB 673, 676 (1958).
99. *International Union of Electrical Workers* vs. *NLRB,* 46 L.R.R.M. 2534, 2536 (D.C. Cir., June 30, 1960).
100. Koretz, *supra,* note 4, at 413.
101. For a more detailed discussion see Sinsheimer, "What May Properly Be Done by Employers and Unions in Relation to Elections Before the National Labor Relations Board," *supra,* note 4.
102. *Chicopee Mfg. Co.,* 107 NLRB 106, 107 (1953).
103. *Supplee-Biddle-Steltz Co.,* 116 NLRB 458, 460 (1956).
104. E.g., *Avildsen Tools and Machines, Inc.,* 112 NLRB 1021 (1955), in

which the Board found one of the employer's statements to be an illegal threat, and the others to be privileged "predictions."

105. Wollett and Rowen, *supra*, note 4, at 395.

106. See Wirtz, *supra*, note 4, at 598-99; Wollett and Rowen, *supra*, note 4, at 395-99, 401-02.

107. Wirtz, *supra*, note 4, at 611.

108. 107 NLRB 427, 430 (1953).

109. *Higgins, Inc.*, 106 NLRB 845 (1953).

110. *Diamond State Poultry Co.*, 107 NLRB 3 (1953).

111. *NLRB* vs. *Federbush Co.*, 121 F. 2d 954, 957 (2d Cir. 1941).

112. Cox, *Law and the National Labor Policy* 44 (1960).

113. *Ibid.*

114. See 48 Lab. Rel. Rep. 126 (May 29, 1961).

115. 1959 *Report of the Committee on Development of the Law under National Labor Relations Act, supra,* note 94, at 29.

116. *Ibid.*

3

THE OBLIGATION TO BARGAIN

IN GOOD FAITH

ROBBEN W. FLEMING

Professor of Law, University of Illinois

The duty to bargain, which was not even included in the Wagner Act as originally submitted to the Congress,[1] is now universally recognized as one of the key concepts in collective bargaining. Policy decisions of the next decade in this area will exert enormous influence on the future course of collective bargaining. One can, with a reasonable degree of confidence, predict that two of the most important questions involved in the duty to bargain litigation of the sixties will be:

1. "To what extent will the new issues which are likely to arise be subject to mandatory bargaining?"—a new phase of an old question, in which "job security" (*Order of R. R. Telegraphers* vs. *Chicago and N. W. R. Co.*[2]), and "internal union affairs" (*Allen Bradley Co.* vs. *NLRB*[3]) are likely to be in the forefront; and

2. "Insofar as such demands are held to be subject to voluntary bargaining, what role will the government play?"—which, in turn involves an analysis of the *Borg-Warner*[4] and *Insurance Agents'*[5] cases.

That the above questions are likely to receive primary attention in the years immediately ahead is not to say that all other questions will be unimportant. For example, roving reconnaissance parties will surely continue to probe for kinds of information which must be furnished in bargaining,[6] and conclusions as to whether a given attitude or approach to collective bargaining constitutes "good faith" will always have to be drawn.[7] Nevertheless, the important policy question appears to be what role the government is going to play in shaping collective bargaining, and that question resides within the suggested framework.

An elaborate history of the origin and development of the good faith bargaining requirement would contribute little to the present analysis. A brief history is, however, both warranted and necessary.

A Look at the Past

Though the Wagner Act was introduced in the 74th Congress without subsection 5 of Section 8, the language was added by the Senate Committee after Lloyd K. Garrison, chairman of the old National Labor Board, insisted that it was necessary in order to make the right of self-organization effective.[8] Even so, the legislative history of the subsection leaves considerable doubt as to what the Congress had in mind. Senator Wagner once asserted that the Act would "not compel anyone to make a compact of any kind if no terms are arrived at that are satisfactory to him,"[9] but later told the Senate that an employer would be obligated "to negotiate in good faith with his employees' representatives; to match their proposals, if unacceptable, with counterproposals; and to make every reasonable effort to reach an agreement."[10] And Senator Walsh assured his colleagues that the Act would only lead employee representatives to the door of their employer, without going beyond it,[11] but at the same time expressed confidence that "the employer will deal reasonably with his employees."[12]

As a matter of fact, administrative boards, operating in the labor-management relations area, had for some years prior to the Wagner Act been dealing with the concept of a duty to bargain. The Railway Labor Board, created by the Transportation Act of 1920,[13] had found that a similar provision in that act required "an honest effort by the parties to decide in conference. If they cannot decide all matters in dispute in conference, it is their duty to there decide all that is possible. . . ."[14] The Board also referred to "good faith" as essential to the parties' negotiations.[15]

Subsequently, under the National Industrial Recovery Act of 1933, section 7(a) required that each code of fair competition include a provision "that employees shall have the right to organize and bargain collectively through representatives of their own choosing."[16] The National Labor Board, in making its first official attempt to define the "right" thus conferred, decided that it involved an implicit reciprocal duty in employers to bargain,[17] and that this duty involved something more than a bare requirement that the employer meet and confer with employee representatives.[18] "True collective bargaining involves more than the holding of conferences and the exchange of pleasantries. . . . While the law does not compel the parties to reach an agreement, it does contemplate that both parties will approach the negotiations with an open mind and will make a reasonable effort to reach a common ground of agreement."[19] This "incontestably sound principle" was followed by the National Labor Relations Board while it operated under a joint resolution in the year before the Wagner Act was passed,[20] and by similar boards after the passage of the act. Indeed, as Justice Brennan was to say so many years later in the *Insurance Agents'* case, practically, it could hardly have been otherwise.[21]

Whatever doubts remained with respect to the above were laid to rest with the passage of the Taft-Hartley Act. A new section, 8(d), was made to read:

> For the purpose of this section, to bargain collectively is the performance of the mutual obligation of the employer and the representative of the employees to meet at reasonable times and confer in good faith with respect to wages, hours, and other terms and conditions of employment, or the negotiation of an agreement, or any question arising thereunder, and the execution of a written contract incorporating any agreement reached if requested by either party, but such obligation does not compel either party to agree to a proposal or require the making of a concession. . . .[22]

At the same time section 8(b)(3) imposed upon labor organizations a duty to bargain corresponding to that of the employer.[23]

Having decided that the law required the parties to do more than meet in order to fulfill the good faith bargaining requirement, the board and the courts could not escape a further definition of what constituted good faith. Moreover, this question could arise in quite different contexts. The most common situation, and the one with which we are here primarily concerned, would involve negotiations over a first or renewed contract. But it could occur after the signing of a contract, either because the union wished to bargain about an item not included in the contract,[24] or over a grievance growing out of a difference as to the meaning of the contract.[25]

In its early decisions under the Wagner Act, the NLRB decided that "good faith" in bargaining meant a sincere desire to reach an agreement, though this definition was variously phrased.[26] The bargainer's state of mind was the decisive factor, but mental state had to be inferred from totality of conduct. Affirmative and negative guideposts were soon set up. An employer must actively participate in the negotiations,[27] not just listen and reject union proposals.[28] He must also make counterproposals when demands of the union were not satisfactory to him.[29] On the negative side, the employer could not engage in stalling tactics,[30] could not suddenly shift his position when agreement was near,[31] could not reject provisions routinely placed in most contracts, such as recognition or arbitration clauses,[32] or withhold agreement on trivial matters, such as the use of company bulletin boards.[33] Certain types of conduct, like refusal to sign an agreement once reached, were held to be so clearly inconsistent with good faith as to be *per se* violations of the act.[34]

"Good faith" bargaining could hardly exist in a vacuum. The parties had to be bargaining about something. The act said that the union represented the employees with respect to "wages, hours, and other terms and conditions of employment."[35] Suppose the bargaining demand could not reasonably be said to fall within that classification? Or suppose it did, but to comply would result in the violation of some other law? These were problems which the NLRB could not avoid, and the result was a classification system which categorized bargaining demands as illegal, voluntary, or mandatory. Illegal demands were disposed of with relative ease. If, for instance, the union sought a type of union security outlawed by the Taft-Hartley Act, the employer could refuse to bargain without being guilty of an unfair labor practice.[36] But the difference between voluntary and mandatory subjects, and the results which should flow from such a distinction, were not always clear. As early as 1939 the NLRB held that an employer could not insist that the union organize the employer's competitors before an agreement was signed, because this was not within the area of bargaining required by the above language.[37] And in 1940 the Board ruled that an employer's proposal that a union post a performance bond was outside the area of mandatory bargaining and could not be insisted upon as a condition precedent to the agreement.[38] These rulings were subsequently sustained by the courts.[39] On the other hand, "wages, hours, and other terms and conditions of employment" were held to include such items as Christmas bonuses,[40] the rental of company-owned houses,[41] the price of meals furnished by the employer,[42] and free time for coffee breaks during working hours.[43]

Mandatory subjects, said the Board, could be bargained to an impasse without being guilty of an unfair labor practice, but voluntary subjects, which were outside the statutory language, could not. This was the general status of the law when the *Borg-Warner*[44] case came before the Supreme Court in 1958. And it is to that case, and the analytical framework which it provides for the disposition of future cases, that we must now turn.

THE BORG-WARNER FRAMEWORK

Shortly after the UAW was recognized as the bargaining agent for the Wooster Division of Borg-Warner in 1952, it presented bargaining demands. The Company, in turn, submitted counter-proposals, two of which called for: (1) a "ballot" clause, calling for a pre-strike vote of employees (union and non-union) as to the employer's last offer, and (2) a "recognition" clause which excluded the international, which had been certified, and substituted the local. The NLRB held that insistence upon either of these clauses amounted to a refusal to bargain, and ordered the company to cease insisting upon either clause as a condition precedent for accepting a collective bargaining agreement.[45] When the Board sought to enforce its order the Court of Appeals set aside that portion of the order relating to the ballot clause, but upheld the Board's order as to the recognition clause.[46] The Supreme Court then agreed with the Board on both counts.[47]

Little time need be wasted on the "recognition" clause aspect of the case, for none of the tribunals thought that the company could maintain its position in this respect. The Board's certification ran to the international union, the act obliged the company to sign an agreement once reached with the bargaining agent, and there was no ground for refusing to do so.

The ballot clause, however, raised quite a different question. The clause provided that, as to all non-arbitrable issues (which eventually included modification, amendment or termination of the contract), there would be a 30-day negotiation period after which, before the union could strike, there would have to be a secret ballot taken among all employees in the unit (union and non-union) on the company's last offer. In the event a majority of the employees rejected the last offer, the company would have an opportunity, within 72 hours, of making a new proposal and having a vote on it prior to any strike.

From the very first, the union made it clear that the ballot clause was wholly unacceptable. The company nevertheless insisted. A strike ensued which was ultimately settled by an agreement which contained both of the controversial clauses. Prior to the signing of the agreement the international filed unfair labor practice charges, contending that insistence by the company on inclusion of these clauses constituted a refusal to bargain. The trial examiner specifically found that neither side was guilty of bad faith, but nevertheless concluded that the company was guilty of a *per se* unfair labor practice. He reasoned that both of the clauses which were in contention were outside the scope of mandatory bargaining, and that the company's insistence upon them over the union's opposition amounted to a refusal to bargain as to mandatory subjects of collective bargaining.

Though the Supreme Court ultimately sustained the NLRB, four of the justices thought the ruling on the ballot clause was wrong. In large part this was because of a deep-seated feeling that Congress intended "to assure the parties to a proposed collective bargaining agreement the greatest degree of freedom in their negotiations, and to require the Board to remain as aloof as possible from regulation of the bargaining process in its substantive aspects."[48]

The *Borg-Warner* decision has been subject to much criticism,[49] and for that reason, and its importance to the future, it requires further analysis.

Given the *Borg-Warner* facts with respect to the ballot clause, it would seem that the Board, and subsequently the courts, had open at least three alternative lines of decision: (1) to hold that the ballot clause was a mandatory subject of bargaining within the meaning of "wages, hours, and other terms and conditions of employment"; (2) to hold that the clause was non-mandatory, but that insisting upon bargaining about it was not, *per se*, an unfair labor practice, thus requiring that the decision as to the presence or absence of an unfair labor practice be based upon the *total* situation; or (3) to hold, as the Board and the Supreme Court did, that insistence upon such a clause was *per se*, an unfair labor practice. Of these various alternatives the Sixth Circuit, from which the appeal came, thought that the first was the best. In other words, it thought that the ballot clause could quite easily be brought within the area of mandatory bargaining. There was precedent for this;[50] management and labor ideas as to the proper scope of bargaining had undergone considerable change in recent years,[51] and the ballot clause looked to the court like a variation of the no-strike clause which had already been held to be bargainable.[52] Finally, the Circuit Court thought that the case was clearly distinguishable from the *Corsicana Cotton Mills* case[53] in which the company had insisted that the contract contain a provision to the effect that non-union employees should have a right to attend union meetings and vote upon the provisions of the contract negotiated by the union as bargaining agent. In the present case non-union employees would be permitted to express their views on but one phase of the contract, and one which was of vital importance to them.[54]

That the Supreme Court might have taken the view that the ballot clause was a mandatory bargaining subject is hardly open to doubt. Though directing his dissent toward another point, Justice Harlan noted his disagreement with the Court's conclusion on this point.[55] For the moment, however, discussion of the court's decision on this point can better be delayed. The question inevitably arises, and can be thrown in better perspective, when we discuss current job security and internal union affairs bargaining demands.

The main thrust of the Harlan dissent in *Borg-Warner* was directed at the majority's conclusion that the insistence upon the ballot clause was, *per se*, an unfair labor practice. To so hold when the demand was admittedly legal would, argued the dissent, ignore the trial examiner's affirmative finding that the employer had bargained in good faith, and place the Board in the position both of unduly restricting the scope of bargaining, and coming to the aid of the party having the weaker bargaining power.

Most of the criticism of the *Borg-Warner* decision has been directed at its alleged interference with the scope of collective bargaining. In the actual case, the realities of bargaining were that the Borg-Warner company was the stronger of the two antagonists. Thus when the union refused to discuss the ballot clause, the company simply sat tight, weathered a month-and-a-half strike, and then obtained the contract it wanted—including the ballot clause. In the absence of interference by the NLRB or the courts, the company achieved what it wanted in bargaining. It did this while continuing to engage in what the trial examiner found was good-faith bargaining. The Board's decision, sustained by the Supreme Court, had the effect of changing the bargaining results, for it ordered the company to cease and desist from insisting upon inclusion of the ballot proposal in the contract. Viewed from the vantage point of sound collective bargaining, was this a good or a bad result? There will be a temptation to answer this question on the basis of whose ox is being gored. Thus company representatives may be inclined to feel that the result is quite outrageous, while unions may be entirely satisfied. It is not difficult to demonstrate that this is hardly an adequate basis for reaching a conclusion. Take an example which has recently been in the news. The UAW has been complaining that at the very time that Ford insists upon the necessity for holding the line on wage increases it has been passing out liberal bonuses to its executives.[56] Suppose in bargaining the UAW took the position that the new contract must contain a clause in which the company agreed to refrain from giving any bonuses to executives during the life of the new contract. Presumably such a bargaining demand would be legal, in the sense that there is no reason why the company could not agree to such a clause if it wanted to. At the same time the demand could hardly be said to fall within the mandatory bargaining area, since it would have nothing directly to do with "wages, hours, and other terms and conditions of employment." A reasonable argument could be made by the UAW that it could not be expected to exercise restraint on the wage front at the same time that the company passed out handsome bonuses to executives. Therefore the union would not necessarily abandon a good faith bargaining posture by insisting upon inclusion of the clause in the contract. Could the union bargain to an impasse on this issue? Under the majority rule in *Borg-Warner* it could not, for insistence upon a non-mandatory subject would, *per se*, constitute a refusal to bargain. Under the minority rule, such insistence would not necessarily be an unfair labor practice; the decision would presumably hinge on consideration of other factors before a final answer could be given. Would industry representatives be outraged by application of the majority's decision to this set of facts? Would labor people be pleased with it?

If the Ford-UAW example seems far-fetched and unlikely, take another case which is surely within the ken of human experience. Suppose a financial tycoon with a well established reputation for buying up companies, milking them, and then dumping them, buys a small company which a union has just organized. Fearful of what is about to happen to them, the union demands in bargaining that the company adhere to past practices with respect to executive compensation. There would appear to be nothing illegal about such a demand, the union could certainly demonstrate a good faith concern in the subject area, and yet there would be no doubt that the demand was not within the mandatory classification in so far as bargaining is concerned. Quite conceivably the union would have the bargaining strength to enforce the demand. The *Borg-Warner* rule would prevent it from doing so. Would company representatives still feel that this was an outrageous result? Would unions still think it appropriate?

The point of this analysis is, of course, that quite apart from the voluntary-mandatory dichotomy, which will be discussed at greater length elsewhere, the *Borg-Warner* rule does have the effect of restricting bargaining. In the actual case the company had the power, while bargaining in good faith on a legal matter, to achieve its bargaining demand. The Board and the Supreme Court would not let it do so. In the hypothetical example, the union might well have achieved its bargaining objective, while bargaining in good faith on a legal demand. The *Borg-Warner* rule could prevent it from doing so. It can be said that any other rule would simply place a premium on bargaining power, and is therefore undesirable. This may be true, but exactly the same criticism could be made with respect to subject matter in the mandatory category, and in such a case neither the Board nor the courts would interfere. In fact, the essence of the American Labor-management policy is freedom to exert economic pressure on each other. Rarely is the strength of the parties in perfect balance. Therefore, the policy contemplates sheer bargaining power as one of the principal determinants of a settlement. But it can be argued that even if this is so, bargaining power ought to be confined to the limits of mandatory subject matter. Otherwise the base for industrial strife is unduly broadened. By analogy, one can argue that we have a minimum wage law which prevents a powerful company from imposing extremely low wages on a weak union, and restrictions on union membership demands which prevent a powerful union from imposing objectionable union security requirements on a weak and unwilling company. By defining collective bargaining in relation to "wages, hours, and terms and conditions of employment," perhaps Congress meant to limit the use of bargaining power to those areas. There are two difficulties with this conclusion. The first is that the phrase "wages, hours, and terms and conditions of employment" is so broad a term that it is impossible to say exactly what Congress had in mind. And the second is that when 8(d) was written into the Wagner Act, at the time of the Taft-Hartley amendments, Congress was concerned with the intrusion of the Board into bargaining matters.[57] It was for this reason that 8(d) included the "wages, hours, and terms and conditions of employment" phrase. An order from the Board which would take away what the Borg-Wagner company had gained in collective bargaining would seem to be inconsistent with the Congressional intent. On the other hand, one cannot be certain that Congressmen who would disapprove the *Borg-Warner* rule as applied in that case, might not like it if applied to a union in the exercise of its superior bargaining power.

So long as it is clear that the *Borg-Warner* rule has the effect

of imposing government regulation over what might otherwise
qualify as good-faith collective bargaining, a judgment as to the
desirability of the rule is perhaps better withheld pending further
examination of the mandatory subject matter category.

BARGAINING ISSUES OF THE FUTURE

Bargaining demands which are already known, or are appearing
on the horizon, make two things clear: (1) The Board and the courts
are going to have to go through a searching re-examination of
what constitutes a proper subject for mandatory bargaining; and
(2) Insofar as such subjects are held to be non-mandatory, the
implications of the *Borg-Warner* rule are going to have to be faced.

The *R. R. Telegraphers* case[58] illustrates the kind of issue which
may be expected to arise with increasing frequency in the period
immediately ahead. In that case the Northwestern Railroad sought
to abandon some of its stations. The plan would necessarily result
in the loss of jobs for some of the station agents and telegraphers
who were members of the union. The union thereupon sought to
negotiate a collective bargaining agreement which would include
the rule that no position in existence on a certain date could be
abolished or discontinued except by agreement between the carrier and the union. The District Court thought that the contract
proposal related to "rates of pay, rules, and working conditions,"
the Circuit Court of Appeals said that this conclusion was "clearly
erroneous," and the Supreme Court agreed with the District Court.
In doing so it said:

> The employment of many of these station agents inescapably hangs
> on the number of railroad stations that will either be completely
> abandoned or consolidated with other stations. And, in the collec-
> tive bargaining world today, there is nothing strange about agree-
> ments that affect the permanency of employment.[59]

Four of the justices, however, did not agree. They said:

> It is not to be doubted that a carrier and a labor union, representing
> the carrier's employees, lawfully may bargain about and agree
> upon matters in mitigation of hardships to employees who are
> displaced by railroad unifications or abandonments; but they may
> not agree, nor may any regulatory body order, that no jobs shall
> be abolished, and thus defeat unifications or abandonments required
> in the public interest.[60]

The minority went even further and said that the union's demand was not a lawfully bargainable subject, that the carrier could not lawfully accept it, and that a strike to force its acceptance would be one to force a violation of the law.[61]

This decision is of particular interest because of the present emphasis in collective bargaining on job security. Technological changes are altering historic employment patterns, with a general exodus from production to service industries. In 1960 blue-collar jobs for men dropped by 1,300,000 but white-collar jobs rose by 600,000.[62] Approximately 400,000 railroad jobs have been abolished in the last five years, and the unions fear that mergers now under discussion will add another 200,000 to this total.[63] More steel was poured last year by 460,000 production workers than 540,000 had produced ten years earlier, and 200,000 aircraft workers were dropped in the shift from planes to missiles.[64]

In an effort to protect their members, unions have devised a wide assortment of bargaining demands. These range from insistence that no plant be moved without the consent of the union, to guarantees against plant closings, to rigid retention of employees and preservation of wage rates despite any changes which may take place, to transfer rights including guarantees against loss in the sale of the employee's home or cancellation of his lease. Several agreements along such lines have already been reached.[65] One of the most recent involves the American Cable and Radio Corporation and the Communications Workers of America.[66] The new contract provides that no worker shall be laid off or downgraded as a result of technological change. If fewer employees are required because of automation, the company is obliged to place the dislodged workers in other jobs carrying an equivalent title and pay rate. Another clause in the contract protects the workers in the event the long-rumored merger between American Cable and RCA Communications takes place. Workers could then choose between keeping their present jobs and pay, or taking advantage of any benefits which might be provided in the Federal legislation which would be required in order to authorize the merger.

Which, if any, of these demands are within the mandatory bargaining requirements of the Act, and what will be the result of holding that they are voluntary? Before attempting to answer the first question it may be well to pause and examine a recent decision of the NLRB. In the *Fiberboard* case[67] the employer had bargained with the union for a unit of some 50 maintenance and powerhouse employees since 1937. Just before the existing 1959 contract was to expire, the employer decided to contract out its maintenance work. He thereupon advised the union that bargaining on a new contract would be pointless. The union had not previously been informed of the employer's intention, although the feasibility of contracting out such work had been under consideration by the employer for some time. An unfair labor practice charge was filed against the employer, alleging that he was under a duty to bargain with the union about contracting out work. In a split decision the NLRB held that the employer's duty to bargain legitimately covered matters affecting employees while employed, as well as termination and post-termination rights and obligations, but that it did not cover the question of whether the employment relationship should exist. The Board added that Congress did not intend to compel bargaining over basic management decision, such as whether and to what extent to risk capital and managerial effort.

If the dissent in the *R. R. Telegrapher's* case is right (and the analogy is not perfect because of other legislation in the railroad field), many of the above demands of unions might be said to be against the public interest—assuming there is a public interest in "efficiency." And under the *Fiberboard* decision there is surely a fine line between bargaining that employment will not be diminished during the life of a contract by the closing of a plant, and bargaining that employment will not be diminished by subcontracting after a contract has expired. If the later is nonmandatory because Congress did not intend to compel bargaining over basic management decisions, the former is hardly less so. Yet these are among the significant bargaining issues of the period ahead. Unions will be derelict in serving their members if they do not put forth demands designed to protect job security. Moreover, "the fact that trade unions may restrict the rate at which new machinery and processes are introduced does not necessarily mean that the product of industry is being limited, as employers, left to themselves, may make changes at a rate faster than the optimum."[68] If bargaining demands having to do with job security are not within the mandatory bargaining area of "wages, hours, and terms and conditions of employment," the net result will be that one of the most important bargaining problems of the period will be outside the main stream of the very legislation which was designed to encourage collective bargaining. Presumably there is nothing illegal about such demands; therefore if they are not mandatory they must be classified as voluntary. The agreements already cited indicate that many managements will willingly bargain over such issues. Others may not. What then? Does the *Borg-Warner* rule mean that unions, by insisting, will be guilty of a *per se* unfair labor practice even though the demands are legal, are advanced in the utmost good faith, and are clearly related to the basic needs of the membership? Finally, if such demands are non-mandatory, and will result in an unfair labor practice charge if pushed to an impasse, will collective bargaining legislation be serving its basic purpose?

There is another line of cases, represented by *Allen Bradley* vs. *NLRB*,[69] which seems destined for the Supreme Court, and which may clarify the duty to bargain. In those cases[70] the union threatened to, and did, fine members who crossed the picket line during a strike. In the principal case some of the affected employees then filed unfair labor practice charges with the NLRB, contending that the union had violated Section 8(b)(1)(A) of the Labor Management Relations Act by depriving them of their Section 7 rights to refrain from organizational or other activities. This charge was dismissed by the NLRB because of the provision to Section 8(b)(1)(A) that the language of the paragraph "shall not impair the right of a labor organization to prescribe its own rules with respect to the acquisition or retention of membership therein. . . ."[71] At the same time other employees filed a similar charge with the Wisconsin Employment Relations Board, alleging a violation of the state act. Though the Board sustained the charge, it was ultimately reversed by the Wisconsin Supreme Court on preemption grounds.[72] This series of events, which took place between 1956 and 1959, caused the company to adopt a new tactic. When bargaining rolled around in 1959 it demanded that one of the two following alternative clauses be included in the contract:

> Neither the Company nor the Union nor its members will interfere with, restrain or coerce by discipline, discharge, fine or otherwise, any employee in the exercise of his rights guaranteed by Section 7

of the Labor-Management Relations Act, including the right to refrain from any or all of the specified activities.

Or

Neither the Company nor the Union nor its members will inter-fere with, restrain or coerce by discipline, discharge, fine or other-wise, any employee in the exercise of his right to self-organization, to form, join or assist labor organizations, to bargain collectively through representatives of his own choosing, and to engage in other concerted activities for the purpose of collective bargaining or other mutual aid or protection, or his right to refrain from any or all such activities.[73]

In submitting these proposals the company stated that it was open to discussion as to the phraseology, but that it would stand firmly on the principle set forth in the clauses. The union took the position that this was not a proper subject for collective bargain-ing because it pertained to internal union affairs. The company clearly bargained in good faith in all other respects.

When the company insisted upon inclusion of clauses like the one set forth above, the union filed unfair labor practice charges. Relying principally on the *Borg-Warner* case, the NLRB held for the union.[74] The Seventh Circuit refused to enforce the Board's order on the ground that this case was distinguishable from *Borg-Warner* in that the clauses in question were a subject of manda-tory bargaining. The Court said:

. . . the reasoning of the Court [in *Borg-Warner*] evidently was based on the premise that the manner and means by which the Union decided to call a strike was of no concern to the employer, that it was of concern only to the employees and their union. In contrast, the subject matter of the proposal in the instant case is of mutual concern to the employee and his employer. The situation is more akin to the 'no-strike' clause which the Court in Borg-Warner recognized as concerned with 'relations between the employer and the employees' and, therefore, a proper matter for collective bar-gaining. The purpose of such a clause was to prevent a strike by the employees during the period covered by the agreement so that the employer might retain the benefit of their services. The purpose of the clauses proposed here was to permit employees to work both for their benefit and that of the employer.[75]

One need only go back into history a bit to illustrate the dubiety of the distinction between the non-mandatory ballot clause in

Borg-Warner and the mandatory discipline clause in *Allen Bradley*. In 1948 Allis Chalmers and its employees suffered a costly strike at the company's West Allis plant. The local union leadership, then dominated by Harold Christoffel, who was commonly believed to be a Communist, engaged in the most outrageous ballot-stuffing practices in calling the strike.[76] After several years of continuing conflict, Christoffel was dislodged and the local union placed under an administrator from the international union. Thereafter, in 1950, the parties signed a contract which contained the following "democratic processes" clause:

> The Union shall conduct elections of the Bargaining Committeemen, and other Union representatives designated in this agreement, and the Local Union delegates to the International Union Convention in accordance with the general safeguards of the International Union Constitution and Local Union By-Laws, on the date of signing this agreement, including adequate notice of nominations and elections, adequate opportunity to nominate candidates, reasonable eligibility requirements for nominees, an adequate protection against fraud and error in the determination of election results. . . . The said elections shall be conducted by secret ballot by the Union on the Company's premises. The Company shall furnish suitable facilities. Members losing time from work in voting shall be paid at average earned rate. A voting schedule shall be arranged in accordance with the practices of the National Labor Relations Board in effect on the date of signing this agreement.[77]

The purpose of the clause was obviously to prevent a repetition of the 1948 experience. Both parties desired this. Suppose they had not. Suppose the company had simply insisted on such a provision in bargaining. Would it have been guilty of an unfair labor practice because this was not a mandatory bargaining subject? If so, can one easily distinguish the *Allen Bradley* case? If, in that case, as the Circuit Court said, "The purpose of the clauses proposed here was to permit employees to work both for their benefit and for that of the employer,"[78] did the democratic processes clause have a different purpose?

There are cases, of course, in which the employer quite clearly interferes with the internal processes of the union. A recent example involved a situation in which the employer insisted upon including in the new contract stipulations which were designed to limit the union's right to select the members of its bargaining and grievance committees.[79] But there is a gray area, particularly as it relates to the procedures for calling a strike and any continuation of work during the strike, in which it is hard to say that contractual clauses do not relate to working conditions. What more basic working condition is there than whether there is going to be any work at all?

Until it is overturned or modified, *Borg-Warner* must be regarded as the law. Critics will feel that it represents an unduly restrictive interpretation of the phrase "wages, hours, and terms and conditions of employment," and that it places the weight of government behind the *status quo*. The danger in an approach having these dual characteristics is that collective bargaining will not remain viable. And if the history of collective bargaining demonstrates anything, it is that change and adjustment are essential to its life cycle.

At least two alternative routes away from *Borg-Warner* are available. The first lies in the direction of liberalizing the interpretation of the "wages, hours, and terms and conditions of employment" phrase. The end result then more nearly becomes *Allen Bradley* than *Borg-Warner*. The price of this approach is enlargement of the mandatory bargaining area, with accompanying governmental pressure towards such bargaining. This may displease Congress which, at the time of the Taft-Hartley amendments in 1947, fairly clearly thought the NLRB was intervening too much in telling the parties what they must bargain about.[80] Such a ruling would doubtless hasten the inclusion of marginal subjects in contracts, for if a subject is once brought into the mandatory bargaining area it becomes more difficult to resist some kind of a compromise without engaging in an unfair labor practice. Liberalization of the scope of mandatory bargaining could, of course, be accompanied by maintenance of the present *Borg-Warner* rule with respect to voluntary subjects. For those who believe in maximum flexibility in the realm of collective bargaining this approach might be thought to combine the worst feature of the present rule with error in exactly the opposite direction. In other words, to expand the mandatory bargaining area is to extend the government's influence over subjects about which the parties *must* bargain. To maintain the *Borg-*

Warner rule is to use the government's influence *against* good faith bargaining on voluntary subjects.

A second route away from *Borg-Warner*, assuming the courts want to take it, is to interpret the phrase "wages, hours, and terms and conditions of employment" conservatively, but find that going to an impasse on voluntary subjects of bargaining is not, *per se*, an unfair labor practice. The principal opponents of this view may be those who fear the power of strong unions over weak managements, or vice versa. Of the two, management opponents may be the more vociferous for fear of further inroads into the so-called management prerogatives.

BARGAINING TACTICS

The *Insurance Agents'* decision,[81] in which union harassing tactics such as the refusal to solicit new business, reporting late at district offices, engaging in "sit-in" mornings rather than doing customary duties, etc., were held not to be inconsistent with good faith bargaining on the part of the union, was not a great surprise. Previous cases has suggested the likelihood of such a result.[82] Much of the comment which the case has evoked has been directed at one of the two following questions: (1) What other tactics may the parties, particularly the employer, use without being guilty of an unfair labor practice? and (2) Will the Frankfurter dissent ultimately come to be the law in such cases?

That the NLRB has changed its rulings since the *Insurance Agents'* decision, is clear. Thus in 1959 the Board would routinely hold that when a union enforced an overtime ban during contract negotiations this was harassing conduct which made the union guilty of an unfair labor practice for refusing to bargain in good faith.[83] By 1960, when a union directed employees to refuse to work overtime and to engage in intermittent work stoppages during bargaining negotiations in order to force the company to agree to a contract, the Board reversed its trial examiner, because of the recent decision in the *Insurance Agents'* case, and held that such tactics were not, in and of themselves, a violation of Section 8(b)(3).[84] In a very recent case one wonders, in fact, whether the Board hasn't gone too far in complying with the Supreme Court's decision. In the *Cheney Lumber Co.* case[85] the union struck in violation of a no-strike clause. The trial examiner thought that this was a refusal to bargain in good faith, but the Board reversed him on the authority of *Insurance Agents'*. It is true that the Taft-Hartley Act does not contain, as does the Wisconsin Employment Peace Act, a specific unfair labor practice grounded on failure to comply with the collective bargaining contract.[86] But is there not a difference between ordering a union to *cease and desist* from engaging in the contract violation, when such a violation is not made an unfair labor practice, and *crediting* the union with good faith in bargaining when it is in violation of the existing contract during negotiations for a new contract?

The fact that unions may now engage in harassing tactics without committing an unfair labor practice has naturally caused speculation as to what tactics the employer might use with like immunity. There have been few cases so far which test the point, and there is little to be gained by restating other analyses of the general problem which have already appeared.[87] The 9th Circuit has suggested in the *Great Falls Employers' Council* case[88] that what is sauce for the goose may also be sauce for the gander. In that case the union was dealing with an association of retail food stores. When the union struck one of them the others promptly locked out their employees. No one doubted that under such economic pressure the lockout was legal, but this was not the crucial point. The locked out employees applied for unemployment compensation under the Montana law. Anticipating that such claims might be granted (though in fact they were subsequently denied), the employers recalled their locked-out employees on a two-day a week basis. This enabled them to earn approximately $16 a week, which apparently disqualified them from unemployment compensation. The union claimed, and the NLRB agreed, that such manipulation of tenure and terms of employment infringed on the employees collective bargaining rights under Section 8(a)(1) and (3). Relying heavily on the *Insurance Agents'* decision and quoting from it, the Circuit Court refused to enforce the Board's order, saying that it was none of the business of the Board "to define through its processes what economic sanctions might be permitted negotiating parties in an 'ideal' or 'balanced' state of collective bargaining."[89]

The remaining question in *Insurance Agents,'* and the one which touched off the Frankfurter dissent, was how far the Court intended to go in promulgating a *per se* rule that a partial strike could not be evidence of a failure to bargain in good faith.[90] Mr. Justice Frankfurter obviously thought the majority intended such a rule. This he thought was wrong, for it would be preferable to hold that the Board could consider such harassing tactics as one link in the chain which might support a finding of bad faith. If the majority did hold as the dissenting members of the court suggest, the rule of the dissent would seem far better. Dealing with partial strikes and harassing tactics is going to be tricky business at best, and any foreclosure of the Board's flexibility by establishing a *per se* rule that harassing tactics cannot constitute an unfair labor practice would be unfortunate.

The long run importance of the *Insurance Agents'* case has to do with neither the harassing tactics, as such, nor the question of whether a *per se* rule was established. The important question relates to the role which the government is going to play in collective bargaining. Note with care some of Mr. Justice Brennan's language in the majority opinion:

> . . . Congress [at the time of the passage of the Wagner Act] was generally not concerned with the substantive terms on which the parties contracted. . . . And in fact criticism of the Board's application of the 'good faith' test arose from the belief that it was forcing employers to yield to union demands if they were to avoid a successful charge of unfair labor practice. . . . Since the Board was not viewed by Congress as an agency which should exercise its powers to arbitrate the parties' substantive solutions of the issues in their bargaining, a check on this apprehended trend was provided by writing the good-faith test of bargaining into Section 8(d) of the Taft-Hartley Act.[91]

> The same problems as to whether positions taken at the bargaining table violate the good-faith test continue to arise under the Act as amended [by the Taft-Hartley Act]. . . . But it remains clear that #8(d) was an attempt by Congress to prevent the Board from controlling the settling of the terms of collective bargaining agreements.[92]

It is apparent from the legislative history of the whole Act that the policy of Congress is to impose a mutual duty upon the parties to confer in good faith with a desire to reach agreement, in the belief that such an approach from both sides of the table promotes the over-all design of achieving industrial peace. . . . Discussion conducted under that standard of good faith may narrow the issues, making the real demands of the parties clearer to each other, and perhaps to themselves, and may encourage an attitude of settlement through give and take. The mainstream of cases before the Board and in the courts reviewing its orders, under the provisions fixing the duty to bargain collectively, is concerned with insuring that the parties should have wide latitude in their negotiations, unrestricted by any governmental power to regulate the substantive solution of their differences.[93]

Why is the above language so important? Because it is basically inconsistent with the approach which the same court took in the *Borg-Warner* case. And which of the two approaches the court takes in the future is of great importance to the collective bargaining process.

Assume, if you wish, that the illegal, mandatory, and voluntary categories into which the NLRB and the courts have so long divided bargaining demands are now too well established to be abandoned. Assume also that the company's ballot demand in *Borg-Warner* was, as the court said, a voluntary bargaining subject. Did this necessarily mean that if carried to an impasse the demand was an unfair labor practice? Doesn't the court say in the *Insurance Agents'* case that Congress was not concerned with the substantive terms on which the parties contracted? And that Section 8(d) was a check on a trend which Congress thought it saw in the Board to force the acceptance of demands made in bargaining? By saying that the ballot demand was voluntary and could not be carried to an impasse, the Court, in effect, forced the company to withdraw a demand. Is there a difference between forcing one party to accept a demand, and forcing another party to withdraw a demand, insofar as the degree of governmental interference is concerned? If Congress did not want the Board to force bargaining, is there any more reason to believe that it wanted the Board to prevent bargaining, so long as such bargaining was legal and in good faith? Didn't the Court's decision in *Borg-Warner* arbitrate a substantive solution which had been reached in bargaining? Wasn't Section 8(d) used to control the settling of the terms of the collective bargaining agreement? Is *Borg-Warner* reconcilable with the mainstream of cases before the Board and in the courts, which is concerned with insuring that the parties should have wide latitude in their negotiations, unrestricted by any governmental power to regulate the substantive solution of their differences?

Placed side by side, the two cases look like this: *Borg-Warner* said that the company could not carry a voluntary bargaining demand to an impasse, even though the demand was perfectly legal and it was bargained in good faith. Allowing the company to carry the issue to an impasse might prevent a settlement (though in fact it had not), but the other alternative was governmental interference with the bargaining process. Of the two alternatives, the court seemed to feel that the latter was preferable. The *Insurance Agents'* case dealt with harassing tactics employed by the union in support of a mandatory bargaining demand. The conduct was legal, and the union bargained in good faith. Allowing the union to continue the tactic might have the effect of forcing the employer to subsidize his own strike—a result which on the surface seems to be inconsistent with our theory of collective bargaining. The alternative was government interference with the bargaining process. Of the two alternatives, the court seemed to feel it was better not to interfere. The incongruity of the two results shows up in a hypothetical case which combines the two fact situations. Suppose in the insurance case the agents had used the same harassing tactics in support of a voluntary bargaining demand. The Board would then find itself in the dubious position of tolerating the harassing tactics because the Supreme Court had told it to give the parties wide latitude in bargaining, but then restraining the union from insisting in good faith on a legal demand because it was in the voluntary category.

SUMMARY AND CONCLUSIONS

When Congress added Section 8(5) to the Wagner Act it probably did not foresee the extent to which it was opening the door to governmental intervention in the collective bargaining process. Yet such intervention was, at least to a degree, inevitable. It was unrealistic to suppose that the parties could be required to bargain collectively if, in fact, the law simply escorted them to the bargaining door and then said, "What happens behind those doors is not inquired into. . . ."[94]

Whatever may have been the intentions of the Congress with respect to the duty to bargain, there was in existence at the time a substantial body of precedent interpreting similar language. Armed with this authority, emanating from railroad labor law, the World War I War Labor Board, and predecessor New Deal Boards, the newly created NLRB soon developed a good faith bargaining concept which involved more than a bare requirement that the employer meet and confer with employee representatives.

Once the criteria for good faith bargaining were established, a new question arose. What did the parties have to bargain about? The formula which the NLRB used, with court approval, to resolve this problem involved a classification of demands as illegal, mandatory, or voluntary. Illegal demands created no great difficulty, but the difference between mandatory demands, which were directly related to the statutory language of "wages, hours, and terms and conditions of employment," and voluntary demands, which were not, has been a source of trouble. Voluntary demands could not be carried to an impasse, but mandatory demands could. The problem was spotlighted when the Supreme Court held, in the *Borg-Warner*[95] case, that the legal, voluntary demand, though bargained in good faith, constituted an unfair labor practice when carried to an impasse. Four justices dissented and they were joined by many academic critics who thought that the Court was unnecessarily interfering with the bargaining process.

The implications of the *Borg-Warner* decision have emerged from a series of other cases dealing only tangentially with the duty to bargain. The *R. R. Telegraphers'*[96] decision involved the permanency of the employment of station agents whose jobs were about to be abolished. Four of the justices thought that this was not a lawful bargaining matter. In a similar vein, the NLRB held, in the *Fiberboard* case,[97] that on the expiration of the existing contract an employer could subcontract maintenance work without bargaining with the union despite the fact that such work had, for more than twenty years, been under the jurisdiction of the union. The Board's rationale was that the mandatory duty to bargain did not cover the question of whether the employment relationship should exist.

Given the emphasis of present and foreseeable bargaining demands on job security, the above decisions are of great significance. One need but glance over some of the current bargaining demands to see the scope of the problem. Consider some of the following:

1. That no existing company plant be closed or moved during the life of the collective bargaining contract;
2. That no personnel be severed or reduced in earnings as the result of the installation of new equipment;
3. That displaced personnel be given transfer rights to other company plants, including moving pay, a "settling-in" allowance, and guarantees against losses in the sale of houses or termination of leases;
4. That displaced employees be given re-training allowances, even where such re-training can only provide jobs with another employer;
5. That production workers be put on a salaried basis, rather than paid by the hour;
6. That a flexible work week be established and payments made into a fund which would stabilize pay on the basis of forty hours per week;
7. That pension funds be invested in low-cost housing for union employees; and
8. That foreign production of the company's product be limited or eliminated.

Some of the above demands would surely be classified as mandatory. Others are almost certainly in the voluntary category. Many impinge upon what we have traditionally thought of as "management's prerogative." Yet in the changing and very real world of bargaining, all may be close to the felt needs of the parties. In his recent challenge to the AFL-CIO, Jimmy Hoffa called the displacement problems arising out of automation as serious as war, and indicated in no uncertain terms that the Teamsters were prepared to fight.[98]

Deciding which of these current demands falls into the mandatory category will not be an easy task. Job security and internal union affairs proposals pose extremely delicate issues. Holding that a demand is mandatory results in governmental pressure to bargain. Congress has recorded its reluctance to have the parties so pressured. For that reason both the Board and the courts may feel obliged to go slow, though history certainly suggests that the mandatory category will be expanded.

Insofar as any of the above demands is held to be voluntary, the NLRB will, under the *Borg-Warner* decision, prevent the demand from being carried to an impasse. The result will be governmental interference with the bargaining process. In the *Insurance Agents'* case,[99] which was concerned with tactics rather than the duty to bargain, the court went to great lengths to explain the impropriety of governmental interference with bargaining. Among other things, it pointed out that when Congress inserted Section 8(d), defining collective bargaining, in the Taft-Hartley Act, it did so in large part because it did not like having the NLRB tell the parties what they must bargain about. Is there a difference between telling the parties what they must bargain about, or turning the coin over, and telling them what they cannot insist on bargaining about, though the subject is perfectly legal?

The classification of bargaining demands into illegal, mandatory, and voluntary categories is now probably too well established to be upset. And there is no particular reason why it should be. There is little or no argument about the illegal category. Congress certainly meant that there was a limit to subjects about which the Board could order the parties to bargain. The serious question that is left is whether the Board or the Courts should intervene to prevent an impasse over a voluntary subject when the bargaining is being conducted in good faith. The essence of the argument presented herein is that so long as the parties are in good faith, and the demand is legal, the Board and the Courts should keep their hands off. Even if this is done there will remain a difference between mandatory and voluntary bargaining subjects in that the government will not step in to require the parties to bargain about the latter. But neither will it prevent them from doing so, by ordering one party not to go to an impasse. The risk that such an approach will broaden the base for industrial strife will be more than compensated for by allowing the parties maximum flexibility to adjust to changing times and conditions.

Notes

1. *Hearings before the Senate Committee on Education and Labor on S. 1958,* 74th Cong., 1st Sess., pt. 2, at 137 (1935).
2. *Order of R.R. Telegraphers* vs. *Chicago and N. W. R. Co.,* 362 U.S. 330 (1960).
3. *Allen Bradley Co.* vs. *NLRB,* 286 F. 2d 442 (7th Cir. 1961).
4. *NLRB* vs. *Wooster Division of Borg-Warner Corp.,* 356 U.S. 342 (1957).

5. *NLRB vs. Insurance Agents' International Union, AFL-CIO,* 361 U.S. 477 (1960).

6. *Sylvania Electric Products, Inc.* vs. *NLRB,* 48 L.R.R.M. 2313 (1st Cir. 1961).

7. *International Typographical Union, AFL-CIO* vs. *NLRB,* 81 Sup. Ct. Rep. 855 (1961).

8. See note 1 *supra.*

9. 79 *Cong. Rec.* 7571 (1935).

10. *Ibid.*

11. 79 *Cong. Rec.* (7659-60) (1935).

12. *Ibid.*

13. 41 Stat. 456 (1920).

14. *In Re Int'l Ass'n of Machinists,* 2 RLB 87 at 89 (1921).

15. *American Train Dispatchers Ass'n* vs. *Baltimore & Ohio R. R.* 4 RLB 787 (1923).

16. 48 Stat. 198 (1933).

17. *National Lock Co.,* 1 NLB 15 (1935); *Hall Baking Co.,* 1 NLB 83 (1934).

18. *S. Dresner & Son,* 1 NLB 26 (1934); *Edward G. Budd Mfg. Co.,* 1 NLB 58 (1933).

19. *Connecticut Coke Co.,* 2 NLB 88-89 (1934).

20. *Houde Engineering Corp.,* 1 NLRB (old) 35 (1934).

21. 361 U.S. at 484.

22. Labor-Management Relations Act (Taft-Hartley Act) #8(d), 61 Stat. 142 (1947) 29 U.S.C. 158 (d) (1958).

23. Labor Management Relations Act (Taft-Hartley Act) #8(b)(3), 61 Stat. 141 (1947), 29 U.S.C. 158(b)(3) (1958).

24. *E. G. Jacobs Mfg. Co.,* 9 4 NLRB 1214 (1951), *enf. granted.* 196 F. 2d 680 (2d. Cir. 1952). See Cox and Dunlop, "The Duty to Bargain Collectively During the Term of an Existing Agreement," 63 *Harv. L. Rev.* (1950), 1097, 1099-1101.

25. *Hughes Tool Co.,* 56 NLRB 981 (1944).

26. *Sands Mfg. Co.,* 1 NLRB 546 (1936); *Atlas Mills,* 3 NLRB 10 (1937); *Highland Park Mfg. Co.,* 12 NLRB 1238 (1939).

27. *Highland Park Mfg. Co.,* 12 NLRB 1238 (1939); *Scandore Paper Box Co.* 4 NLRB 910 (1938).

28. *Gagnon Plating & Mfg. Co.,* 97 NLRB 104 (1951).

29. *J. H. Rutter-Rex Mfg. Co.,* 86 NLRB 470 (1949); *Weiner, d.b.a. Benson Produce Co.,* 71 NLRB 888 (1946).

30. *NLRB vs. National Shoes, Inc.* 208 F. 2nd 688 (2d Cir. 1953); *Stanislaus Implement and Hardware Co.,* 101 NLRB 394 (1952), *enf. granted.* 226 F. 2d 377 (9th Cir. 1955).

31. *NLRB vs. Nesen,* 211 F. 2d 559 (9th Cir., 1954); *L. G. Everist, Inc.* 103 NLRB 308 (1953); *J. W. Woodruff, Sr.,* 90 NLRB 808 (1950), *enf. granted,* 193 F. 2d 641 (5th Cir. 1952).

32. *Montgomery Ward & Co.,* 37 NLRB 100, 121 (1941), *enf. granted,* 133 F. 2d 676 (9th Cir. 1943); *Reed & Prince Mfg. Co.,* 96 NLRB 850 (1951), *enf. granted,* 205 F. 2d 131 (1st Cir. 1953), *cert. denied.* 346 U.S. 887 (1953).

33. *Reed & Prince Mfg. Co., supra,* note 8.

34. *NLRB vs. Highland Park Mfg. Co.,* 110 F. 2d 632 (4th Cir. 1940).

35. *Supra,* note 22.
36. *NLRB* vs. *National Maritime Union of America,* 175 F. 2d 686 (2d Cir. 1949).
37. *George P. Pilling & Son Co.,* 16 NLRB 650 (1939), *enf. granted,* 119 F. 2d 32 (3rd Cir. 1941).
38. *Jasper Blackburn Products Corp.,* 21 NLRB 1240 (1940).
39. *NLRB* vs. *Dalton Tel. Co.,* 187 F. 2d 811 (5th Cir. 1951); and *NLRB* vs. *Darlington Veneer Co.,* 236 F. 2d (4th Cir. 1956).
40. *NLRB* vs. *Niles-Bement-Pond Co.,* 199 F. 2d 713 (2d Cir. 1952).
41. *NLRB* vs. *Bemis Bros. Bag Co.,* 206 F. 2d 33 (5th Cir. 1953).
42. *Weyerhaeuser Timber Co.,* 87 NLRB 672 (1949).
43. *Fleming Mfg. Co.,* 119 NLRB 452 (1957).
44. *Supra,* note 4.
45. 113 NLRB 1288.
46. 236 F. 2d 898 (6th Cir. 1956).
47. *Supra,* note 4.
48. 356 U.S. at 356.
49. Cf., Wollett, "The Borg-Warner Case and the Role of the NLRB in the Bargaining Process," 12 *N.Y.U. Conf. Lab.* 39 (1959).
50. *Allis-Chalmers Mfg. Co.* vs. *Labor Board,* 213 F. 2d 374 (7th Cir. 1954).
51. 236 F. 2d at 903.
52. *Ibid.*
53. 236 F. 2d at 904.
54. *Ibid.*
55. 356 U.S. at 353.
56. No. 412 CBNC Part 1, March 17, 1961, p. 1.
57. H. R. Rep. No. 245, 80th Cong., 1st Sess. 19-20.
58. *Supra,* note 2.
59. 363 U.S. at 336.
60. *Ibid.,* at 357.
61. *Ibid.,* at 355.
62. *The New York Times,* April 6, 1961, p. 18, col. 8.
63. *The New York Times,* April 6, 1961, p. 18, col. 7.
64. *The New York Times,* April 7, 1961, p. 16, col. 3.
65. No. 416 CBNC Part 1, May 12, 1961, p. 1.
66. *The New York Times,* June 19, 1961, p. 18, col. 3.
67. *Fiberboard Paper Products Corp.,* 130 NLRB No. 161 (1961).
68. Slichter, *Union Policies and Industrial Management,* p. 5 (1941).
69. *Supra,* note 3.
70. E. g., *Local 248, UAW* vs. *Wisconsin Board,* 105 N.W. 2d 278 (1960).
71. 127 NLRB No. 8 (1960).
72. *Wisconsin Board* vs. *Lodge 78, IAM,* 105 N.W. 2d 278 (1960).
73. 286 F. 2d at 444.
74. *Supra,* note 71.
75. 286 F. 2d at 445.
76. *Allis-Chalmers Workers' Union, Local 248, UAW* vs. *WERB,* 8 L.R.R.M. 1148 (1941).
77. 1950-55 Collective Bargaining Agreement between the Allis-Chalmers Mfg. Co. and Local 248, United Automobile, Aircraft and Agricultural Implement Workers of America, Article II, Section G.
78. 286 F. 2d at 445.

79. *American Vitrified Products Co. and Local 967, United Brick Workers,* 127 NLRB No. 92 (1960).

80. *Supra,* note 57.

81. *Supra,* note 5.

82. E.g., *Textile Workers Union of America, CIO* vs. *NLRB,* 227 F. 2d 409 (DC Cir. 1955), cert. granted 350 U.S. 1084 (1955), but vacated 352 U.S. 864 (1956).

83. *Local 2, Amalgamated Lithographers and Buffalo Employers Group,* 124 NLRB No. 36 (1959).

84. *Local 220, IUE and Package Machinery Co.,* 127 NLRB, No. 174 (1960).

85. *Lumber & Sawmill Workers Union (Cheney Cal. Lumber Co.),* 130 NLRB, No. 34 (1961).

86. Wisconsin Statutes, Ch. 111, #111.06(f) (1955).

87. Green, "Employer Responses to Partial Strikes: A Dilemma?," 39 *Texas L. Rev.* (1960), 198 and Mittenthal, "Partial Strikes and National Labor Policy," 54 *Mich. L. Rev.* (1955), 71.

88. *NLRB* vs. *Great Falls Employers' Council,* 277 F. 2d 772 (1960).

89. *Ibid.,* at 777.

90. See note, "Labor Management Relations—NLRB May Not Equate Partial Strike to Harass Employer with Failure to Bargain in Good Faith," 109 *U. Pa. L. Rev.* (1960), 134.

91. 361 U.S. at 485.

92. *Ibid.,* at 487.

93. *Ibid.,* at 488.

94. 79 *Cong. Rec.* 7660 (1935).

95. *Supra,* note 4.

96. *Supra,* note 2.

97. *Supra,* note 67.

98. *The New York Times,* July 4, 1961, p. 8, col. 1.

99. *Supra,* note 5.

4

THE UNION SECURITY ISSUE

PAUL E. SULTAN

Professor of Economics, Claremont Graduate School

The union security issue was created at the very inception of labor organization in America, and the cycles of conflict it has since engendered have followed (with a time lag) the waves of union growth. Today, even if one accepts the permanence of union organization and the maturity of bargaining relations, those contract terms making explicit union security are continuing sources of controversy. What elements contribute to the enduring quality of this problem?

The persistence of the conflict can in part be explained by the complexity of the issues involved. For example in orthodox economic theory, competition was presumed to dominate market structures. Unfortunately the nineteenth-century blueprint of the competitive society provides a poor description of twentieth-century reality. But we have not yet fully fashioned the devices for balance and control where the discretionary exercise of power shapes, rather than is shaped by, impersonal market forces. In this setting, the union security issue represents the clash between those inspired by the historic ideals of the competitive society and those awed by the size—and resigned to the permanence—of large scale industrial organization.

Superimposed on this field of controversy is the dispute over the relevance of political democracy to union-management power relations. The notion seems well established that the mechanism of democracy is as relevant to economics as it is to politics. Perhaps we have been drawn to this conviction because of the hope that somehow democracy *within* the organization can provide that degree of restraint and control no longer assured by external market pressure. But those concerned with political freedom in a market setting often fail to grasp the inextricable relationship of such freedom to power; too often these are regarded as opposite rather than complementary elements in the bargaining relationship. As a case in point, in the three-way interdependence of the worker, union and management, the union-management economic (power) relationship can be and is affected by the union-membership political (democratic) relationship. We have not yet fully explored the manner in which the extension of the latter democratic relationship may disrupt the former power relationship, but obviously the individual worker's freedom cannot be analyzed in any context that ignores the reality of market power. If this relationship be acknowledged, how does one measure and then establish that balance between individual rights and group discipline that would offer workers the optimum of political influence and economic gain? And would that optimum be consistent with alternative maximizing goals, such as the maintenance of price level stability or increased economic growth?

Finally, we have an aversion to issues in which merit can be found on both sides, blinded as we are with the notion that virtue is undivided and that the task of analysis is to identify the villain in the piece. Unable to conceive, then, of the conflict of good against good, a kind of Gresham's law has operated, with the bad arguments driving out the good, with emotionalism swamping rationalism. Indeed, one weary student of the subject decided to determine the weight of evidence by placing the mass of material received from partisans on his bathroom scale.[1]

In this chapter we shall focus on only a few aspects of this intricate problem. We shall make a statistical survey of the form and extent of such security agreements, review those forces intensifying interest in them today, survey a few of the judicial interpretations of state right-to-work statutes, and single out for attention the agency shop or bargaining fee arrangements. And finally we shall weigh the advantages of union security agreements, both in terms of the power balance between unions and management and the political relations of union membership to union leadership.

THE FORMS AND SCOPE OF UNION SECURITY

Since 1954, the proportion of contracts containing union security clauses has levelled off at 81 per cent. But this stability should not obscure significant shifts in the form these have taken in the last fifteen years. For example, the 1947 Taft-Hartley ban on the closed shop caused a rapid growth in the union-shop agreement (17 per cent in 1946 to 49 per cent in 1949-1950). And since 1950, union-shop coverage has increased steadily by displacing maintenance-of-membership agreements. By 1958-1959,[2] the union shop represented over 90 per cent of all security arrangements. However, a fifth of these did exempt certain groups from membership requirements—in some cases those who were not members at the effective date of the agreement, or those whose religious convictions prevented such membership.

Union-shop provisions are more frequently found in manufacturing than non-manufacturing enterprise. Eleven industries had union-shop provisions that covered over 90 per cent of all major agreements with unions. These include: apparel, lumber, printing and publishing, rubber, leather and leather products, stone, clay, and glass products, primary metals, fabricated metal products, mining and crude petroleum production, wholesale trade and retail trade. Three industries, tobacco, products of petroleum and coal, and communications had union-shop coverage of less than 25 per cent. There is no apparent relationship between the proportion of contracts containing union-security agreements and the proportion of production workers in various industrial groups covered by union agreements. For example, in the 90 per cent union-shop group above, the proportion of production workers covered by a union agreement for lumber was 44 per cent; printing and publishing 65 per cent; rubber 81 per cent; leather 49 per cent; stone, clay and glass 78 per cent; primary metals 89 per cent; fabricated metals 71 per cent.[3] These comparisons do not support the hypothesis that union-security agreements are most often negotiated in industries where the union is already fully represented. They also suggest the proportion of the job territory yet available to those workers rejecting union membership as a condition of employment.

The 19 per cent of agreements not containing a union security clause represent, implicitly or explicitly, a "sole bargaining" relationship, for the exclusive bargaining principle is embodied in federal law. And some contracts, while making no provision for union security, do contain a clause to encourage membership. Such a harmony clause might read:

> The employer states to the union that it has no objection to and it believes that it is in the best interests of the employees, the union, and the employer, that all employees within the unit become and remain members of the union.

Union check-off arrangements have increased in coverage from 20 per cent of collective bargaining agreements in 1942 to 77 per cent of agreements in 1958-1959. Seventy-six per cent of sole bargaining contracts contained check-off provisions, while 70 per cent of the union-shop and membership-maintenance contracts contained this provision. Thus, the less secure the union, the greater the impulse to negotiate such an agreement. It is not surprising, therefore, that 85 per cent of workers under major agreements in right-to-work states were covered by such provisions, as against 68 per cent under agreement in states without such laws.[4]

The penetration of union organization in the nineteen right-to-work states is indicated by the 2,147,343 union members affiliated with AFL-CIO unions living in such states. In 1958, this represented 16 per cent of the total United States AFL-CIO membership.[5] In 1958-1959, 19 union-shop agreements were still operative in right-to-work states. These agreements, covering 37,500 workers, were negotiated in Indiana prior to June 1957, the effective date of Indiana's right-to-work law.

THE CONTEMPORARY CHALLENGE TO UNIONISM

It may seem strange that at this late date in our industrial history, union leadership should still regard almost every innovation in labor legislation as a threat to union existence, or that it should fear that "capitalist encirclement" in the community threatens its survival. Yet a crisis does confront American unionism. While the

challenge to union influence today is hardly a life-or-death struggle, it does compound that anxiety (some would call it a neurosis)
characteristic of American union leadership and naturally intensi-
fies leadership interest in security arrangements.

Clearly the 57 volumes and 19,914 pages of testimony collected
by the McClellan committee served to build political pressure for
reform, a pressure probably not fully relieved by the Labor Management Reporting and Disclosure Act of 1959. The survival qualities of Hoffa—described in the press as leading the 1961 Teamsters
convention with one hand on the gavel and the other on the switch
to all floor microphones—has fascinated the public, but has also in-
tensified its anxiety about union power and roused its competitive
instincts for control. Even though the Democratic platform in the
1960 convention called for the repeal of Section 14(b) of the Taft-
Hartley law, Kennedy was noticeably silent on this issue during the
campaign. Given the Congressional alliance of southern Democrats
and Republicans, it is unlikely that legislation involving changes
in the status of union security agreements will soon be forthcoming
from Congress. Thus, "labor victories" at the polls may involve for
unions at best a holding action against the rising tide of public
concern about union power.

Several of the changing characteristics of the labor force involve
a defense-in-depth against union organizational drives. An ever-
increasing proportion of the labor force is made up of women who
often regard themselves as temporary labor-force participants.
Where these are secondary wage earners, the substantial increment
of family income they provide does much to reduce the appeals
of union militancy. The higher education levels achieved by new
job entrants, while occasionally leading to an academic sympathy
for the principles of unionism, often infuses the job entrant with
the conviction that unions are necessary agencies to protect the
untutored and unskilled worker, but certainly not himself. The
dispersion of new home construction and the conservatism of
suburbia diminish the prospects for participation in and loyalty
to union ideals. Automation leads to "depopulation" in the plant
and offers those "baby sitting" for machinery a more dignified work
environment, and a semi-engineering or technical status. In such
a plant the decline in labor costs to total costs enables management

to be more enlightened in its personnel policies, and more generous in wage policies. Even the secular increase of structural unemployment has failed to evoke the usual view of unions as the champions of trampled worker rights. Ironically, attention given to the work-rules issue has encouraged the view that unions have engineered this plight. Indeed, the list of national ills attributed to union monopoly power seems infinitely expandible to cover such problems as cost-push inflation, unfavorable trade balances, the gold drain, or even the lag in our missile race with Russia.

The internal structure of union administration poses problems too. The dedication and missionary zeal of union leadership baptized under fire by the Great Depression is not readily simulated in new union leadership. As the professional takes over, as the bureaucratization of union organization is extended, as increasing reliance is made on the expert, the union itself becomes an impersonal mechanism. The centripetal forces that increase organizational efficiency clash with those centrifugal forces represented by the increasing diversity of membership viewpoint. In effect, the union is challenged from within and without. Union organizing drives have been stalled in their tracks.

The dispersion and smaller size of unorganized plants, the entrenched hostility to union ideals in the south—complicated with the race issue—the expanding proportion of white collar and service workers to manual workers,[7] all have combined with the above mentioned factors to prevent any substantial expansion in real union membership. Union interest in security clauses is not, therefore, surprising. Where negotiated, they promise at least the possibility that membership growth will pace labor force growth. But even this is only a possibility, for manpower demands are increasing in those areas in which unions have had the most difficulty in gaining recognition, let alone security.

On the other side of the balance sheet, there is today much more cautious consideration given to support of right-to-work statutes. In 1958, six states—California, Colorado, Idaho, Kansas, Ohio, and Washington—voted on right-to-work proposals. In all but Kansas the provision was placed on the ballot as a result of initiative petitions and in all states but Kansas, the resolution was defeated. Opposition to such statutes is clearly stiffening. Of the

19 states with such laws in 1962, 12 were secured in the forties
(11 in 1947), 5 from 1950 to 1955, and only 2 (Indiana and Kansas) in the 1956-1962 interval.[8] Republican candidates have reap-
praised their support for such state provisions, fearing that identification with the issue will mobilize union opposition to them.
Intensive union efforts to secure the registration of voters undoubtedly assured the defeat of many Republican candidates in
1958. From a political viewpoint, however cool the public attitude
towards organized labor, support of such a measure represents a
calculated risk.

Right-to-work committees have been undaunted by such timidity
and continue to operate at both the national and state level. Thus,
at the present time a delicate balance of political power seems to
exist, with union prospects for securing repeal of Section 14(b),
allowing state right-to-work enactments, not much more likely
than the enactment of a national right-to-work statute.

The Status of State Right-to-Work Statutes

In the test cases of the North Carolina, Nebraska, and Arizona
right-to-work statutes before the Supreme Court, the union movement argued that right-to-work laws

> . . . adversely affect not only contract right and liberties protected
> under the Fourteenth Amendment and the contract clause, but also
> impair the fundamental right of assembly as exercised by working
> men when they seek to form and maintain unions.

Because right-to-work statutes limit the freedom of a group to
refuse to work with non-union men, they jeopardize the freedom of
association guaranteed in the First Amendment. Such a refusal was,
in the union view, the heart of workmen's association, for the freedom enjoyed by labor is derived from union power; union power
is derived from effective collective action; and the freedom of collective action is thus implicit in the freedom of assembly. The
denial of union security in the name of protecting the rights of
the non-unionist would mean only that the minority was being
protected at the expense of the majority.

The Supreme Court was not impressed with such reasoning. It
upheld the constitutionality of right-to-work laws declaring:

> It is difficult to see how enforcement of this state policy could
> infringe the freedom of speech of anyone, or deny to anyone the

right to assemble or to petition for a redress of grievances. . . .
There cannot be wrung from a constitutional right of workers to
assemble to discuss improvement of their own working standards,
a further constitutional right to drive from remunerative employment all other persons who will not or can not participate in union
assemblies.[9]

In a separate decision in *AFL* vs. *American Sash and Door Co.*,
Justice Frankfurter observed that

> The right of association, like any other right carried to its extreme,
> encounters limiting principles. . . . At the point where the mutual
> advantage of association demands too much individual disadvan-
> tage, a compromise must be struck. . . . When that point has been
> reached—where the intersection should fall—is plainly a question
> within the special province of the legislature.[10]

It is thus established that Congress has the right to permit states
to restrict union security agreements.

It is one thing to uphold the constitutionality of right-to-work
laws, but quite another to define the range of union activity not
in conflict with such statutes and the range of remedies available
to state courts not in conflict with the Federal preemption doctrine. Can a union, for example, undertake informational picketing
to advertise that non-union men are employed in a plant? Can a
union picket to secure representation rights, even though it avows
no intention of requesting any form of a union security? Can
individual non-union workers covered by a collective bargaining
agreement invalidate the union's sole bargaining clause by claiming statutory sanction for individual bargaining? And if this be
true, can a union then advance the claim for membership-only
bargaining? These, among others, have been issues facing the
courts in right-to-work states. The few field studies made on the
effects of this legislation suggest that court interpretations have
tended to transcend the original purpose of such statutes.

In several states, the "unlawful purpose" doctrine has been utilized to establish the legality of union picketing. In *Construction
and General Labor Union Local 688* vs. *H. I. Stephenson*, house-
mover Stephenson was confronted with pickets at the erection site
of one of his buildings, protesting the employment of non-union
labor and the failure of employees on the job to join their union.
An injunction was issued with the employer attorney reasoning

that the right to picket, like all other rights attendant to free speech, must at times be subordinated to the police power of the state. Even peaceful picketing may be banned if it is conducted for the purpose of achieving unlawful goals. The Supreme Court of Texas accepted the "illegal purpose" motivating union picketing:

> There was . . . a substantial basis in the record . . . to conclude that the immediate purpose of the picketing was to compel Stephenson to discriminate in favor of union members and against nonunion men in hiring his employees, in violation of Article 5207a [the Texas Right-to-Work Law].[11]

In *Thurman* vs. *Shearin*, employees struck their employer for improved contract terms. The strikers were replaced and union picketing against the employer then restrained because it was held to be in violation of the right-to-work statute:

> This [strike] plainly is for the purpose of coercing the complainants to bargain with a nonrepresentative union, and to sign a contract with a union, which would interfere with the right of complainants' employees to choose their own bargaining representative.[12]

On occasion the courts have looked beyond the actual content of union proposals to view the union constitution. In *Self* vs. *Taylor*, the court noted that the union constitution contained the mandate that union men not work with non-union men. Union picketing to secure recognition and/or bargaining concessions was enjoined.[13] Similarly in *Texas State Federation of Labor* vs. *Brown and Root*,[14] the employer contended that union picketing was an automatic violation of the right-to-work law because all contracts, in spite of the content of the agreements with the employer, would be administered according to those union constitutional provisions and bylaws requiring the closed shop. In this case, an original ten-day restraining order was renewed eighteen times and allowed to run six months. Again the court decided that the true purpose of the union was to force a violation of the right-to-work statute because the union wanted *all* the men employed by Brown and Root to be union members.

In *Plumbers Union* vs. *Graham* the Supreme Court ruled on the legality of picketing in the light of the Virginia right-to-work statute, holding that it was unlawful for a union to picket to compel an employer to discourage non-union workers or to picket to compel an employer to require that employees join the union as a condition of employment.[15] In his dissent,[16] Justice Douglas pointed to the difficulties of distinguishing that picketing motivated to advertise the facts of the situation, which would be privileged, and that motivated to deprive non-union men of employment. Unfortunately, both motives often operate simultaneously and the task of distinguishing motives may be tenuous or impossible.

The Supreme Court has attempted to resolve the thorny issue of picketing by raising the issue of Federal preemption. While 14(b) of the Taft-Hartley Act allows states the freedom to restrict union security agreements, it does not allow the states freedom to curb a union strike or picketing. In *Farnsworth & Chambers Co. vs. Local Union 429*,[17] the Supreme Court denied the authority of a state court to enjoin picketing designed to secure a union security agreement as one of its purposes. But in an earlier decision, *Algoma Plywood & Veneer Co. vs. WERB*,[18] the Court had decided that the State of Wisconsin could properly grant relief for discharged employees pursuant to a union security agreement that violated state law. In *Sheet Metal Workers International Association vs. Nichols*,[19] the Arizona Supreme Court denied that the *Farnsworth* decision nullifies the *Algoma* ruling. It pointed to the conference committee report submitted to the House of Representatives on the intention of Section 14(b):

> It was never the intention of the NLRA . . . to preempt the field . . . so as to deprive the States of their powers to prevent compulsory unionism. . . . To make certain that there should be no question about this, section 13 was included in the House bill. The conference agreement in Section 14(b), contains a provision having the same effect.[20]

Thus the Arizona Supreme Court denied that the preemption doctrine prevented the state courts from assuming jurisdiction of the case. It reversed, however, the remedies granted by a trial court of $15,000 compensatory and $35,000 punitive damages to an employee who alleged that an oral union security agreement between an employer and union had deprived him of employment. The court rejected the hearsay nature of the evidence utilized to establish that such an agreement between the employer and union did, in fact, exist.

Because most state right-to-work statutes contain the provision that employees shall have the right *to join* or not join unions, several tests have been made to determine if the former freedom can be used to bar discrimination for union activity. In *Sandt* vs. *Mason*[21] three employees were fired for union membership, but the Supreme Court of Georgia ruled that the remedial provisions of the statute were not applicable to that portion of the act which barred such discrimination. In *Willard* vs. *Huffman*[22] the North Carolina court ruled that violations of the law would be established if the plaintiff were discharged *only* for union membership activities. The burden of proof rested with the discharged individual to establish that union activity was the "motivating" or "moving cause" for the discharge and not some other reason. In *Miami Laundry Co.* vs. *Linen, Dry Cleaning Drivers, Local 935*[23] a union charged that employees had been discharged for union membership. The court dismissed the case with the argument that the rights involved in the Florida statute are personal rights, and therefore could not properly be defended by the union. In *Lunsford* vs. *City of Bryan*, Lunsford was discharged, allegedly for inefficiency, but he contended that such action was based on his interest in joining the International Association of Fire Fighters. The jury in the trial court found that since Lunsford was not a member of the union when he was fired, he could not be protected by the union right-to-work law. The City of Bryan contended:

> These statutes do not say that union activity, intention to join a union, union sympathy or anything other than "membership" is protected. For the courts to write into these statutes any such broader meaning of the term "membership" would be indeed to open a Pandora's box.[24]

The Civic Court of Appeals upheld this contention but it was subsequently reversed by the Supreme Court of Texas.

These cases reveal the diverse interpretations made of right-to-work laws. There is some consensus, however, that such laws have not seriously altered the balance of power between unions and management in local labor markets. As J. R. Dempsey observes in his *The Operation of Right-to-Work Laws:*

> Evidence is most probably not sufficient to support the extreme

charges of unions that a Right-to-Work Law is destructive of collective bargaining by not allowing the union to represent all the workers.[25]

Several considerations might support this conclusion. First, it must be appreciated that union security is normally negotiated after a union is recognized, and hence a presumption of union support or strength exists as a precondition for the negotiation of such contracts. There has not been a flood of litigation over the right-to-work issue, suggesting that the law may not be so disruptive to traditional bargaining relations as originally feared. Indeed, Fred Myers considers the issue in this conflict to be more symbolic than practical.[26] Second, it is sometimes difficult to distinguish that part of court reasoning that relates to additional state statutes, such as a ban on secondary boycotts, when a court proscribes picketing for recognition or picketing urging the employment of union members. It is also difficult to predict with certainty those remedies still available to state courts to enforce compliance of the state statutes. Third, in some cases the activities banned by the state courts would also be banned by federal statute. This is clearly the case where union demands involve discrimination in the placement of union members on jobs. Fourth, there seems general agreement that provisions of the law are often ignored by both unions and management, particularly when such provisions as the hiring hall arrangement have served to the mutual advantage of both management and unions. In any event, given the complex of forces effecting bargaining relations, it is methodologically difficult, if not impossible, to verify the effect of such legislation on union power, growth, industrial unrest, industrial plant location or even union democracy, however plausible one's speculation. A complex of forces affects the union management power balance, and it is indeed difficult to untangle or isolate the specific influence of such legislation.

The Agency Shop Issue

In the 1958-1959 Labor Department survey of union security clauses, only 15 of the 1,631 agreements studied (covering bargaining agreements involving 1,000 or more workers) contained agency shop provisions; 3 of these were combined with a modified union shop, 8 were in maintenance-of-membership provisions and 4 were with sole bargaining agreements.[27] In spite of such modest representation, interest in and extension of such agreements will undoubtedly develop in the future. This is likely because the "fee only" obligation to unions meets several criticisms of compulsory union membership. Interest in this arrangement has been stimulated by the realization that such clauses are not prohibited in all right-to-work states. In 1960, the Steelworkers secured an agency shop clause to be operative in those states where union shop provisions are banned but agency shop provisions allowed. Their contract specifies that employees who would otherwise be required to maintain membership be required to pay to the union

> . . . each month a service charge as a contribution toward the administration of this agreement and the representation of such employees. . . . The service charge for the first month shall be in an amount equal to the union's regular and usual initiation fee and monthly dues and any general and uniform assessment, and for each month thereafter in an amount equal to the regular and usual monthly dues and any general and uniform assessment.[28]

Agency shop agreements made their appearance in a few contracts during World War II and were sanctioned by the War Labor Board when agreed to by management and unions.[29] Interest increased when, in 1946 following a prolonged strike between the Ford Motor Company and the United Automobile Workers in Canada, Justice I. C. Rand of the Canadian Supreme Court was called upon to arbitrate the dispute. In place of the union shop sought by the union, he awarded a compulsory dues check-off.

In making his award Justice Rand cautioned upon the widespread application of his formula, feeling that the extension of union security had to be made in the light of the complex of forces that affect labor-management relations. But employee contributions to support the bargaining functions of the union were justified because of the benefits derived from such bargaining. He added: "It is irrelevant to try to measure benefits in a particular case. . . ."[30] Furthermore, while admitting that union leaders were not free of those "human frailties from which only a few saints escape," the solution to abuses within the union movement was greater democratization of the union. And such democratization might be encouraged by the fee arrangement, even though membership itself remained at the option of the employee:

> The obligation to pay dues should tend to induce membership, and this in turn to promote that wider interest and control within the union which is the condition of progressive responsibility.[31]

Even though a uniform checkoff was granted to the union so that it might "function properly," restrictions were placed on the abuse of union power. If a wildcat strike developed which was not repudiated and suppressed by the international, the company could fine involved employees a maximum of $3 a day, and suspend the check-off arrangement for a maximum of six months.[32] In addition, all employees, whether union members or not, were free to participate in strike elections to be conducted by secret ballot by the Department of Labor in the Province. Section 8 added that "Any employee shall have the right to become a member of the union by paying the entrance fee and complying with the constitution and by-laws of the union." Thus in gaining the assured flow of revenue to support bargaining functions, the union was held more strictly accountable for wildcat walkouts, denied the opportunity to discriminate in admission policies, and required to allow all employees to vote in strike elections.

The award appealed to both unions and management for by August of 1951, a sampling of Canadian collective bargaining agreements revealed that 5 per cent of these, covering 13 per cent of the workers surveyed, provided for the compulsory check-off of regular union dues for all employees in the bargaining unit where membership in the union was not required. In 1956 these proportions had increased to 18 per cent and 22 per cent respectively.[33]

A modification of the Rand formula was developed by the British Columbia Board of Conciliation in July 1951, when Chief Justice Sloan recommended, in a dispute involving the International Union of Mine, Mill and Smelter Workers, that all employees subject to the compulsory check-off also have the right to vote in the election of local union officers. In the Province of Quebec, on the other hand, the Civil Court ruled invalid the Rand formula because the Quebec civil code clearly specified that no two parties could sign a contract engaging a third party against his or her opposition. There must be proven consent. But this did not prevent a Montreal Conciliation Board, headed by Jacques Fournier, from resolving a dispute involving the Building Service Employees in two Montreal hospitals. The Board granted the substance of the Rand formula, but ordered that *employers* be held liable for union dues which an employee might refuse to pay.[34]

The Canadian evolution is not unique. For example in Switzerland, the government had traditionally considered union security clauses to be necessary for effective union bargaining. But in the late twenties, the principle was modified when it was contended that socialist unions could compel financial tribute from workers who were opposed to socialist principles. The Swiss courts reasoned that in such a situation, "It is contrary to good morals when the defendant union compels the plaintiff, by threats of losing his job, to belong to the union while he is of other political conviction."[35] So long as the union was not politically neutral, it would be unlawful for a union to displace workers from their jobs.

In 1949, a federal tribunal evolved the formula calling for "contributions of solidarity," a proposal endorsed by the Swiss parliament in 1956. Workers did not have to join a union, but were required to make a contribution to meet the costs of collective bargaining since collective bargaining agreements benefit all employees. Such contributions from non-members could not, however, be excessive. It was assumed they would approximate 50 per cent of union dues. Further, such revenues must be used for collective bargaining purposes or for those welfare purposes benefiting all employees.[36]

In the United States, the NLRB in April, 1950, ruled on the subject of the agency shop, declaring that support money provisions were a valid form of union security.[37] In 1952 the Board declared that Congress did not intend to illegalize the practice of obtaining support payments from non-members.[38] In the same year, the general counsel sustained a regional director's refusal to issue a complaint against an employer who had discharged six men for failure to pay dues under an agency shop contract.[39]

What are the issues involved in the attack on agency shop agreements? First, it must be established if states have the authority, under the permissive arrangements of Section 14(b) to ban such fee arrangements. Secondly, do states with statutes that bar union membership as a condition of employment by implication also bar such fee arrangements?

Turning to the first question, Section 14(b) of the Taft-Hartley law provides that "nothing in this act shall be construed as authorizing the execution or application of agreements requiring *membership* in a labor organization as a condition of employment in any State or Territory in which such execution or application is prohibited by State or Territory law."[40] Given the literal translation of this section, it has been argued that ten states have transcended the authority granted them by 14(b) in framing statutes that restrict the financial support rendered to a union.[41]

Even though the proponents of right-to-work legislation are generally eager to establish the burdensome obligations of union membership, while the opponents of such statutes stress the "dues-tendering" limits of that obligation, in the agency shop debate the partisans switch sides. For now the proponents of right-to-work legislation argue that the form of union shop contemplated by the Taft-Hartley Act is hardly distinguishable from the agency shop, and hence by implication the latter falls within the orbit of 14(b). Since these forms are in substance identical but for the formality of joining the union, the prohibition of financial payments to the union is consistent with the prohibition of compulsory union membership. As George Rose reasons, the payment of dues is the support unions seek under union security agreements. Therefore "it appears rather unrealistic for unions to contend that entering into a so-called 'agency shop' agreement, whereby employees are not required to join the union but to pay dues and fees to the union, is not a violation of the right-to-work laws."[42]

There is persuasive evidence to support this position. In sustaining the legality of the amendments to the 1951 Railway Labor Act, the Supreme Court pointed out: "We only hold that the requirement for financial support of the collective-bargaining agency by all who receive the benefits of its work is within the power of Congress."[43] In *Radio Officers Union* vs. *NLRB*, the Court said "Congress intended to prevent the utilization of union security agreements for any purpose other than to compel payment of union dues and fees."[44] The Texas Supreme Court, in *Sandsberry* vs. *International Association of Machinists,* pointed out that under a union security clause "The unwilling employee need assume no pledge of conformity nor promise of obedience, nor even make application for membership to retain employment under the union shop contract."[45]

Under the Taft-Hartley version of the union shop, membership obligations are limited to the tendering of dues and the regularly required initiation fees. In *Union Starch & Refining Company* vs. *NLRB,*[46] the Board was sustained in its contention that employees could not be discharged (so long as they had offered to pay their dues and initiation fees) for a refusal to participate in any initiation ceremony, sign any loyalty pledge to the union, or attend union meetings. Several additional cases have made even more explicit the narrow demands the union can make on members under the threat of the member's employment. A union cannot deduct from union dues amounts assessed against members to support strike action, and then demand the discharge of the member for being in arrears of his dues payment.[47] A union cannot demand the discharge of an employee expelled from a union for conduct unbecoming a union member,[48] an employee who has been expelled and refused to pay a fine to the union,[49] an employee failing to pay a fine for refusing to picket,[50] or an employee who fails to pay strike fund assessments or general assessments either separately or along with union dues and fees.[51]

We have, then, what J. A. McClain has labelled a debtor-creditor relationship between union members and unions.[52] Cannot one infer that the agency shop, which requires only support money from members and non-members alike, approaches in substance the provisions of the Taft-Hartley union shop? From the viewpoint of the civil libertarian, the freedom to stand apart from the membership of an organization, even if that membership involves no actual participation requirement, may be a vital one. But in a practical sense, the determinant of union power and efficiency is not likely to be based on the forced inclusion in the organization of unwilling workers, but rather from the uninterrupted flow of revenue to finance union activity. To the union the technical freedom of the employee to avoid membership may be a quite satisfactory *quid pro quo* for sustained financial support of the union, particularly since the obligations of membership have been so narrowly construed by the NLRB and Court rulings.

Even though the agency shop may appeal to those concerned with individual worker rights because it allows the personal detachment of the employee from union affairs, the freedom *to stand apart* from union organization does not usually involve the symmetrical freedom *to become involved* in union affairs. It should be remembered that in the Taft-Hartley Act, the Railway Labor Act and Rand formula, *if* a union takes a worker's dues under a union shop agreement, the employee then has the option of exercising his full membership rights in the union. It is not clear that the option of membership is available to all employees under agency shop clauses. Thus, the worker may be denied admission to a union, or even expelled from the union, and not be relieved of his obligation to pay support money to the organization. In this context, the financial obligations in sustaining union organization may not reinforce, but perhaps encourage indifference to the civil liberties of individuals, whether these persons be in or out of the organization. When NLRB member Kimball questioned the legality of the agency shop arrangement in the first GM case in Indiana, he observed:

> If, as in the instant case, those who would pay an equal fee for the Union to carry out its function as the exclusive bargaining agent are denied equal rights to participate in and benefit from the bargaining process, they would have a second-class status, and thus would be deprived of a fundamental right guaranteed in the Act.[53]

The absence of the financial inducements to modify discriminatory admission requirements is hardly a small point, particularly when one realizes that the major effort in the Labor Management Reporting and Disclosure Act to legislate democracy or establish labor's Bill of Rights contains nothing to restrict a union's discriminatory admission requirements.[54]

It is sometimes contended by agency shop critics that those states not making explicit a ban on support payments to the union neglected to do so only because they could not conceive of a distinction between membership in and financial support of unions. The National Association of Manufacturers, for example, declares that this distinction makes a mockery of efforts to protect the individual employee against representation he does not want. "This situation clearly points up the need for hard-won state Right-to-Work Laws to be carefully drafted."[55] But the issue is not created only because of sloppy draftsmanship, for in a few states the explicit ban on financial payments to a union was rejected to favor the more general clause banning membership as a condition of employment.[56]

The point has also been raised that Section 302 of the Taft-Hartley Act prohibits employer contributions to unions, except for membership dues. Employers cannot legally collect service fees from non-union members simply because these are not membership dues.[57] Such service fee payments may be found lawful, however, when authorized by an employee's written permission for such a deduction. But what if the employee refuses to sign such a statement? The only option available to the union would be to collect bargaining fees directly from the employee.[58]

Interest in fee arrangements has increased substantially since 14(b) opened the door to state regulation of union security agreements. Ten states have statutes which expressly ban the payment of dues to a union as a condition of employment. These include Alabama, Arkansas, Georgia, Iowa, Mississippi, North Carolina, South Carolina, Tennessee, Utah, and Virginia. The remaining nine states—Arizona, Florida, Indiana, Kansas, Nebraska, Nevada, North Dakota, South Dakota, and Texas—have statutes which are silent on the matter of fees and charges. The issue then arises whether a union membership ban involves a bargaining fee ban. What is the status of the agency shop in these nine states?

In Arizona, a Superior Court enjoined union picketing designed to secure, among other things, the agency shop. The Trial Court observed:

> It would require a most narrow and unrealistic construction of the existing laws to sanction a contract that would require employees not belonging to a union to contribute an assessment equal to the union dues to obtain or retain employment. . . . This Court's duty, under the evidence herein, becomes clear with respect to a holding that the agency shop clause violates the law of this State.[59]

Similarly, a Florida Appellate court ruled that an agency shop clause violates the Florida right-to-work law.[60]

In Indiana, the validity of the agency shop is of considerable significance, for Indiana is the only industrial state with such a statute. In *Meade Electric Company, Inc.* vs. *Hagberg*,[61] the Indiana Superior Court of Lake County in 1958 upheld the legality of the agency shop. The court contended that if prohibition of such a clause were intended, it would have been made explicit. Since the Indiana right-to-work provision was a penal statute, its provisions must be strictly construed. Thus it was unwilling to enlarge on the definition of membership to include the payment of dues to a union. It observed that such arrangements seemed fair because of union obligations to represent all employees, whether union members or not, and suggested that in any event it would not have jurisdiction to enjoin attempts to obtain the agency shop because of the federal preemption doctrine. In June of 1959, the Appellate Court upheld the contention of the lower court without endorsing the lower court opinion that federal preemption would invalidate any state proposal to restrict agency shop agreements.

The status of such agreements was confused by a NLRB decision in the spring of 1961.[62] In a three-to-two decision, the majority agreed that General Motors was free to refuse bargaining for an agency shop contract for its firms located in Indiana. Chairman Leedom ruled that since GM and the UAW were not free to require union membership as a condition of employment, ". . . so they were not free to require, as a condition of employment of such employees, any lesser form of union security, such as an agency shop." While Leedom did not rule on the legality of the agency shop in a state with no right-to-work law, member Kimball offered that such agreements were illegal, whether in a right-to-work state or not.[63]

But an appeal for a reconsideration of this decision proved successful. In September 1961, the Board reversed its ruling of February in the same year.[63] In the rehearing, both parties agreed that the issue should involve only the legality of the agency shop in the light of Federal law, without consideration being given to state right-to-work statutes. In its four-to-one ruling, the Board now held that Section 8(3) of the NLRA—which allows that membership can be a requirement negotiated in a collective bargaining agreement— was intended to be "permissive" and not "exclusive" in character.

In effect, the Board held that the union shop represented a *maximum* form of union security allowed, and that lesser forms of union security, such as the agency shop, were permissible. The Board noted that the existing national agreement between the UAW and GM required that the union "accept into membership each employee covered by this agreement who renders to the Union the periodic dues and initiation fee uniformly required as a condition of acquiring or retaining membership in the Union."

In his vigorous dissent, member Leedom rejected the contention that non-members did, in fact, enjoy the full right to membership or the full rights of membership. In his view, non-members could not, *as a matter of right,* be eligible to vote on how their support money was to be spent, entitled as a matter of right to receive the Union's publication, to receive strike benefits, to participate in the union's educational fund, or to have any of the other benefits guaranteed union members. He pointed to the testimony of the UAW counsel that under an agency shop agreement, "probably a non-member would not vote in the strike vote." Building his case on the "disparity of benefits provided as between union members and non-union members," Leedom concluded that the requirement that non-members pay dues could hardly be considered a "lesser form" of union security, for there was then exacted from the non-member "all the requirements of membership without the benefits which derive from membership." He further reasoned that an employee, given this "Hobson's choice," would be driven to membership: "For who can say as a verity that a man forced to buy a cake will not eat it?"

But the majority, looking to the practices of the UAW and the contract terms proposed, emerged with the conclusion that support money payments were a legitimate demand of the union so long as all employees had the option of joining the union. It would seem that the union must surrender any discriminatory standard for determining admission of employees as the *quid pro quo* for such a clause. But what would be the status under such a contract of a union member who is expelled from his union and persists in exercising his option of "becoming" a union member? Any union security agreement cannot easily be reconciled to a union's arbitrary admission requirements. Nor can the agency shop be easily reconciled to the "private fraternal association" concept of unionism.

The Kansas Supreme Court has reversed a trial court's dismissal of a suit seeking to enjoin the application of an agency shop contract.[64] In this case three employees were threatened with a discharge for failure to pay the equivalent of union dues and assessments. In declaring the agency shop illegal, the Kansas court reasoned that since Kansas policy was constitutional in origin, it could be construed liberally.

In Nebraska, the state attorney general declared the agency shop to be unlawful.[65] The Nebraska statute provides that a person may not be denied employment because of membership in or *affiliation with* a labor organization. The attorney general deduced that since membership must involve something more than affiliation, the presence of the affiliation proviso would bar fee bargaining arrangements. Similarly, in Nevada the attorney general has ruled that agency shop contracts aré devices to avoid the clear mandate of Nevada law.[66] The requirement that non-union workers pay sums equal to union dues was the very thing the law was intended to prevent.

But in North Dakota, the attorney general, relying on the Indiana *Meade Electric* vs. *Hagberg* decision, ruled that agency shops were permitted under that state's right-to-work law. But such fees must be based solely on the cost of representation.[67] On the other hand, the attorney general in South Dakota pointed to the prohibition of agreements which directly or *indirectly* interfere with the right to work to support his opinion that the agency shop was an illegal form of union security in South Dakota.

Finally in Texas, the attorney general has declared, in response to a letter from the Senate Committee on Labor and Management Relations, that the agency shop clause in union contracts violates the laws of Texas.[68]

Our scorecard indicates, therefore, that the negotiation of an agency shop agreement is a permissible form of union security in the light of federal labor law. In the nineteen states with right-to-work statutes, court cases involving a test of the agency shop have developed in Florida, Kansas, and Indiana, with only the Indiana courts allowing the agency shop. But only in Kansas has the issue been resolved by the highest state court. Beyond this, the attorney generals of five states—Nebraska, Nevada, North Dakota, South Dakota, and Texas—have offered opinions on the legality of the agency shop, and only in North Dakota has a limited form of this agreement been held to be a legitimate form of union security.

Union Security and Political Action

In 1951 the Railway Labor Act was amended to allow the negotiation of union security agreements of essentially the same type as permitted by the LMRA. The most important exception was that "union shop contracts could be entered into notwithstanding . . . any other statute or law . . . of any state."[69] The Nebraska Supreme Court declared that 2 *Eleventh* violated the First and the Fifth Amendments; it not only denied employees their freedom of association, but required members to pay for many things besides the cost of collective bargaining.

The Supreme Court reversed the Nebraska ruling.[70] Justice Douglas, speaking for the majority, reasoned that "The choice by the Congress of the union shop as a stabilizing force seems to us to be an allowable one." He accepted the benefit theory of unionism: "One would have to be blind to history to assert that trade unionism did not enhance and strengthen the right to work." But he added that the wisdom of the union requirement to make union membership a condition of employment was an issue over which the judiciary had no concern.

On the matter of ideological conformity, he noted the limited obligations of the member to his union, obligations confined to periodic dues, initiation fees and assessments (which did not include fines and penalties), and concluded that "On the present record, there is no more an infringement or impairment of First Amendment rights than there would be in the case of a lawyer who by state law is required to be a member of an integrated bar." Pointedly, the door was left open for further consideration of this issue if evidence were established that union dues were in fact used to force ideological conformity on union members.

In *Machinists* vs. *Street*,[71] findings which the court described as "detailed and specific" on the use of union funds for political purposes were presented to it. The lower courts had reasoned that the exaction of such dues for such purposes were not reasonably necessary to effective collective bargaining and the Supreme Court of Georgia perpetually enjoined the enforcement of a union shop agreement so long as such "unlawful activities" were engaged in by the union.

Speaking for the majority, Brennan surveyed the legislative history of 2 *Eleventh*, observing the emphasis given by railroad unions on the need to spread the costs of the elaborate collective bargaining machinery to all of the benefiting employees, rather than members alone. He could find no Congressional sanction for the use of union funds to force employees to support political causes which they oppose. "We respect this congressional purpose [to spread the cost of bargaining] when we construe 2 *Eleventh* as not vesting the unions with unlimited power to spend exacted money." In his concurring opinion, Douglas reasoned that each individual should

> . . . be allowed to enter his group with his own flag flying, whether it be religious, political, or philosophical. . . . If . . . dues are used, assessments are made, to promote or oppose birth control, to repeal or increase the taxes on cosmetics, to promote or oppose the admission of Red China into the United Nations, and the like, then the group compels an individual to support with his money causes beyond what gave rise to the need for group action.

But having agreed that membership in the group should not be conditioned on the individual's acceptance of the group's philosophy, the Court had difficulty in suggesting the appropriate reconciliation between majority and dissenting interest. ". . . We think the courts in administering the Act should select remedies which protect both [minority and majority] interests to the maximum extent possible without undue impingement of one on the other." How was this to be achieved?

The Court majority believed that to bar the union shop in such cases would sweep too broadly, but in suggesting remedies that lower courts might apply revealed the awsome task of establishing the optimizing ideal suggested above. The Court hoped to avoid "curtailment of the traditional activities of railroad unions" by suggesting the restriction of that portion of union revenues expended for political purposes that originated from persons who had made known their objection to such use. Thus, an injunction might be secured to return to the individual a proportion of his own dues, represented as that fraction of union expenditures for political activities to the union's total budget.

Black, in his dissent, pointed out that such a "parsimonious limitation" could hardly protect workers from the "flagrant violation" of their First Amendment rights, and involved much greater trial and accounting burdens on both unions and workers than justified by the relief afforded:

> It may be that courts and lawyers with sufficient skill in accounting, algebra, geometry, trigonometry and calculus will be able to extract the proper microscopic answer from the voluminous and complex accounting records of the local, national and international unions involved.

He favored the simple alternative of banning union shop agreements where union funds were used for political purposes. Whittaker could see no way to meet the union response to a protesting member that the funds used for political purposes were not drawn from his dues, but from a non-objecting member. But even more difficult would be the task of drawing a clear line between what is and what is not "proscribed activity." He too, because of these difficulties, favored the solution of the Georgia courts.

But Frankfurter, joined by Harlan, assaulted the basic premise underlying the majority opinion of the court. In a slashing attack, he declared that the notion that economic and political concerns were separable was "pre-Victorian." Political activity was indissolubly related to the economic and social effectiveness of unions:

> The absence of any showing of concern about unions' expenditures in political areas . . . only buttresses the conclusion that Congress intended to leave unions free to do that which unions had been doing. It is surely fanciful to conclude that this verbal vacuity implies that Congress meant its amendment to be read as providing that members of the union may restrict their dues solely for financing the technical process of collective bargaining. . . . None of the parties in interest at any time . . . not one suggested that the statute could be emasculated in the manner now proposed. . . . it is significant that a construction now found to be reasonable never occurred to the litigants.

And he wondered if efforts to secure the fair representation of minority interests in union politics would not be redundant if unions were constitutionally forbidden, because of minority opposition, to spend money in accordance with the majority's desires.

Clearly, the remedies suggested by this decision are unworkable. Congress may feel compelled to make more explicit the content of membership obligations under union security agreements, but this clarification is not likely to occur in the near future. Meanwhile unions will undoubtedly take the initiative to confront the court with the same issue, but so framed that it must be resolved in its constitutional terms alone. And right-to-work proponents will attempt to make more general the implications of the ruling by its extension to other than the railroading segment of the economy. On balance the union movement can find little comfort in the content of the existing decision, for there was more disagreement within the Court on the devices to restrict the use of union funds than whether, in fact, such restrictions should be made.

Some Power Implications of the Controversy

To those familiar with the long history of those contracts negotiated by employers in which *non*-membership was a condition of employment, the role of the employer as the champion of employee freedom of choice on the matter of union membership may seem somewhat incongruous. The lustre on the shield of others in the right-to-work crusade seems somewhat tarnished because of the evident anxiety of these organizations to avoid identification with other agencies concerned with those broader forms of employment discrimination based on race, creed, or color. Thus, if the inspiration for the right-to-work movement is the evil of discrimination, it is puzzling that the attack should be given such a narrow focus. It is not surprising, therefore, that some should suspect that the target is not discrimination itself, but union power that allows such union discretion to arise in the first place. It is not irrelevant to speculate, therefore, on the way in which the extension of minority interests within the labor force might affect the power balance between unions and management.

If one accepts the cynical view that employer interest in right-to-work often reveals a circuitous device to weaken union power, how is this accomplished? A union certified by a narrow majority of employees is nevertheless legally obligated to represent all employees in the bargaining unit. The limited financial base for representation and bargaining activities may frustrate union success. Much union staff time is taken up in "selling" union membership to potential members. Such activity may divert energies from more constructive duties. Union leadership may become increasingly harassed, for not only does dissension exist within the union over the burden of carrying the "free rider," but officers and business agents feel it is politically expedient to push every grievance, regardless of its merit. With a loss of a security clause, the cost of administration for the union may increase at the very time that the financial base to support such activity is reduced.

More important than this is the possibility of an open challenge to union control during an impasse in bargaining or during a prolonged strike. Non-members may be more willing to contemplate returning to the job, and the smaller the proportion of employees falling within the orbit of union discipline and the union's communication media, the greater is the risk that a strike may fail. This consideration is particularly crucial if the number of non-members within the plant, combined with non-members wanting work in the plant, is greater than the number of employed union members that go out on strike.

The relevance of right-to-work to strike strategy is evident in a recent court ruling that employers were free to negotiate for a right to work clause in their union contracts.[72] The NLRB has usually prevented an employer from negotiating a contract provision involving internal union affairs. The Supreme Court has supported the NLRB ruling that a contract proposal requiring a pre-strike secret vote of employees could not be a mandatory subject for bargaining.[73] Such an issue involved internal union affairs and the disciplinary powers of the union were reserved to the union in Section 8(b)(1)(A) of the NLRA. But in the instant case, *Allen Bradley Co.* vs. *NLRB,* the federal appellate court in Chicago ruled that an employer was free to negotiate a contract term that would limit the right of the union to discipline or fine its members for engaging, or *not* engaging, in union activities. The employer was moved to insist on such a clause because in a previous strike with the union, the union had imposed fines against members who had crossed picket lines to work. While the NLRB refused to support the union in the collection of those fines, the state courts did. The purpose of the clause was to bar such a penalty in the future. Even though the Taft-Hartley Act amendments restricted union pressure involving the job security of members in order to achieve compliance with union rules, this ruling seems to place the capacity of a union to impose discipline during a strike in jeopardy. An area previously considered off-limits to the employer has now been opened up to employer bargaining. Thus, while a union may have success in preventing the state from enacting legislation that would restrict its freedom to bargain for security, the union may find that such freedom may not in fact lead to security agreements but contract terms that limit the capacity of the union to consolidate membership support behind union policies.

Finally, the existence of a right-to-work statute may give the employer a psychological edge in a contest for employee support. During an organizing campaign, the employer may stress the incapacity of the union to retaliate against anti-unionists, regardless of the outcome of the election. Paraphrasing the Lewis strategy of the thirties, the employer may advertise: "Our state laws proclaim your freedom not to join a union."

Beyond the strategy of gaining recognition, day-to-day relations with the union may prove more disruptive. The necessity of being sensitive to individual grievances, responsive to every faction in the local can lead to a situation one writer described as minority rule. In preparing for bargaining sessions, union representatives will accumulate the aggregate of demands made by all factions rather than screen these in terms of what is economically feasible. Management will be assigned the total blame for modest concessions at the conference table. Such spirited bargaining may result not only in sharper conflicts, but greater instability in the cost-price structure. Right-to-work legislation is not likely, therefore, to lead to either tranquility in union-management relations, or stability in cost-price relations.

But if belligerence creates problems for the employer and the public, its opposite may create problems for the membership. Given the new look in bargaining negotiations—sometimes called hard bargaining—union officers may be tempted with some variant of the theme: If you can't beat them, join them. Such an accommodation may take the form of a union security clause. The subtle transformation of union policy from militancy to maturity, from conflict to cooperation, may enjoy the sanction of all who have not fully contemplated its impact on individual employee interests.

Put in more general terms, once the union conceives of its stability in terms of the stability of management, both may cooperate with each informally to satisfy the organizational imperatives they both face. The accommodation process can very easily involve policies that antagonize portions of the labor force. In such a case both management and the union may be the target for employee criticisms. It should be appreciated that there is no legal prohibition against a union recommending that an individual be fired so long as that request is not related to unionism. For example, a union can request the discharge of members expelled for Communistic activities, of employees drinking on the job, for activities that endanger the safety of other employees, or for general incompetence. In traditional analysis of union-management relations, there has been no lack of evidence of the subterfuge management may employ to "get" an employee who has been the spearhead of union organizational activities. The problem of establishing that the discharge of such employees was inspired by incompetence rather than union activity has been a thorny one indeed. But if both the union and management agree informally that certain troublemakers should be discharged, the chances of those so discriminated against may be limited. Management and the union may be joint depositors in the bank of evidence against the individual. Such a person may not only lack a forum in which to give expression to his difficulties, but lack the personal resources to continue single-handedly a struggle against the legal talent of two organizations. Such a situation is certainly isolated today, but the picture of small individuals caught between the common interests of two power mechanisms is one that bears consideration for the future. The adjustment of the union to the economic necessities or rhythms of corporate life may be labeled "maturity" or "responsibility" in the bargaining relationship, but it is an adjustment that may deny the individual with divided or dual disloyalties a sanctuary and—in extreme cases—his employment.

The seriousness of this possibility has yet to be established. But it does suggest that the union is going to have to make greater efforts to satisfy not only the majority of the workforce, but the peculiar interests of dissident minorities. An effort will have to be made, if not to institutionalize, at least to legitimatize, dissent. Our analysis suggests that while non-membership may not be the best control device over union policy, some control mechanism beyond the resistance power of management may yet be necessary. In our concern with the possibility that union-management harmony may be secured at the public expense, we have neglected the possibility that it may also be secured at the individual worker's expense.

NOTES

1. When the author complained to a Teamster official about the implausible economic analysis employed by unions in the 1958 California right-to-work campaign, the unionist explained: "Right to work laws are being sold like a bar of soap and we're going to unsell them like a bar of soap."

2. Rose Theodore, "Union Security and Checkoff Provisions in Major Union Contracts, 1958-59," *Monthly Labor Review*, Vol. 82, No. 12 (December 1959), p. 1351.

3. H. M. Douty, "Collective Bargaining Coverage in Factory Employment, 1958," *Monthly Labor Review*, Vol. 83, No. 4 (April 1960), p. 347.

4. Rose Theodore, "Union Checkoff Provisions," *Monthly Labor Review*, Vol. 83, No. 1 (January 1960), pp. 26, 28.

5. Data derived from membership as reported by state bodies of the AFL-CIO in 1958. See Harry P. Cohany, "Union Membership, 1958," *Monthly Labor Review*, Vol. 83, No. 1 (January 1960), p. 8-9. For 1960 data, see *Monthly Labor Review*, Vol. 84, No. 12 (December 1961), p. 1308. Total membership in right-to-work states changed little from 1958-1960. Texas and Indiana still accounted for about one third of union membership in right-to-work states.

6. For supporting statistics and an interesting analysis see Edwin E. Witte, "The Crisis in American Unionism," Chapter 7 in *The Arbitrator and the Parties*, Washington: Bureau of National Affairs, 1958; see also Solomon Barkin, *The Decline of the Labor Movement*, A Report to the Center for the Study of Democratic Institutions, Santa Barbara: 1961.

7. In 1900 white collar workers accounted for 28 per cent of the non-farm labor force. In 1960 the proportion had increased to 46.6 per cent. From 1900 to 1960, blue collar workers diminished from 57 per cent to 40 per cent of the non-farm labor force. See Carol A. Barry, "White Collar Employment: Trends and Structure," *Monthly Labor Review*, Vol. 84, No. 1 (January 1961), p. 13.

8. David A. Swankin, "State Right-to-Work Legislative Action in 1958," *Monthly Labor Review*, Vol. 81, No. 8 (December 1958), pp. 1380-1381.

9. *Lincoln Union* vs. *Northwestern Co.* 335 U.S. 525, 530-1.

10. 335 U.S. 538, 546.

11. 225 S.W. (2d) 958, 962.

12. Tennessee Chancery Court (February 15, 1956) 37 LRRM 2579, 2581.

13. 235 S.W. (2d) 45, 50.

14. Tex Ct Civ App (1952) 233 SW. 2d 622; Writ of error refused, Tex Sup Ct (1952) 246 SW 2d 938.

15. 345 U.S. 192.

16. *Ibid.*, pp. 202-5. As C. B. Rogers complained, " . . . determination of the lawful purpose' test appears to be little more than a semantic vehicle for giving free run to the economic predilections of the individual trial courts." "Right-to-work Statutes and the 'Unlawful Purpose' Doctrine," *Journal of Public Law,* II (Spring 1953), p. 212.

17. 299 S.W. 2d 8, 353 U.S. 969.

18. 336 U.S. 301.

19. Ariz. Sup. Ct. 1961. 42 Labor Cases par 50, 176, March 8, 1961.

20. H.R. Rep. No. 510, 80th Cong., 1st Sess. 60 (1947), 1 Leg. Hist. 564.

21. 208 Ga. 541, 67 S.E. (2d) 767.

22. NC Sup Ct (1958) 247 NC 523, 101 SE. 2d, 373, 376; NC Sup Ct (1959) 250 NC 396, 109 SE. 2d 233 cert. den'd. U.S. Sup. Ct. (1959) 261 US 893, 80 S Ct 195.

23. 41 So (2d) 305, 307.

24. *Lunsford* vs. *City of Bryan,* 292 S.W. 2d 852; 156 Tex. 520, 297 S.W. 2d 115.

25. J. R. Dempsey, S.J., Milwaukee, Wisconsin: The Marquette University Press, 1961, p. 127.

26. *Right to Work in Practice,* A Report to the Fund for the Republic, New York, 1959, p. 45.

27. "Union Security and Checkoff Provisions in Major Union Contracts, 1958-59," *op. cit.* A Bureau of National Affairs survey of 400 "representative" contracts indicated that 6 per cent of these contained agency shop clauses. 46 LRRA 458, October 17, 1960.

28. AFL-CIO *Collective Bargaining Report,* Vol. 5, No. 3 (April 1960), p. 22.

29. For references to War Labor Board cases that validated union security arrangements involving requirements other than membership as a condition of employment, see *Public Service Co. of Colorado,* 89 NLRB 418, note p. 424.

30. "Award on Issue of Union Security in Ford Dispute," *The Labour Gazette* (January 1946), Ottawa, Canada. Reprint, p. 5.

31. *Ibid.,* p. 6.

32. After one week, employees could lose one year's seniority for every continuous absence for a calendar week. The employer could suspend his checkoff obligations for not less than 2 and not more than 6 months.

33. Memorandum from J. T. Montague to W. R. Dymond, Canadian Department of Labour, Economics and Research Branch, Ottawa, September 24, 1957.

34. As described in "Canada Labour Views," July 3, 1957 and contained in a memo from W. R. Dymond of the Canadian Department of Labour to the author.

35. Quoted by Michael Dudra, "The Swiss System of Union Security," *Labor Law Journal,* Vol. 10, No. 3 (March 1959), p. 167.

36. *Ibid.,* p. 170.

37. *Public Service Company of Colorado,* 89 NLRB 418. This ruling covered terms of an agreement negotiated prior to the Taft Hartley amendments to the LMRA.

38. *American Seating Company,* 98 NLRB 800, 802.

39. Rulings on Appeals from Interim Decision of Regional Directors in Complaint Cases, Case No. 364, August 15, 1952. The General Counsel more recently has ruled that a contract would be illegal if it stipulated withholding severance pay from employees discharged for failing to pay their service fee to the union. Rulings on Appeal from Interim Decision of Regional Directors in Complaint Cases. Case No. SR-33, July 27, 1959.

40. 61 Stat. 136; italics supplied.

41. See Jerome L. Toner, "Right-to-Work Laws and the Common Good," Presidential Address to the Catholic Economic Association, Eighteenth Annual Meeting, December 28, 1959, Washington, D. C. (Processed) pp. 4 and 14; Norman Jones, "The Agency Shop," *Labor Law Journal,* Vol. 10, No. 11 (November 1959), p. 787.

42. George Rose, "The Agency Shop v. the Right-to-Work Law," *Labor Law Journal,* Vol. 9, No. 8 (August 1958), p. 580.

43. *Railway Employes' Department* vs. *Hanson,* 351 U.S. 225, 238.

44. 347 U.S. 17, 41 (1954).

45. 25 Tex. 524, 295 S.W. 2d 412, 416.

46. 87 NLRB 779 (1949), enf'd, 186 F. 2d 1008 (7th Cir. 1951), cert. denied 342 U.S. 815. See also *United Brotherhood of Carpenters,* 115 NLRB 518 (1956).

47. *Peerless Tool & Engineering Co.,* 111 NLRB 853 (1955).

48. *Coal, Gasoline & Fuel Oil Co.,* 113 NLRB 111 (1955).

49. *Kaiser Aluminum & Chemical Corp.,* 93 NLRB 1203 (1951).

50. *Eclipse Lumber Co.,* 95 NLRB 464 (1951), 199 F. 2d 684 (9th Cir. 1952).

51. *Central Pipe Fabricating & Supply Co.,* 114 NLRB 350 (1955).

52. J. A. McClain, Jr., "New Judicial Concepts: Right to Work—Union Membership," *Labor Law Journal,* Vol. 8, No. 3 (March 1957), p. 163. For discussion on the obligation of union membership, see Jerome L. Toner, "The Union Shop Under Taft-Hartley," *Labor Law Journal,* Vol. 5, No. 8 (August 1954), pp. 552-562; Bernard H. Fitzpatrick, "The Starchless Union Shop Issue," *Labor Law Journal,* Vol. 5, No. 9 (September 1954), pp. 595-598, 651; Charles Cogen, "Is Joining the Union Required in the Taft-Hartley Union Shop?" *Labor Law Journal,* Vol. 5, No. 10 (October 1954), pp. 659-662, 735-736; Jerome L. Toner, "The Taft-Hartley Union Shop Does Not Force Anyone to Join a Union," *Labor Law Journal,* Vol. 6, No. 10 (October 1955), pp. 690-695, and Walter L. Daykin, "Union Fees and Dues," *Labor Law Journal,* Vol. 9, No. 4 (April 1958), pp. 289-297.

53. *General Motors Corp.* 130 NLRB 481, 502 (1961).

54. For a critical commentary of the bill on this score, see Benjamin Aaron, "The Labor-Management Reporting and Disclosure Act of 1959," *Harvard Law Review,* Vol. 73, No. 5 (March 1960), pp. 855-866. As Kurt L. Hanslowe makes the point, "One point seems to me to be elemental. The right *to* union membership needs to be enhanced. For the individual employee to make his voice felt in the union requires that he be allowed to join and to participate. The law has done an appalling amount of pussy-footing in failing

to recognize that the union is a sufficiently significant instrument in the working lives of people so as to require modification of the general rule that a voluntary association is free to reject for membership anyone it pleases." "Individual Rights in Collective Labor Relations," *Cornell Law Quarterly,* Vol. 45, No. 1 (Fall 1959), p. 53.

55. Memorandum of the Industrial Relations Division, N.A.M. "A Look at the Agency Shop," December 5, 1960 (Mimeographed), p. 3.

56. In Kansas, Senate Bill No. 116 incorporated a more restrictive language but the bill failed to pass in the 1951 legislative session. The Kansas Supreme Court denied the relevance of this in outlawing the agency shop, considering the argument to be "highly speculative." *Higgins* vs. *Cardinal Manufacturing Co.* 188 Kan. 11, 360 P. (2d) 456.

57. Dale D. McConkey, "Was the Agency Shop Prematurely Scrapped?" *Labor Law Journal,* Vol. 9, No. 2 (February 1958), pp. 150-1.

58. For discussion see Norman Jones, "The Agency Shop," *Labor Law Journal,* Vol. 10, No. 11 (November 1959), pp. 783 and 788.

59. *Baldwin* vs. *Arizona Flame Restaurant,* 82 Ariz. 385, 313 p. 2d 759. In the appeal to the Supreme Court of Arizona, the court declared it unnecessary to rule on the legality of the agency shop on the ground that the point had been abandoned.

60. *Schermerhorn* vs. *Retail Clerks,* Local 1625, Florida Court of Appeals, 1961. CCH, Topical Law Reports, Par. 19,259 (Sept. 29, 1961).

61. *Meade Electric Co.* vs. *Hagberg,* 159 N.E. 2d 408.

62. *General Motors Corp.,* 130 NLRB 481 (1961).

63. 133 NLRB No. 21, Case No. 7-CA-2560, September 29, 1961.

64. *Higgins* vs. *Cardinal Manufacturing Co.,* 188 Kan. 11, 360 P. (2d) 456 (1961).

65. Ruling of State Attorney General Clarence Beck, March 8, 1960. CCH Law Reports, Par 41,025.10; 45 LRRM 104. Italics added.

66. Attorney General Opinion No. 407, September, 1958, reversing the Attorney General Opinion of July 11, 1952.

67. Attorney General Opinion, August 24, 1959; similarly January 13, 1956. CCH Labor Law Reports, N. Dakota, Par 41,025.15; 34 LRRM 2707.

68. Attorney General Opinion (1961) No. WW-1018, March 14, 1961.

69. 68 Stat. 1238, 45 U.S.C. No. 152, Eleventh, Section 2.

70. *Railway Employes' Dept.* vs. *Hanson,* 160 Neb. 669, 71 N.W. 2d 526, 351 U.S. 225.

71. United States Supreme Court, Docket No. 4, October Term, 1960, June 19, 1961. On Appeal from Supreme Court of Georgia. Reversing and remanding (1959) 215 Ga. 27, 108 S.E. (2d) 796, which affirmed *Looper* vs. *Georgia Southern & Florida Railway Co.,* (Ga. 1957).

72. *Allen Bradley Co.* vs. *NLRB* (CA-7, 1961).

73. *NLRB* vs. *Wooster Division of Borg-Warner Corp.* 356 U.S. 342.

5

THE WEAPONS OF CONFLICT:

PICKETING AND BOYCOTTS

DONALD H. WOLLETT

*Attorney and arbitrator; formerly Professor of Law, Louisiana State
University, New York University, and the University of Washington*

WHAT ARE THESE THINGS?

Thirty years ago a state supreme court, seeking escape from the
dilemma which it had created for itself by developing two conflicting lines of cases, solemnly held that a labor union member who pa-
trols with a banner more than 100 feet from an employer's place of
business is not a picket subject to injunction because a picket is
"an out-guard posted before an army to give notice of any enemy
approaching."[1] The reference to a military dictionary is amusing
but not surprising, for the fact is that picketing is a weapon of
economic warfare and can best be understood in those terms.

One of the standard methods of waging war is to undertake to
dry up the enemy's sources of supply or his markets, or both, i.e., to
subject him to quarantine, by enlisting the support of persons who
either have or are likely to have some sort of economic relationship with him. In the context of a labor dispute picketing is the
union's usual, although not its only, technique for recruiting and
mobilizing this "third force." It is, always and without meaningful
exception, part of an effort to boycott.

The behavior to which the term "picketing" is commonly applied
covers a wide range of conduct, the variables being the number

of men, where they are and when they are there, what they say, the size, shape, and type of signs they carry, the language on those signs, the leaflets they hand out (if any), etc. However, all of this behavior has some common qualities.

First, there is always an element of communication. It may be obscured by other aspects of the conduct, as in the case of mass picketing, but it is there.

Second, picketing is intended to reach a specialized audience, *viz.*, persons who either have some sort of economic relationship to the employer or are likely to enter into one.

Third, since picketing is aimed at a narrow group, it occurs in places where and at times when the members of that group can be met face to face.

Fourth, picketing is designed to produce an immediate response. The picketing union does not merely seek acceptance of an opinion or point of view, and it is not content with decision after a reasoned, contemplative judgment. It demands supportive action now.

Finally, the picket, unlike the political speaker who importunes his listeners to vote his way, is in a position to observe whether or not his efforts have produced the desired behavior.

THEORIES OF JUDICIAL CONTROL [2]

Of Means and Ends

Picketing which, regardless of its objectives, involves violence or threats of violence is regarded as "coercive" and subject to restraint. If the peaceful and non-peaceful aspects of the picketing are inextricably entwined, the entire course of conduct may be enjoined.[3] If, however, they are separable, the decree may be tailored so as to permit the peaceful conduct while restraining violence, threats of violence, molestation, and the like. Or it may limit the number of pickets or the places where they may be stationed.[4]

A number of cases, particularly early ones, enjoined picketing on the theory that it was *ipso facto* "coercive." However, on analysis these decisions appear to have rested, not on findings that persons respected the picket line because of fear of physical harm, but on the ground either (a) that it was effective in interfering with advantageous economic relationships, that is, that it did what picketing is always designed to do,[5] or (b) that it had some objective which the court thought was unlawful.[6]

Some courts applied the common law rule that the intentional infliction of harm on another is tortious unless justified.[7] Proof of intentional harm makes a *prima facie* case, which may be overcome by showing that the injury was inflicted in order to advance the economic self-interest of the defendant. Thus, many courts treated picketing as lawful if its purpose was to obtain benefits for the members of the union, i.e., better wages, shorter hours, or improvement of other terms or conditions of employment.[8]

Some courts refused, however, to accept the strengthening of group bargaining power, e.g., the all-union shop, as a legitimate end.[9] And others took the position that, unless a union had members employed by an employer, it was a "stranger" without sufficient interest in the terms and conditions of employment in his plant to justify the infliction of harm; and that, therefore, picketing to gain status as the bargaining representative of employees was unlawful.[10] This position was held even though the evidence showed that the employer was part of an organized industry and his existence as a non-union operation jeopardized working conditions in union shops.

Limiting the Arena of Battle

It was not enough, at least as most courts viewed the matter, that the picketing was peaceful and that its objective was lawful. Either on the theory that economic warfare must be kept within reasonable bounds lest the cost to the community become intolerable, or on the ground that "neutrals" to the dispute should be protected, picketing a place of business operated by an employer other than the one with whom the union had a quarrel was a "secondary" boycott, and generally treated as unlawful.[11]

A "primary" employer, as the term was used, meant one whose labor relations policies the union disputed. A "secondary" employer was one upon whom the union was exerting economic pressure solely because of some kind of business relationship it maintained with the "primary" employer. Reverting to the *prima facie* tort doctrine, it might be said that the union, since it had no quarrel with the "secondary" employer's employment conditions and practices, lacked sufficient interest to justify causing injury to him.

Two notable exceptions evolved. The first was the "economic ally" doctrine, which held that when the "primary" employer, crippled by a strike at his place of business, farmed his work to a "secondary" employer, the latter, by accepting the work, allied himself with the former and could be picketed.[12]

The second, and potentially much broader exception, was the "unity of interest" doctrine, which held that where a "secondary" employer has an identifiable economic stake in the "primary" employer's successful resistance to the union's demands, as, for example, where he retails a product manufactured in a non-union plant, he is not a "neutral" and may be subjected to union pressures.[13]

Although this doctrine might have been extended to include any "secondary" employer making, processing or delivering goods for use by the "primary" employer and any "secondary" employer using the products or services of the "primary" employer, it seems largely to have been restricted to the situation where the "secondary" employer held the "hot" goods for resale.[14]

One further point needs to be made. *All* boycotts, regardless of the location of the pickets, involve pressure by a union which causes (or seeks to cause) one person to stop doing business with another—that is, to bring onto one side of the dispute a person who is not a party to it. In that sense all boycotts are "secondary." But the term has had a different meaning in law, depending not alone on *whose* behavior was affected by the picketing but also on *where* the picketing occurred. Thus, for instance, the Washington court, which was notably intolerant of pressures applied at the premises of "secondary" employers,[15] permitted picketing, if it was otherwise lawful, at the place of business of the "primary" employer even though it caused truck drivers working for "secondary" employers to refuse to make deliveries at the picketed premises.[16]

STATUTORY IMMUNITIES

Prior to 1935 the major objective of American unions was to organize workers and to gain recognition and acceptance as their bargaining representatives. For many reasons, one of which was the absence of legal restrictions on employers' ability to utilize economic power in repressing union activity on the part of their employees, this objective proved extraordinarily difficult to attain.

Strikes were broken by discharging strikers and hiring replacements. Judgments were obtained against striking, picketing, and boycotting either by invoking the Sherman Act[17] or, where the employer had demanded the execution of "yellow dog" contracts as a condition of employment, by standing on the tort of inducing breach of contract.[18]

Moreover, underlying the fabric of the law, statutory or decisional, was the widely-held notion that a union is an interloper or "stranger" to a particular employer, utterly without interest in his employment policies and practices, unless and until it organizes his workers, even though it has organized his competitors and subjected them to a market disadvantage vis-à-vis the non-union employer.[19]

Section 20 of the Clayton Act was an early Congressional effort, at least for purposes of the Sherman Act, to expand the concept of when a labor dispute justifying picketing and boycotting lies between an employer and a union, but it proved to be abortive.[20]

However, a sweeping and effective change occurred in 1932 with the passage of the Norris-LaGuardia Act.[21] Although the statute applied only to the federal courts, many of the important industrial states followed the lead of Congress.[22] Furthermore, while the Norris-LaGuardia Act appeared in terms to do nothing more than prescribe limits on federal judicial power to grant injunctive relief in labor disputes, it was subsequently given a substantive meaning which largely immunized unions from actions under the Sherman Act.[23]

In the absence of violence, picketing was free from the federal injunctive process provided (a) that the plaintiff and the defendant are "engaged in the same industry, trade, craft, or occupation in which [a labor] dispute occurs, or [have] a direct or indirect interest therein,"[24] and (b) that the matter in controversy concerns "terms or conditions of employment, . . . the association or representation of persons in negotiating, fixing, maintaining, changing, or seeking to arrange terms or conditions of employment, *regardless of whether or not the disputants stand in the proximate rela-*

tion of employer and employee." (Emphasis supplied.)[25] Thus, the principles of the Norris-LaGuardia Act pointed the law in a direction almost 180 degrees removed from the course which it had generally followed for the better part of a century.[26]

REASON VERSUS FORCE: EMERGENCE OF AFFIRMATIVE LABOR POLICIES

The policy underlying the Norris-LaGuardia Act (and parallel or similar state legislation) was essentially *laissez-faire, viz.,* that in the main the law should keep its hand out of labor disputes, permitting employers and unions to resolve their conflicts by the use of such economic weapons as they could muster and command. The statute reflected the philosophy that had been urged by Holmes nearly forty years earlier: that the clash between the interests of management and labor is a form of competition which, because "competition is worth more to society than it costs," requires the law to tolerate "the intentional inflicting of temporal damage, including the damage of interference with a man's business, by some means, when the damage is done not for its own sake, but as an instrumentality in reaching the end of victory in the battle of trade."[27]

However, the enactment of the Wagner Act[28] three years later manifested a very different notion of the proper role of government in labor disputes from that of the Norris-LaGuardia Act and set in motion policies that inevitably collided with those of the earlier statute.

Even though limited in scope, the Wagner Act was interventionist legislation. It recognized that disputes over the organization of workers into unions for the purpose of collective bargaining are government business, and directed that such controversies should be resolved in accordance with the wishes of the employees involved. The choice of the majority in an "appropriate bargaining unit" was controlling. Employers were commanded to remain neutral, or substantially so, and to accept the decision of their workers. Unions were left unregulated.

The Taft-Hartley amendments of 1947[29] reaffirmed this basic policy and gave it added support by expressly recognizing the right to reject unions and collective bargaining, and by protecting employee freedom of choice against limited types of union inter-ference. Beyond that, the 1947 legislation set forth the notion that the government also has a stake, justifying intervention and regu-lation, in other kinds of labor disputes.

In addition to prohibiting the inclusion of certain provisions in collective bargaining agreements [30] and providing for a degree of governmental supervision of the process of negotiating and re-negotiating contract terms,[31] it declared that disputes over the interpretation and meaning of labor contracts should be resolved in the courts.[32]

CURRENT LABOR POLICY: MAJOR POINTS OF CONFLICT

Disputes over Organization and Representation

The emphasis of the Wagner Act on employee preference as the controlling factor in determining whether a given union would gain status as the bargaining representative in a particular plant or business establishment clashed with some of the traditions of American trade unionism.

The unions of the United States that lived to see the 1930's had survived in an inhospitable and uncongenial climate: depressions and sated labor markets, deep seated employer hostility, employee apathy and lack of class-consciousness, and indifferent, if not antagonistic, governments. Their vitality and strength lay in mem-bership cohesiveness built around skilled jobs and leadership which, taking as its first obligation the protection and advancement of the members' bread-and-butter interests, claimed and attempted to enforce sovereignty over all work falling within the trade or craft.

These unions, particularly in industries characterized by intense competition, a multiplicity of small employing units, and high labor costs, understood that they could neither hold nor improve the gains made for their members in the unionized segment of the trade against the market competition of unorganized employers enjoying the advantage of lower labor costs. It was necessary either to keep non-union products out of the market or to unionize all of the jobs in the competitive area.

A union's interest in the terms and conditions of employment was not limited to a single employer. It extended, rather, through-

out the trade and compelled the union either to organize the unorganized or, failing that, to expropriate them from the market by
using the weapons of economic warfare. The Norris-LaGuardia
Act manifested an awareness of these facts.

However, the Wagner Act did not. The grouping of jobs designated by the National Labor Relations Board as the "appropriate
bargaining unit" within which the principle of majority free choice
determined whether or not employments would be unionized was
much narrower than the unit of competition. Although multi-
employer units were sometimes found to be appropriate, usually
the unit designation embraced only the jobs of a particular employer. The union might lose an election or otherwise fail to get
support, thereby leaving the jobs outside its hegemony. But the
considerations set forth above might militate against acceptance
of the employees' decision and compel the union to continue to
press for control of the jobs by resort to self-help.

The problem was complicated by the rise of industrial unions,
not only because their interest in the terms and conditions of employment and their need to organize transcended particular trades
or crafts and extended to all employments in the industry, but also
because their jurisdictional claims frequently overlapped those
of the craft unions. Victory for one did not necessarily end the
territorial or job ambitions and requirements of the other.

The result was that a union, even though it clearly lacked the
support of a majority of the employees in an "appropriate bargaining unit," might strike, picket or boycott in an effort to achieve
its purposes through economic pressures. The propriety of such
conduct was even subject to rationalization as consistent with,
rather than contrary to, the principle of majority rule, if the proofs
showed that the great bulk of the employees in the industrial or
trade unit of competition supported the union. The employees in
the NLRB's "appropriate bargaining unit" amounted, in this context, only to a minority group whose recalcitrance tended to weaken
the bargaining power of the majority and threaten their employment standards.

Nevertheless, such conduct was repugnant to the affirmative
policy of the Wagner Act, establishing a peaceable procedure for
the resolution of disputes over organization and representation,

and declaring that the freely expressed wishes of a majority of the employees in the "employer unit, craft unit, plant unit, or subdivision thereof"[33] should be controlling. Transgression of the statutory scheme and conflict between the policies of the Wagner Act and Norris-LaGuardia Act were revealed in starkest form in the situation where the employees elected a union which was duly certified by the NLRB as their bargaining representative, thereby fixing upon their employer the duty to bargain exclusively with it, and a union which the employees had rejected picketed in protest.

Since the picketing union and the picketed employer were engaged in the same industry or trade, and since the matter in controversy concerned the representation of persons in negotiating or seeking to arrange the terms and conditions of employment, the activity arose out of a labor dispute within the meaning of the Norris-LaGuardia Act and was therefore immune from federal injunctive process, although its objective was to upset a determination reached in compliance with Wagner Act procedures and principles and, more than that, would force the employer to commit an unlawful act.[34]

Such a collision of policies was intolerable, and the enactment in 1947, as part of the Taft-Hartley amendments, of Section 8(b)(4)(C) making union inducements to strike for recognition in the teeth of a certification an unfair labor practice, requiring the Board to seek a preliminary injunction in federal court, and freeing the court from the strictures of the Norris-LaGuardia Act, was inevitable.

However, in terms of protecting the integrity of the principle that the free choice of the employees in an "appropriate bargaining unit" should control the disposition of disputes over organization and representation, Section 8(b)(4)(C) was clearly inadequate.

First, if an uncoerced majority of the employees selected a union as their bargaining representative without the formality of an election, they remained subject to the pressures created by picketing of the business by some union which they did not want, even though the employer had recognized their choice and negotiated a contract.

Second, if a majority of the employees voted "no" in an NLRB election, Section 8(b)(4)(C) did not interdict immediate picketing by the rejected union.

Finally, there was nothing in the Taft-Hartley amendments to cover the situation where a union, after having conducted an unsuccessful organizational campaign, or perhaps without having bothered to conduct one at all, put up a picket line with the hope that it would hurt the business enough so that either the employer would capitulate without regard to what his employees wanted or the employees, preferring not to be laid off, would see the wisdom of applying for membership.

Section 8(b)(1)(A) of Taft-Hartley prohibited a union from restraining or coercing employees in the exercise of their right to organize or not to organize—to choose or reject a bargaining representative. But the Supreme Court of the United States concluded that the statutory guarantee of the right to strike included the right to picket, and held that the words "restrain or coerce" embraced only the use of repressive union tactics bordering on violence or involving particularized threats of economic reprisal. They did not, so the Court held, proscribe the more diffuse pressures generated by peaceful picketing.[35]

The inadequacies of the Taft-Hartley amendments in protecting employee free choice made it predictable that Congress would legislate further on the matter. The result was Section 8(b)(7), passed in 1959 as part of the Labor Management and Disclosure Act.[36]

Section 8(b)(7) appears to close the first two of the three gaps discussed above. As to the third, it leaves that open, provided that the picketing does not go on too long. How long is too long is not known except that the period cannot be less than one day and may be as long as 30 days—*unless* (1) the union files a petition for an election or a meritorious refusal to bargain charge,[37] in which case the picketing may go on longer than 30 days; *or* (2) the pickets content themselves with saying that the employer is non-union, employees who work for other people pay no attention to what they say, or the picketing is not aimed at changing the mind of the employer or his employees about the merits of unionism, but is designed to expropriate the business from the market place by causing its customers to take their patronage elsewhere. In this case the picketing may go on indefinitely.[38]

Breach of the Collective Agreement

The NLRB, in the exercise of its primary jurisdiction over unfair labor practices, has developed a line of cases recognizing the "traditional sanctity attached to contracts by our system of jurisprudence."[39] Thus, a strike in breach of a collective agreement is not protected concerted activity.[40] Moreover, it operates to suspend the employer's duty to bargain,[41] and it may constitute an unfair labor practice.[42]

However, the Board's function in this area of labor law is peripheral, for Congress, by the enactment of Section 301 of the Taft-Hartley Act, vested jurisdiction in the courts over actions for breach of a labor agreement.

Section 301 provides that "suits for violation of contracts between an employer and a labor organization representing employees . . . may be brought in any district court of the United States. . . ."[43] The rights and duties are federal rights and duties.[44] While state courts have concurrent jurisdiction,[45] the action is governed by federal substantive law "which the courts must fashion from the policy of our national labor laws."[46]

In terms, Section 301 provides only the remedy of damages, and most federal courts have held that, where the propriety of union self-help is in issue, *viz.*, the complaint alleges breach of a promise not to strike, the controversy arises out of a labor dispute within the meaning of the Norris-LaGuardia Act, thus foreclosing issuance of an injunction.[47]

However, the opinion of the Supreme Court of the United States in *Textile Workers Union of America* vs. *Lincoln Mills of Alabama*[48] directs the courts to look at the policy underlying Section 301 and to fashion a remedy that will effectuate that policy.[49] Moreover, the reasoning of *Lincoln Mills* in support of the holding that agreements to arbitrate are specifically enforceable is built on the premise that Congress intended promises not to strike to be enforceable by effective and meaningful remedies. Accordingly, the Tenth Circuit has held that the Norris-LaGuardia Act, read in the light of the language and underlying purpose of Section 301, does not deprive the federal courts of jurisdiction to enjoin a union from resorting to self-help in violation of a collective bargaining agreement.[50] However, as of this writing the weight of authority appears to be contrary.

TOWARD A CONSISTENT LABOR POLICY: SOME SUGGESTIONS FOR THE REGULATION OF PICKETING AND BOYCOTTING

1. *Where there is a forum available for resolution of the issue in dispute, striking should be prohibited. Use of the secondary weapons of economic warfare, picketing and boycotting, should also be prohibited.*

This proposition is by no means novel. It was adopted by the Taft-Hartley Act in cases involving disputes as to who has jurisdiction over certain types of work.[51] It underlay the decision in *Dorchy* vs. *Kansas* that a state may, without offending the requirements of constitutional due process, prohibit a strike for the purpose of collecting back wages allegedly owed to an employee.[52] The Court reasoned that this purpose was not permissible because each party had the right to insist that the matter in dispute be determined only by a court.

It was expressly recognized as sound policy in *Building Trades Council of Reno* vs. *Thompson* sustaining a judgment for damage done to an employer by striking and picketing to force him to collect and remit a fine allegedly owed by one of his employees to the union of which he had been a member at the time the fine was assessed.[53] The court concluded that this objective did not constitute sufficient justification for the intentional infliction of harm, because the claim of the union was subject to ultimate determination by a court of competent jurisdiction.

Furthermore, the Supreme Court, in determining the applicability of the Norris-LaGuardia Act to strikes in the railway industry, has distinguished between "major" disputes involving controversies over the terms of the collective agreement and "minor" disputes over grievances subject to the jurisdiction of the National Railroad Adjustment Board, holding that strikes as to the latter are enjoinable.[54]

The suggestion that union self-help should be prohibited in any case where the matters at issue are within the jurisdiction of, and subject to determination by, a tribunal—judicial, administrative, or arbitral—obviously goes further than is necessary to correct the inconsistencies in federal labor policy discussed above. It would interdict striking, picketing, and boycotting over employer unfair labor practices, as well as over questions of organization and representation. Moreover, it would prohibit such conduct arising out of a dispute over any contract issue which might properly be the subject of a law suit or an arbitration proceeding pursuant to agreement, even though the contract did not contain a no-strike clause.[55]

The justification for prescribing such a broad remedy lies in a basic policy which, while not articulated, underlies the federal labor statutes—from the Wagner Act, through the Taft-Hartley Act, to the Landrum-Griffin Act: that economic warfare as the method for resolving labor disputes is primitive, barbaric, and—most important—wasteful, not only to the disputants, but also to the community. In terms of the Holmesian philosophy which is manifested in the Norris-LaGuardia Act, it often costs society more than it is worth.

The search, therefore, has been for procedures of settlement that are more orderly, more rational, more apt to serve the interests of the community, and less costly than trial by ordeal. And where standards for settlement could be agreed upon, such methods have been adopted.

With the exception of the war years and an occasional controversy which is thought to involve national health, safety, and welfare, self-help arising out of disputes over what the terms of the labor contract should be has largely been left unregulated. We have been content to have such disputes ultimately resolved by power, rather than by process of law, not because we are unmindful of the costs of economic warfare or the antisocial results which it sometimes produces, but because there are no generally agreed-upon or acceptable criteria for settlement, the interpretation and application of which we are willing to entrust to the organs of government.

But where standards and procedures have been agreed upon

and generally accepted as sensible and fair, as in cases involving questions over representation, or over the rights of employees to engage in union activities without being subjected to coercion or discrimination, or over the meaning of a collective bargaining agreement, there do not seem to be any valid reasons for permitting the parties involved to continue to settle their disputes by self-help.

The point is sometimes made that labor disputes are attended by much greater urgency than other kinds of disputes and that, accordingly, their disposition cannot be committed exclusively to the slow and painstaking processes of the law. The point lacks merit for two reasons. First, the proposal set forth above does not prevent out-of-court settlements by agreement. All it does is to make the position of the negotiator and his willingness to give or take more dependent upon the likelihood of success or failure in law than upon the likelihood of an effective strike or picket line. Second, although there is plenty of call for complaint about the sluggishness of the legal process, administrative as well as judicial, this is not, since the defect is not inherent, a valid ground for objecting to the merits of the proposal. It does, however, point up and emphasize the glaring defects in the administration of our labor laws and the need for immediate and radical changes, particularly in the area of interlocutory relief.

A more serious objection is to the assumption, which is implicit in the proposal, that organizational picketing is a species of restraint and coercion which should be prohibited in order to maintain the integrity of the principle that employee free choice should govern the disposition of questions of representation.

The argument in support of the proposal and the validity of the assumption can perhaps best be made by looking at the other side of the coin. An employer is obligated by Section 8(a)(1) not to restrain or coerce his employees in the exercise of their right to engage or not to engage in union activity. It is well settled that, in evaluating and appraising the effect of an employer's conduct on the free exercise of this right, proofs as to *actual* effect are not essential and, if they are put in the record, not necessarily controlling.[56] It is enough that the NLRB, in the exercise of its expertise, concludes that the conduct has a reasonable tendency to produce the proscribed effect, that is, to restrain or coerce.[57]

The purpose of picketing is to dry up the employer's sources of supply, or his market, or both. It may or may not be effective in accomplishing this objective. But, looking again to the cases involving employer conduct under Section 8(a)(1), the success or failure of actions that tend to coerce is not the criterion upon which a finding of coercion is based. The conclusion, based upon the evidence, that conduct tends to or is reasonably calculated to coerce is sufficient. Picketing, which threatens the job security and income of every employee in the picketed establishment, seems clearly to fall in that category.

If the objective of legislation is to free employees from the coercive and restraining effect of picketing, the approach taken by Section 8(b)(7)(C) must be rejected as unsatisfactory. While there may be differences in degree, picketing tends to be coercive on the first day as well as on the thirtieth, and the fact that the union files a petition for an election neither strengthens nor weakens this tendency.

Furthermore, it makes little difference whether the objective of the picketing is to gain recognition, to organize the employees, or to inform members of the public that the employer is non-union with the hope that they will take their business elsewhere. Regardless of its objective, picketing threatens the business and therefore tends to restrain or coerce the employees who work there. Furthermore, making the legality of picketing turn on such refinements— whether it is recognitional, organizational, or merely informational —places a premium on the finesse of the union or its lawyer in fixing a course of conduct that will not support an adverse finding as to the picketing's objective. Exactly what is said to the employer before and during the picketing, what language is placed on the signs, etc., are all-important. The process is not unlike that involved in counseling an employer as to what he should say in a "captive audience" speech so that he can effectively coerce his employees without appearing to the NLRB to be doing so. The protection accorded employee freedom of choice should not be subject to circumvention by artful manipulation.

It *is* material, in appraising the effect of picketing, as Section 8(b)(7)(C) recognizes, that it does not produce refusals to work. Where this is the fact, the tendency to coerce is obviously diminished. However, in the situation where so-called "publicity" or "informational" picketing has its greatest effectiveness, that is, at or near a retail outlet or similar establishment offering goods or services to the general public, its tendency to coerce is certainly not removed by the failure of employees to give it heed.

Much of the confusion about the nature of picketing and the reluctance to deal with it squarely as a weapon of economic coercion stems from the Supreme Court's decision in *Thornhill* vs. *Alabama*.[58] The case held that the dissemination of information and opinions concerning a labor dispute and the importuning of persons not to patronize or do business with a particular employer are within the area of free discussion protected by the Constitution of the United States against governmental abridgement. The Court concluded, therefore, that a state cannot prohibit *all* methods and means for communicating such facts, ideas and points of view, including picketing, simply because they are put into operation at or near the employer's premises and threaten him with economic harm.

Subsequent decisions of the Court have made it clear that, while picketing is a method for disseminating facts and opinions about labor disputes, it is not to be equated with other modes and means for the communication of such information and ideas. Quite apart from what is said, a picket line as a means of communication "involves patrol of a particular locality" and "may induce action of one kind or another irrespective of the . . . ideas . . . disseminated."[59] Clearly the words spoken on a picket line, even though innocuous on their face, lose "significance as an appeal to reason" and become "part of an instrument of force" where they are set in context of violence.[60] Furthermore, even in the absence of violence, picketing is not immune from regulation where it is an integral part of conduct designed to cause the commission of an unlawful act,[61] to force a non-union enterprise to change its hours of business,[62] or to coerce an employer to require his employees to join a union.[63]

It is the physical characteristics of picketing, as set forth in the introduction to this paper, that distinguish it from other modes and methods of speech and compel the conclusion that the communication of information by picketing may be prohibited in circumstances where dissemination of the same information by some other means, e.g., a newspaper, a leaflet, a handbill, or a televised speech, would be privileged under the First Amendment.[64]

The cases seem to make it clear that picketing which appeals to workers to refuse to perform services may constitutionally be restrained, so far as free speech considerations are concerned, on any ground that has a rational basis. The response of a worker to a picket line usually stems from custom, fear of reprisal, or a belief that no picket line should ever be crossed. Neither what the picket says nor how the worker reacts seems to have much to do with the "free discussion concerning the conditions in industry and the laws of labor disputes" that the Court in the *Thornhill* case regarded an "indispensable to the effective and intelligent use of the processes of popular government to shape the destiny of modern industrial society."[65]

The point may be developed by drawing an analogy again to cases involving the question of whether employer speech amounts to restraint or coercion within the meaning of Section 8(a)(1). Since the effect of an employer's conduct is a "subtle thing" requiring a "high degree of introspective perception,"[66] the trier of fact may not only appraise the content of the speech but may also weigh the circumstances surrounding it, including the place and time of the delivery and the relationship between the speaker and the listener.[67]

Suppose the labor relations director of a company involved in an organizational campaign by a union called the 100 employees affected to a meeting on company time and property and stated as follows: "Generally speaking, I have no objection to unions. But I don't like the XYZ union, which I understand some of you are tied up with. And I suppose some of the rest of you are thinking about getting tied up with it. I don't like the XYZ union because it's a bad outfit. It's an unfair outfit. I hope you won't give it any support. In fact, I'll be disgusted with you if you do. But the decision is yours. The question is: Are you going to be loyal to the company or to the union? I want your answer now, and I want you to give it to me this way: Those of you who support the union leave the room by the rear door where my two assistants are standing; those of you who support the company stay in your seats for the purpose of signing a petition repudiating the union."

The effect of such a "captive audience" speech on the listeners cannot be equated exactly to the impact of picketing. A union, unlike an employer vis-à-vis his employees, does not always have power to cause economic reprisals to be visited upon workers who defy its wishes. However, the analogy is close enough to be useful.

As to the employees who remained in their seats, did they do so because of the persuasive effect of the speaker's remarks, uttered pursuant to his right to discuss freely "the conditions in industry and the causes of labor disputes?" Or did they remain there because, by calling them into a company meeting room during working hours and demanding an immediate decision and response to his plea—under managerial surveillance—he established a *locus in quo* with a greater potential for inducing the action he desired than any of the opinions he expressed?

Constitutional considerations do not foreclose a determination that the latter factors, not the former, produced the response of the listeners, and that such conduct should be prohibited. The same thing should be true as to picketing which is aimed at causing work stoppages.

There remains, however, a good deal of doubt about how far a legislature may go in regulating picketing which directs its appeal solely to customers of the employer, the same kind of picketing which, if it is "informational," is exempt from the interdictions of Section 8(b)(7)(C).[68] Such picketing lacks the threat of economic sanction which inheres in picketing aimed at causing employees to refuse to work. However, it retains the rest of the characteristics which differentiate picketing from other methods of communication.

It is helpful, in considering this aspect of the problem, to consider again the ingredients of the *Thornhill* doctrine. The basic postulate is that labor relations are not matters of mere local or private concern. Like the expression of ideas about religious and political issues, the communication of facts and opinions about questions of labor relations involves matters of public concern. Such speech is, therefore, within the area of free discussion embraced by the First Amendment.

It follows that the setting forth of information and points of view about labor disputes through pamphlets, leaflets, handbills, newspaper advertisements, and speeches on radio or television is largely immune from regulation, even though the result is that some customers or potential customers turn away from the employer involved. The peaceful discussion of matters of public interest cannot be interdicted merely on a showing that others may thereby be persuaded to take action. Influencing others is a prime purpose of speech, and it cannot be restrained solely because it is effective.

The trouble, however, with equating "consumer" picketing with leaflets, advertisements, and radio speeches is that it typically does not involve a free discussion of anything. It usually does not attempt to inform, educate, propagandize, or to advance public knowledge. It has no utility in terms of the "effective and intelligent use of the processes of popular government to shape the destiny of modern industrial society." Its only purpose, and its only function, is to place the employer in quarantine by labeling him as "unfair."

Moreover, its effectiveness depends, in large measure, on two factors, neither of which has anything to do with free communication or discussion: (1) the degree to which the general public holds the predeliction that unions are right and employers are wrong; and (2) the extent to which consumers are unwilling to risk incurring the displeasure of the picketing union.

The slight element of speech involved in "consumer" picketing does not, when weighed against the competing value of protecting employee freedom of choice, appear to compel, as a matter of constitutional law, or to justify, as a matter of policy, carving out an exception to the proposal that picketing should be prohibited where the issue in dispute is the organization and representation of employees (or any other issue subject to determination by a tribunal of competent jurisdiction).

However, a "do not patronize" list should be treated differently. Although it makes the same appeal as "consumer" picketing, it does not demand an immediate, on-the-spot response under the watchful eye of the union. It gives the reader time to think about the matter and to reach and carry out his decision free from surveillance. Therefore it lacks some of the characteristics of picketing that cause it to "induce action of one kind or another, irrespective of the . . . ideas . . . disseminated."

Limiting unions to the use of leaflets, advertisements, speeches, and the like, plus "do not patronize" lists, would, of course, sharply curtail their ability to organize all workers employed in the competitive market in order to protect employment standards in the unionized segment of the industry. However, this result seems justified by (1) the development of unions from small organisms struggling to survive in a hostile environment to large and vital organizations wielding power and influence, and (2) the importance of protecting the integrity of the body of law developed over a period of 25 years implementing the principle, by now generally accepted in the industrial community, that the wishes of the majority of the employees in an appropriate bargaining unit, expressed without restraint or coercion, should control the disposition of questions of organization and representation.

2. *Where no forum is available for resolution of the matter in dispute, striking should be permitted unless its objective is to force a transgression of law. The same rule should govern as to picketing and boycotts provided that as to employers other than the one with whom the union has a dispute, the union may interfere with their business only to the extent that they are performing strikers' work, operations directly related thereto, or operations directly related to the use or marketing of the products of the strikers' work.*

Disputes over what the terms of the collective agreement should be, arising out of the process of negotiation or renegotiation, are not, except for an occasional arbitration agreement, submissible to any tribunal with authority to render a final and binding determination.[69] This type of dispute may, because of the lack of acceptable criteria for settlement and unwillingness to entrust the job of fixing the terms and conditions of employment to political agencies, ultimately have to be settled by the process of economic warfare.

Obviously unions must be permitted to use their prime weapon, the strike, in an effort to influence the employer's position at the bargaining table. It has been less obvious, at least to the NLRB, that employers must also be permitted to use their prime weapon, the lockout.

The NLRB has taken the position that "an employer may close down his plant to avoid unusual operative problems or economic losses over and beyond the ordinary loss of business or customers attendant upon any strike, provided that, in the Board's judgment, the fear of an imminent strike is reasonable. . . . [T]he Board has manifested a marked disposition to find that the exceptional circumstances justifying a lockout do not exist."[70]

Where the motive of the employer in shutting down his plant is to punish his employees for engaging in, or threatening to engage in, a strike, or to frustrate their desire to organize and bargain collectively, the basis for holding that his conduct constitutes an unfair labor practice is clear. Where, however, an employer is bargaining in good faith with the union in an attempt to reach agreement on the terms of a contract and, in an effort to exert his bargaining power and to get an agreement which is more favorable to him than might otherwise be the case, he closes down his plant, there is no identifiable principle of federal labor policy that justifies holding that his conduct is unlawful.

Accordingly, just as the union is free to strike, the employer should be permitted to lock out. The employees have a right to have the employer bargain with their union representative in good faith. They do not have a right to have him eschew the use of the economic weapons at his command so that they can make a better bargain.

As to rules which should govern picketing and boycotting, it is necessary at the outset to identify the relevant policy considerations.

Strictly speaking, there is no position of neutrality in a labor dispute for any person who has an economic relationship with the "primary" employer at the time the dispute begins or who has an opportunity to enter into such a relationship while it is still going on. There are differences in the degree of involvement and interest in the outcome of the dispute, but maintaining or establishing any relationship will to some extent give support to the employer, while terminating or foregoing it will to some extent give support to the union.

This being so, the protection of neutrals is not a very satisfactory ground upon which to build a policy governing picketing and boycotting. The sounder basis, in the case of disputes which are not

submissible to a forum and where the notion is that it is better
to let the parties resolve their conflict by doing battle than to impose settlement on them, is to permit limited, but not total, warfare by restricting the arsenal of weapons which each may use
to those which have approximately equal force and effectiveness.

The objectives should be twofold: (1) to limit the costs to the
community in the event of open conflict; and (2) to maximize the
possibility, insofar as practicable, that the parties will accom-
modate their differences through peaceable means by making it
unlikely that either can win an economic war—that is, gain more
than he loses.

Of course, no statutory standards, regardless of how sound they
may be generally, will serve these ends in all cases. Sometimes the
nature of the industry and the bargaining structure are such that
a strike, even though unaccompanied by picketing and boycotting,
is so costly to the community that it cannot be tolerated. Furthermore, any effort to limit the parties to the use of approximately
equal weapons is futile where the economic power of one is vastly
superior to that of the other.

The following principles afford some guide lines.

a. Since the employees have a right to strike in an attempt to
improve their terms and conditions of employment, they have
a right to undertake, by peaceful means, to insure that the
strike is effective, that is, that it inflicts harm on the employer. It follows that the strikers may interfere with or discourage performance of the work which, but for the strike,
they would be performing by:

(1) inducing or encouraging other employees, no matter by
whom they are employed, not to perform such work;

(2) inducing or encouraging other employees, no matter by
whom they are employed, not to perform services which
are directly related to and necessary for the performance
of such work;

(3) inducing or encouraging other employees, no matter by
whom they are employed, not to perform services which
are directly related to and necessary for the use or
marketing of the products of such work;

(4) inducing or encouraging prospective purchasers not to
use such work or to purchase the products of such work.

b. The employees do not have the right to inflict harm on any employer other than their own, except as permitted under No. 1 above, by inducing or encouraging his employees to refuse in the course of their employment to perform services, or by inducing or encouraging any person to refuse to purchase his goods or services.

c. Since the employer has a right to lock out in an attempt to improve the terms and conditions under which his business is being operated, he has a right to undertake, by peaceful means, to insure that the lockout is effective, that is, that it inflicts harm on the employees. It follows that the employer may interfere with or discourage performance of work by locked out employees which, but for the lockout, they would be performing for him, by inducing or encouraging other employers not to hire them. Furthermore, since the strike is a two-edged sword which must, in order to function as the motive power for agreement, inflict harm on employees and employers alike, the employer has the same right in a strike situation to attempt to dry up the strikers' other sources of income.

Under these proposals the question of whether the union's objective in inducing a work stoppage was to cause one employing entity to stop doing business with another would be immaterial.[71] Thus, there would be no occasion to do what the NLRB has done in "common situs" and "ambulatory situs" cases, namely, to invent artificial rules governing the time and place of picketing and the language on the signs and to substitute them for findings of fact as to the union's state of mind.[72]

The characterization of picketing as "primary" or "secondary" would also be unimportant.[73] Again manifesting its disposition to convert facts with probative value into fixed rules enabling mechanical case dispositions, the Board has moved from the position that picketing at the premises owned by a struck employer is *exempt* from the statutory interdiction, even though it is extended to a gate reserved for the employees of an independent building contractor and causes them to refuse to work,[74] to the view, at least until the Supreme Court's recent remand of the *Electrical Workers'* case,[75] that such picketing is *within* the statutory interdiction.

Under the proposals set forth above, the controlling inquiry in

all cases—"primary" situs, "common" situs, or "ambulatory" situs—
would be the character of the work performed by the employees to
whom the picketing reached. Its legality would depend upon
whether they were performing (1) strikers' work, (2) operations
directly related thereto, or (3) operations directly related to the
use or marketing of the products of that work.[76]

So far as "consumer" picketing is concerned the union would be
permitted to engage in "products" picketing at the site of the distributor rather than merely being permitted to spread "publicity
other than picketing," which is the scope of the exception set forth
in the 1959 amendments to Section 8(b)(4). It should be noted,
however, that the picketing would have to be limited to inducing
or encouraging refusals to buy the particular product. It could not
be used to set in motion a boycott of the distributor or retailer.[77]

Furthermore, while the union could picket the distribution outlet
for "hot" goods or "struck" work in order to induce or encourage
persons not to buy or use it, it could not, in the event of such
purchase or use, punish such persons for refusing to accede to its
wishes. For example, a union, in dispute with a manufacturer of
neon signs over the terms and conditions of employment, could
engage in "products" picketing at the premises of a distributor of
such signs. But it could not picket a handbag shop that, despite
the picket line, made a purchase. Such picketing would tend either
to produce refusals to work or refusals to patronize which would
not be within permissible limits, for the work done at the handbag
shop is not directly related to and necessary for the performance,
use, or marketing of the "struck" work and the products sold there
are not the result of such work. The handbag shop is an actual,
not a prospective, customer and should, since it is not in a position
to influence the outcome of the dispute, be free from the union's
economic pressure.[78]

A harder case arises when the customer purchases a service
instead of a product. Suppose, for instance, a union of maintenance
electricians is on strike against an employer whose business is
servicing burglar alarms. A jewelry store contracts to have its
burglar alarms serviced by the struck employer. May the union
picket the jewelry store? The answer is yes if and when the work
is done there, for the union may induce or encourage employees

not to do work which, but for the strike, its members would be doing.[79] But suppose the servicing work is performed elsewhere. May the union still picket the jewelry store in an effort to induce or encourage its proprietor not to use non-union services? The answer would be no, for the reasons set out above. However, the rationale is not as persuasive. The service contract calls for the continuous use of non-union work. Hence the jewelry store is still in a position to influence the outcome of the dispute by terminating the contract. However, on balance it seems preferable to draw the line as indicated.[80]

The usual problems would doubtless arise as to the "incidental" effects of otherwise permissible picket lines, in either (1) producing work stoppages by employees who were neither doing the strikers' work nor facilitating its performance, use, or marketing, or (2) causing boycotts of distributors or retailers rather than merely refusals to use or purchase a particular product or service. In general these cases would be resolved against the union by following the formula of proof which has been developed under Section 8(a)(3), which makes it an unfair labor practice for an employer to discriminate against his employees in order to discourage or encourage union membership.

Persons are presumed to intend the normal and probable consequences of their conduct. The normal and probable consequence of a picket line is that it will induce or encourage refusals to work or to patronize. Therefore, in the absence of rebuttal evidence, e.g., that the pickets told employees or customers that they were free to work or to patronize, the inference is that the union intended to produce these consequences.[81]

However, the presumption that the picketing union intended to induce or encourage refusals to work or patronize may be overcome by evidence. In *Local 261, United Wholesale and Warehouse Employees (Perfection Mattress & Spring Co.),*[82] the union picketed a retail store, urging customers not to buy a "struck" product, its admitted purpose being to cause the retailer to stop doing business with the manufacturer. The evidence showed that no work stoppage in fact occurred, that the picketing did not reach to service and delivery entrances but was limited to public entrances to the store, that it did not begin until after the store's employees had gone to work and that it ended before they quit for the day, and that the language on the picket signs was addressed entirely to the store's customers. The Board's finding, on this evidence, that the picketing "induced or encouraged" work stoppages appears to make the presumption irrebuttable and is, therefore, contrary to the suggested rule.[83]

The Board's finding that the picketing also constituted "restraint or coercion" within the meaning of Section 8(b)(4), as amended in 1959, appears to be sound, since the legislative history indicates that the amendment was aimed at secondary "products" picketing and the proviso permits only "publicity other than picketing." However, such a finding would not necessarily be correct under the proposed rule. The presumption would be that secondary "products" picketing was designed to cause customers to refuse to patronize the retail outlet. But the union could overcome the presumption with proofs that it intended only to cause customers to refuse to buy the "struck" product.

The line laid down by the foregoing proposals follows the notion that the involvement of third parties should not go beyond what is necessary in order to permit the employees to insure the effectiveness of their strike by following the work and its product.[84] The suggestion with respect to employer boycotts of strikers is simply a converse application of this principle, permitting the employer, since the dispute involves the terms of the contract rather than the statutory right of employees to organize and bargain collectively, to counter the employees' interference with his market by interfering with theirs.

CONCLUSION

The thesis of this paper is that the laws regulating the use of self-help by unions are out of phase with the federal labor policies that have developed since 1935 and that these inconsistencies should be corrected. The old shibboleths, e.g., "government by injunction" should be discarded in favor of the general proposition that, where acceptable procedures and standards are available for the resolution of labor disputes, they should be utilized, to the exclusion of economic warfare, with a full range of effective remedies available as necessary to prevent the disputants from

resorting to self-help. Obviously implementation of these suggestions demands not only many changes in substantive law but also
radical modifications of existing procedures, particularly in connection with the availability of preliminary relief to unions, as
well as employers, in cases involving unfair labor practices.

Where a forum for disposition of the issue in dispute is not
available, the policy of non-intervention should be continued,
with the parties free to resort to limited warfare, using those weapons which will make for a fairly even contest.

NOTES

1. *Sterling Theaters* vs. *Central Labor Council*, 155 Wash. 217, 223, 283
Pac. 1081, 1083 (1930). The court quoted Duane's Military Dictionary.
2. There is no attempt in the next two sections of this paper to treat the
decisional and statutory developments in a comprehensive or encyclopedic
way. The effort is only to highlight trends and mark major developments.
3. *Milk Wagon Drivers Union of Chicago* vs. *Meadowmoor Dairies, Inc.*,
312 U.S. 287 (1941).
4. *American Steel Foundries* vs. *Tri-City Trades Council*, 257 U.S. 184
(1921); *Adams* vs. *Cooks & Waiters*, 124 Wash. 564, 215 Pac. 19 (1923).
Weyerhaeuser Timber Co. vs. *Everett District Council of Lumber & Sawmill
Workers*, 11 Wn. 2d 503, 119 P. 2d 643 (1941).
5. *Jensen* vs. *Cooks' & Waiters' Union*, 39 Wash. 531, 81 Pac. 1069
(1905); *St. Germain* vs. *Bakery & Confectionary Workers' Union No. 9*, 97
Wash. 282, 166 Pac. 665 (1917).
6. *Safeway Stores* vs. *Retail Clerks Union, Local No. 148*, 184 Wash. 322,
51 P. 2d 372 (1935).
7. *Bowen* vs. *Matheson*, 96 Mass. 499 (1867).
8. Mathews, *Labor Relations and the Law* (1st Ed. 1953, Little, Brown &
Co,. Boston), p. 17. But see *Vegelahn* vs. *Guntner*, 167 Mass. 92 (1896).
9. See *Plant* vs. *Woods*, 176 Mass. 492 (1900).
10. *Duplex Printing Co.* vs. *Deering*, 254 U.S. 443 (1921); *Keith Theatre*
vs. *Vachon*, 134 Me. 392, 187 Atl. 692 (1936). But see *Exchange Bakery &
Restaurant, Inc.* vs. *Rifkin*, 245 N. Y. 260, 15 N. E. 130 (1927).
11. *Pacific Typesetting Co.* vs. *Int'l Typographical Union*, 125 Wash. 273,
216 Pac. 358 (1923).
12. *Iron Molders' Union* vs. *Allis-Chalmers Co.*, 166 Fed. 45 (7th Cir.
1908).
13. *Goldfinger* vs. *Feintuch*, 276 N. Y. 281, 11 N. E. 2d 910 (1937).
14. See *Feldman* vs. *Weiner*, 173 Misc. 461, 17 N. Y. S. 2d 730 (1940);
and *People* vs. *Bellows*, 281 N. Y. 67, 22 N. E. 2d 238 (1939).
15. *United Union Brewing Co.* vs. *Beck*, 200 Wash. 474, 93 P. 2d 772
(1939).
16. *Wright* vs. *Teamsters*, 33 Wn. 2d 905, 207 P. 2d 662 (1949).
17. *Loewe* vs. *Lawlor*, 208 U. S. 274 (1908); *Lawlor* vs. *Loewe*, 235 U. S.
522 (1915).
18. *Hitchman Coal & Coke Co.* vs. *Mitchell*, 245 U.S. 229 (1917).

19. *Alco-Zander Co.* vs. *Amalgamated Clothing Workers,* 35 F. 2d 203 (E. D. Pa. 1929).

20. *Duplex Printing Co.* vs. *Deering,* 254 U.S. 443 (1921).

21. 47 Stat. 70.

22. New York, Pennsylvania, New Jersey, and Wisconsin were among the states that enacted such legislation. See *Senn* vs. *Tilelayers Protective Union,* 301 U.S. 468 (1937). But state courts often gave a narrower interpretation to their statutes than the federal courts gave to the Norris-LaGuardia Act. Compare *Lauf* vs. *Shinner,* 303 U.S. 323 (1938), with *Goodwins* vs. *Hagedorn,* 303 N. Y. 300, 101 N. E. 2d 697 (1951).

23. *United States* vs. *Hutcheson,* 312 U.S. 219 (1940).

24. Section 13(b).

25. Section 13(c).

26. *Lauf* vs. *Shinner,* 303 U.S. 323 (1938); *New Negro Alliance* vs. *Sanitary Grocery Co.,* 303 U.S. 552, 304 U.S. 542 (1938); *Cf. Wilson & Co.* vs. *Birl,* 105 F. 2d 948 (3rd Cir. 1939).

27. *Vegelahn* vs. *Guntner,* 167 Mass. 92, 44 N. E. 1077, 1080, 1081 (1896) (dissenting opinion).

28. 49 Stat. 449.

29. 61 Stat. 136.

30. E.g., the closed shop and, by amendment in the Labor Management Reporting and Disclosure Act of 1959, 73 Stat. 519, most kinds of "hot cargo" clauses [Section 704 (b), which added Section 8(e) to the Labor Management Relations Act].

31. Section 8(d). See also, e.g., *NLRB* vs. *Wooster Division of the Borg-Warner Corp.,* 356 U.S. 342 (1958).

32. Jurisdictional disputes between groups of employees over the question of who should perform certain kinds of work were also committed to a forum for disposition. Section 8(b)(4)(D).

33. Section 9(b).

34. Cf. *Fur Workers Union, Local 72 (CIO)* vs. *Fur Workers Union (AFL),* 105 F. 2d 1 (D. C. Cir. 1939), aff'd, 308 U.S. 522 (1939).

35. *NLRB* vs. *Drivers' Local Union 639,* 362 U.S. 274 (1960).

36. 73 Stat. 519, 544.

37. See *Hod Carriers Union (C. A. Blinne Construction Co.),* 49 LRRM 1638 (1962), and *Typographical Union (Charlton Press, Inc.),* 49 LRRM 1650 (1962).

38. It is the "new" NLRB's view, upon reconsideration, that "informational" picketing aimed at consumers is protected by the proviso to Section 8(b) (7)(C) even though it is also intended to organize the employees or to gain recognition, unless it has the effect of causing refusals to perform services. However, "informational" picketing which lacks an organizational or recognitional purpose is outside the reach of Section 8(b)(7) even though it causes refusals to work. *Local Joint Executive Board of Hotel and Restaurant Employees (Crown Cafeteria),* 49 LRRM 1648 (1962), and *Local 89, Chefs, Cooks, Pastry Cooks and Assistants (Stork Restaurant),* 49 LRRM 1653 (1962). Apparently this is also true as to "standards" picketing where the union's sole purpose is to advertise the fact that the company is not meeting area standards of employment. Cf. *Hod Carriers Union (Calumet Contractors Ass'n),* 48 LRRM 1667 (1961). The same rule apparently obtains where the objective is to protest alleged employer unfair labor practices, *Local 200, Teamsters (Bachman*

Furniture Co.), 49 LRRM 1192 (1961), or to force reinstatement of a discharged employee, *Automobile Workers Union (Fanelli Ford Sales, Inc.)* 49 LRRM 1021 (1961).

39. *United Elastic Corp.*, 84 NLRB 768, 773 (1949).

40. *Joseph Dyson & Sons, Inc.*, 72 NLRB 445 (1947); *Scullin Steel Co.*, 65 NLRB 1294 (1946).

41. *United Elastic Corp.*, 84 NLRB 768 (1949). *United Electrical Workers* vs. *NLRB*, 223 F. 2d 338 (D.C. Cir. 1955).

42. *United Mine Workers of America (Boone County Coal Corp.)*, 117 NLRB 1095 (1957), enf. denied, 257 F. 2d 211 (D.C. Cir. 1958). Cf. *Boeing Airplane Co.* vs. *NLRB*, 174 F. 2d 988 (D.C. Cir. 1949).

43. 61 Stat. 156.

44. *Textile Workers Union of America* vs. *Lincoln Mills*, 353 U.S. 448 (1957).

45. *McCarroll* vs. *Los Angeles County District Council of Carpenters*, 49 Cal. 2d 45, 315 P. 2d 322 (1957), cert. denied, 355 U.S. 932 (1958).

46. *Textile Workers Union of America* vs. *Lincoln Mills*, 353 U.S. 448, 456 (1957).

47. *A. H. Bull S. S. Co.* vs. *Seafarers' Union*, 250 F. 2d 326 (2nd Cir. 1957), cert. denied, 355 U.S. 932 (1958); *Sinclair Refining Co.* vs. *Atkinson*, 48 L.R.R.M. 2045 (7th Cir. 1961); *W. L. Mead, Inc.* vs. *Teamsters Union*, 217 F. 2d 6 (1st Cir. 1954); *Sound Lumber Co.* vs. *Lumber & Sawmill Workers*, 34 L.R.R.M. 2494 (N.D. Calif. 1954); *Duris* vs. *Phelps Dodge Copper Products Corp.*, 87 F. Supp. 229 (D. N.J. 1949); *Alcoa S. S. Co.* vs. *McMahon*, 173 F. 2d 567 (2nd Cir.), cert. denied, 338 U.S. 821 (1949).

48. 353 U.S. 448 (1957).

49. *Ibid.*, at p. 456.

50. *Teamsters Union* vs. *Yellow Transit Lines*, 282 F. 2d 345 (10th Cir. 1960), cert. granted, 364 U.S. 931 (1961). *Accord: Johnson & Johnson* vs. *Textile Workers*, 46 L.R.R.M. 2368 (D. N.J. 1960).

51. See *NLRB* vs. *Radio & Television Broadcast Engineers' Union*, 81 Sup. Ct. 330 (1961).

52. *Dorchy* vs. *Kansas*, 272 U.S. 306 (1926).

53. *Building Trades Council of Reno* vs. *Thompson*, 234 P. 2d 581 (1951). Compare *Bakery Sales Drivers Union No. 33* vs. *Wagshal*, 333 U.S. 437 (1948).

54. *Bro. of R.R. Trainmen* vs. *Chicago R. & I. R.R.*, 353 U.S. 30 (1957).

55. However, the latter point is of no moment since it is usually held that a promise to submit certain types of disputes to arbitration implies a promise not to strike over those matters.

56. *Blue Flash Express Co.*, 109 NLRB 591 (1954).

57. *Republic Aviation Corp.* vs. *NLRB*, 324 U.S. 793 (1945).

58. 310 U.S. 88 (1940).

59. *Bakery and Pastry Drivers and Helpers* vs. *Wohl*, 315 U.S. 769, 776 (1942) (concurring opinion).

60. *Milk Wagon Drivers Union of Chicago* vs. *Meadowmoor Dairies, Inc.*, 312 U.S. 287, 293 (1941). See also *Youngdahl* vs. *Rainfair, Inc.*, 355 U.S. 131 (1957). Compare *Newell* vs. *Chauffeurs Local Union*, 181 Kan. 898, 317 P. 2d 817 (1957), reversed, 356 U.S. 341 (1958).

61. *Giboney* vs. *Empire Storage & Ice Co.*, 336 U.S. 490 (1950). See also *Int'l Brotherhood of Electrical Workers* vs. *NLRB*, 341 U.S. 694 (1951).

62. *Int'l Brotherhood of Teamsters* vs. *Hanke,* 339 U.S. 470 (1950).

63. *Int'l Brotherhood of Teamsters, Local 695* vs. *Vogt, Inc.,* 354 U.S. 284 (1957).

64. *Hughes* vs. *Superior Court,* 339 U.S. 460 (1950).

65. *Thornhill* vs. *Alabama,* 310 U.S. 88 (1940).

66. *Radio Officers Union* vs. *NLRB,* 347 U.S. 17, 51 (1954).

67. Section 8(c) of the Taft-Hartley Act prohibits the NLRB from giving controlling weight to these factors in cases involving the question of whether an employer's "captive audience" speech violates Section 8(a)(1). *Livingston Shirt Corp.,* 107 NLRB 400 (1953). However, it does not prevent the Board from determining that such a speech so substantially interferes with employee freedom of choice that it will not be permitted within the 24-hour period immediately prior to an election. *Peerless Plywood Co.,* 107 NLRB 427 (1953). *Compare General Shoe Corp.,* 97 NLRB 499 (1951), and *George J. Meyer Mfg. Co.,* 111 NLRB 154 (1955). In any event, the statutory restriction on the power of the NLRB, since it is not compelled by constitutional requirements, is irrelevant to the issue under discussion.

68. Isaacson, "Organizational Picketing: What Is the Law?—Ought the Law to be Changed?" 8 *Buffalo L. Rev.* 345, 352-353 (1959).

69. The fact-finding and cooling-off procedures of the Railway Labor Act and the emergency dispute provisions of the Taft-Hartley Act merely defer the exercise of self-help and do not involve final and binding determination.

70. Wollett and Aaron, *Labor Relations and the Law,* (Boston: Little, Brown & Co., 2nd Ed., 1960), p. 436 and cases cited and discussed thereafter.

71. See *NLRB* vs. *Local 50, Bakery and Confectionary Workers,* 245 F. 2d 542 (2d Cir. 1957).

72. *Sailors' Union of the Pacific (Moore Dry Dock Co.),* 92 NLRB 547 (1950); *Baltimore Building and Construction Trades Council, Local 16 (Stover Steel Service),* 108 NLRB 1575, remanded in *Piezonki* vs. *NLRB,* 219 F. 2d 879 (4th Cir. 1955); *Washington Coca-Cola Bottling Works, Inc.,* 107 NLRB 299 (1953). For a critical view of the Board's approach to these problems, see *Sales Drivers, Local 859* vs. *NLRB,* 229 F. 2d 514 (D.C. Cir. 1955), cert. denied, 351 U.S. 972 (1956). The "new" Board has shown a disposition to abandon the mechanistic approach to these cases. *Int'l Bro. of Electrical Workers (Plauche Electric, Inc.),* 49 LRRM 1446 (1962).

73. Compare the proviso to Section 8(b)(4)(B), which states that "nothing contained [herein] shall be considered to make unlawful, where not otherwise unlawful, any primary strike or primary picketing."

74. *United Electrical Workers (Ryan Construction Corp.),* 85 NLRB 417 (1949).

75. *Local 761, Int'l Union of Electrical Workers* vs. *NLRB,* 81 Sup. Ct. 1285 (1961).

76. Compare with the dimensions of the "economic alliance" doctrine as adopted in *NLRB* vs. *Business Machines and Office Appliance Mechanics,* 228 F. 2d 553 (2d Cir. 1955), cert. denied, 351 U.S. 962 (1956). See also *Int'l Die Sinkers Conference,* 120 NLRB 1227 (1958).

77. Compare *Goldfinger* vs. *Feintuch,* 276 N. Y. 281, 11 N. E. 2d 910 (1937), with *Feldman* vs. *Weiner,* 173 Misc. 461, 17 N.Y.S. 2d 730 (1940).

78. *People* vs. *Bellows,* 281 N. Y. 67, 22 N. E. 2d 238 (1939).

79. *People* vs. *Muller,* 286 N. Y. 281, 36 N. E. 2d 206 (1941).

80. But see *NLRB* vs. *Business Machine and Office Appliance Mechanics,*

228 F. 2d 553 (2d Cir. 1955), cert, denied, 351 U.S. 962 (1956), holding that, under Section 8(b)(4) prior to the 1959 Amendments, a union of service employees could picket companies that sent their typewriters to be repaired by employers who had become "economic allies" of the employer with whom the union had a dispute. The NLRB, in interpreting the "publicity" proviso to Section 8(b)(4), has refused to differentiate between "products" and "services" and has held that employers who distribute, handle, or advertise goods are "producers." See, e.g., *IBEW Local 712 (Golden Dawn Foods)*, 49 LRRM 1220 (1961). This position is consistent with the rule suggested in the text insofar as it permits a union to urge persons not to buy products that have been serviced by an employer with whom it has a dispute. But it is inconsistent insofar as it permits the union to boycott *all* products sold by the distributor or retailer.

81. See *Local No. 505, Int'l Brotherhood of Teamsters (Carolina Lumber Co.)*, 47 L.R.R.M. 1502 (1961).

82. 81 L.R.R.M. 1121 (1960).

83. The "new" Board's position on this point is consistent with the suggested rule. *Upholsterers Frame and Bedding Workers Twin City Local No. 61 (Minneapolis House Furnishing Co.)*, 132 NLRB No. 2 (1961). See also *Fruit and Vegetable Packers & Warehousemen, Local 760 (Tree Fruits Labor Relations Committee)*, 132 NLRB No. 102 (1961).

84. As to "hot cargo" or "struck work" clauses, the logic of the proposals permits them where the employer agrees not to require his employees to perform (1) work that, but for the strike, the strikers would perform, or (2) work that is directly related to and necessary for its performance or the use or marketing of its products.

6

COLLECTIVE BARGAINING AND

THE ANTITRUST LAWS

GEORGE H. HILDEBRAND

*Professor of Economics and of Industrial & Labor Relations,
Cornell University*

The passage of the Sherman Act in 1890 symbolized a certain continuity in the Anglo-American tradition. Within the common law, there was the well-established principle that contracts in restraint of trade were not enforceable. Coupled to it was the native American doctrine of economic egalitarianism, exalting the free man and making competition "the servo-mechanism of economic life."[1] The doctrine means that every man has the right of access to a market, and that combinations of private power do not conform to the natural competitive order; hence they are forever suspect. The Sherman law put the federal government behind these ideas, providing a means of public prosecution against transgressors. But who were they?

The activities of unions in the labor market have never fitted comfortably with competitive precepts. Yet they accorded well with the economic egalitarianism of that day. It was then a case of the little man against the trusts. Unionism gave the worker a means to cope with the rapidly growing power of capital, and so commanded popular appeal. However, the remedy it afforded required combination—combination to eliminate competition among workingmen in dealing with their employers. To exert this power, the union must attain monopoly in the labor market.

As the Webbs pointed out in *Industrial Democracy* over half a century ago, to make its monopoly fully effective, the union cannot limit itself to a single employer alone but must extend its power to embrace all of the employers in the industry. Thus its goal is really a double one: to end competition among workers at the level of the firm, and to "take wages out of competition" as among competing firms in a common industry or trade. Accordingly, control of the labor market implies indirect control of the product market as well.

So arises a paradox: While the union expresses the egalitarian tradition, it practices monopoly. To practice monopoly effectively, it must seek privileges and immunities under law, although these stand condemned by the tradition itself. In consequence, the partisans of unionism and collective bargaining were driven from the outset to proclaim a dual standard: monopoly in the labor market stands on a different footing from monopoly in the product market.[2] What follows is in good part a history of how this dual view ultimately won out to become the foundation of national labor policy.

DOMINANCE OF THE COMPETITIVE VIEW, 1890-1932

Before the Clayton Act of 1914

The Sherman law makes no references to unions and is most elastic in its coverage of proscribed activities. Hence it was an obvious threat from its inception. Section 1 outlaws "*Every* contract, combination in the form of trust *or otherwise*, or conspiracy, in restraint of trade or commerce" (emphasis supplied). Section 2 makes it a misdemeanor to monopolize, to attempt to monopolize, or to "combine or conspire" with others for such ends. Did this language apply to labor unions?

An answer was not long in forthcoming. In May 1894, Eugene Debs' American Railway Union struck against the Pullman Company. The strike quickly spread to the railroads. To reopen the lines, the Attorney General procured an injunction against Debs and his associates. They violated the order, were arrested, and the case came before the circuit court on a writ of *habeas corpus*.[3]

There Debs' counsel argued the inapplicability of the Sherman

Act because supposedly it was directed solely against capital: "The evil aimed at is one of a contractual character, and not of force and violence." Rejecting this contention as too narrow and seizing upon the phrase "or otherwise" in Section 1, Justice Woods held that the statute embraced all illegal conspiracies in restraint of trade. By leadership of the strike, Debs and his associates had engaged in a massive conspiracy to restrain interstate commerce, using unlawful means in pursuit of this illegal design. Conceding in the abstract the right of men to quit, individually or collectively, the court reasoned that a sympathetic strike of this magnitude, accompanied as it was by violence and intimidation, contravened the Sherman law. Both the purpose and the method were tainted. More important, the court read the ARU's purpose not as bringing maximum economic pressure to bear against Pullman in a struggle involving the labor market, but as the larger one of conspiring to restrain trade in interstate railroad services. This judicial identification of the union's purpose as restraint of trade was to become decisive in the "boycott cases" that were to follow.[4]

The first of these involved the well-known Danbury Hatters.[5] Loewe, a hat manufacturer, operated an open shop. In July 1902, the United Hatters sought to organize his plant, and Loewe was encouraged to resist by offer of financial aid from competitors.[6] The union then struck, also placing his products on the AFL's nationally circulated "unfair list." Loewe went to court on the claim that this secondary boycott violated the Sherman law, winning a judgment against the individual members of the union for over half a million dollars. The case came to the Supreme Court for review, where Loewe succeeded in convincing the court (1) that the federal court had jurisdiction because the boycott "interfered" with his out-of-state orders and shipments, (2) that the Sherman law applied to union activities, and (3) that the Hatters had committed "restraint of trade or commerce" in violation of the act.

In deciding for Loewe in the two cases, the Supreme Court for the first time extended the concept of "restraint of trade" to the activities of a labor union. It did so by interpreting the term as embracing interference by a union with the interstate *shipment* of a commodity, as distinguished from the common-law principle of manipulation of commodity prices by producers or distributors. By rendering "interference" a "restraint," the justices outlawed the secondary boycott under the Sherman Act.[7] In consequence, union resort to any form of economic pressure stood in jeopardy, even where the purpose was to win a labor dispute, and not to manipulate the product market against consumers.

The ominous implications of the first *Loewe* decision drove the AFL into a campaign for statutory immunity. Sections 6 and 20 of the Clayton Act of 1914 seemingly fulfilled this purpose. By proclaiming with magniloquent phrasing that "The labor of a human being is not a commodity or article of commerce," the lawmakers apparently achieve the mundane purpose of distinguishing the labor from the product market, buttressing their intent with the unequivocal declaration that labor organizations and their members shall not "be held or construed to be illegal combinations or conspiracies in restraint of trade, under the antitrust laws." Through Section 20, they regulated the use of injunctions in labor disputes in a manner wholly gratifying to the federation, purportedly protecting the strike, picketing, and the boycott, provided that these activities were lawfully conducted in disputes over terms and conditions of employment. Unhappily for the unions, the Supreme Court continued to travel in a different direction from that taken by Congress, as the *Duplex* case was soon to show.[8]

Between the Clayton and Norris-LaGuardia Acts.

Duplex was one of four manufacturers of printing presses. Between 1909 and 1913, the International Association of Machinists had organized the three other producers, winning a minimum scale and the eight-hour day. Duplex refused to recognize the union. Because it enjoyed lower wages and a ten-hour day, two of its competitors notified the IAM that Duplex must be brought up to standard or they would have to withdraw recognition. The union thereupon struck Duplex in August, 1913, at its Battle Creek, Michigan, plant, backing up the action with a boycott involving appeals and threats to customers, sympathetic strikes by other crafts, and refusal to install or repair Duplex presses. Duplex sought an injunction, but lost in the Circuit Court of Appeals on a holding that Section 20 forbade one.

The Supreme Court saw otherwise. Section 6, the majority declared, granted limited, not general, immunity for "legitimate" objects "lawfully carried out." Section 20 provides qualified immunity, but only "to those who are proximately and substantially concerned as parties to an actual dispute respecting the terms and conditions of their own employment, past, present, or prospective."

In so concluding, the court chose to interpret the union's conduct as an illegal trade restraint, rather than as an effort to protect its national standards in the labor market. Its resort to the boycott and sympathetic strikes extended the dispute to embrace "strangers" or outsiders who, in the court's view, had no legitimate economic interest at stake. Justice Brandeis' dissent went directly against this construction. The union was waging a labor dispute in defense of gains won in collective bargaining. Because the machinists were a national union, the "outsiders" did have a legitimate interest in the outcome, while their participation in no way contravened the protections extended in Section 20. It was not for the court to outlaw such disputes merely because they entail economic losses. Such was the function of the lawmakers alone, and they had not exercised it.

The underlying fact in these cases and in others to follow was the effort of national unions to organize and to bargain collectively with firms serving interstate product markets. These activities inevitably provoked disputes that interrupted the free flow of interstate commerce and also on occasion affected the prices of the products so moving. Naturally this posed the question of intent: was it the union's purpose to manipulate product prices, or was this merely incidental to the primary purpose of monopolizing the labor market alone? Since price impacts were usually manifest and unavoidable, it was easy to identify them as the union's real purpose, even if intent were difficult to prove. However, once the identification was made, the courts would have been in the uncomfortable position of outlawing a great many strikes, now that national product markets were so common—notwithstanding the explicit exemptions conferred by Congress. Since the Clayton amendments rejected the whole notion that "normal" union activities should be construed as efforts to suppress commodity competition by restraint of trade, the courts were driven to the test of intent, as distinguished from effects.[9]

The issue was posed clearly in the *Coronado* cases.[10] Coronado was one of eight subsidiaries controlled by the Bache-Denman Coal Company. Coronado had bargained collectively with the union until April 1914, when it was struck in retaliation for a decision by the Bache-Denman receivers to adopt the open shop. The union attempted to block shipments of the company's coal, and considerable violence and destruction of property followed. The company then sued for damages under the antitrust laws, charging the union with conspiracy to restrain trade. After losing in the district court, it prevailed in the court of appeals, winning an award of $345,600, which was later modified. Eventually the case landed in the Supreme Court, which found in its first decision (1922) that there was no evidence of a conspiracy to restrain trade; also that the international was not liable for any damages. The case was then remanded to the district court for further proceedings.

In his opinion, Chief Justice Taft made the question of intent the central issue. The purpose of the strike, he found, was to organize the company's mines, to improve wages and working conditions, and to lessen the competition from non-union coal as a means to this end. The case differed sharply from *Loewe*, or so Taft thought, where the clear purpose was to interfere with interstate commerce. Coronado was a local strike, "local in its origin and motive, local in its waging, and local in its felonious and murderous ending." Too little output was involved to make price manipulation either a plausible motive or likely effect.[11]

This seemed to leave open the question whether large but unintended price effects would still constitute an illegal restraint of trade in the course of a labor dispute, but it did appear to justify the organizational strike, provided that secondary boycotts or sympathetic strikes were not used in its behalf. At least the latter qualification would make consistent the reasoning employed by the court in the *Loewe, Duplex,* and *Coronado* cases, where the underlying problem—incomplete organization of the labor market—was the same.

Coronado reinstituted a damage suit against the union in lower court, claiming new evidence of a conspiracy to block interstate trade in non-union coal. The district court directed a verdict for the defendants and was sustained on circuit. This brought the case to the Supreme Court a second time. Relying upon the testimony of a former local union official, the court now found that District 21 and its affiliated locals were parties to a conspiracy in illegal restraint of trade, but that the national union was not. It thus reversed the district court in part, remanding the case for a third trial in which District 21, its locals, and certain individuals were defendants. The ensuing proceeding ended in a hung jury, and the case was finally settled out of court for $27,500.[12]

Noting that the daily tonnage of the Coronado company was considerably larger than had been indicated to the court in the 1922 proceeding, Chief Justice Taft based his opinion upon a finding of a direct intent of the union to restrain interstate trade in non-union coal. In his words,

> The mere reduction in the supply of an article to be shipped in interstate commerce by the illegal or tortious prevention of its manufacture or production is ordinarily an indirect and remote obstruction to that commerce. But when the intent of those unlawfully preventing the manufacture or production is shown to be to restrain or control the supply entering and moving in interstate commerce, or the price of it in interstate markets, their action is a direct violation of the Anti-trust Act.

"Direct intent" was therefore the test, a distinction that seemed to recognize the inherent logic of collective bargaining in national labor and product markets by apparently exempting organizational and bargaining activities whose trade effects were indirect, remote, and incidental. However, from the union point of view this approach was still fraught with danger, for two reasons. First, indirect and incidental effects upon trade presumably still could be illegal under antitrust provided that they were substantial, as the decision of the lower court had actually held in the *Debs* case long before. In fact, this possibility opened up an avenue by which national-emergency strikes might have been enjoined under antitrust, if this route had not been closed off by later legislation.

Second, those national unions that were hampered by incomplete organization of their labor markets actually *were* seeking to eliminate the competition of low-cost non-union sources of product—even if this were not always their declared purpose—simply to protect standards won in collective bargaining. If they sought this purpose through organizational strikes, they still could be held liable for an illegal restraint of trade, undertaken tacitly or overtly to manipulate product price.

The whole question of trade restraint by unions came up again with the *Bedford Cut Stone* case.[13] Bedford was one of twenty-four producers in the Indiana limestone district who had joined together in an open-shop drive. Before 1921, the group had bargained collectively with the Journeymen Stone Cutters' Association, a small craft union whose members engaged in quarrying, cutting, and installing stone. In that year, the employers terminated relations with the association, closing employment to its members, and organizing unaffiliated local unions to which they extended recognition. This was a deliberate attack upon the very existence of the association, which it met with a strike, by listing Bedford stone as "unfair," and by ordering its members not to work or install the product under penalty of expulsion for non-observance. Pressure was thus directed at the Bedford producers through local contractors who bought the stone for installation. The boycott was interstate. No violence or destruction of property occurred, nor were there sympathetic strikes.

The producers sued for an injunction under antitrust, on a conspiracy charge involving restraint of trade. Losing in the lower courts, they took the case to the Supreme Court, where they won a reversal. Speaking for the majority, Justice Sutherland found that the union's motive, while locally applied, was an attempt to organize the Bedford quarrymen by an illegal restraint of interstate commerce. "A restraint of interstate commerce," said Sutherland, "cannot be justified by the fact that the ultimate object of the participants was to secure an ulterior benefit which they might have been at liberty to pursue by means not involving such restraint," citing *Duplex* as precedent. The first *Coronado* decision did not apply because the issue then posed was a local "production strike," and not a restraint of trade. The second verdict in that case did apply, because intent to restrain trade was proved. Justice Sutherland then summed up as follows:

> Where the means adopted are unlawful, the innocent general character of the organizations adopting them or the lawfulness of the ultimate end sought to be attained, cannot serve as a justification.

This decision apparently made any form of boycott affecting

interstate commerce an illegal restraint under antitrust. It could not be used even in self-defense, and it mattered not that the end-purpose was legitimate or the means used entirely peaceable.

Brandeis dissented, with Holmes concurring. They could see nothing illegal in the association's counterattack against its declared enemies, and pleaded for a rule of reason in judging its acts. There was no parallel with the *Duplex* case, either in the activities complained of, or in the scope and purpose of the combination. Nor was there a parallel either with *Loewe,* in which there was a general consumer boycott; or with *Brims,* where the union colluded with employers to fix prices.[14] Here was simply an effort at self-protection by a small craft. It should have been upheld.

The *Brims* case stands on a different footing from all the others, because it turned upon a collusory agreement between the carpenters union and employer groups engaged respectively in manufacture and installation of millwork in the Chicago area. The deal was a clear-cut and deliberate restraint of interstate trade, for the express purpose of raising prices. It was invoked because the local manufacturers had found their market undercut by non-union millwork coming from out of state, while the carpenters they employed felt the same adverse pressure. To end this competition, the parties devised a three-cornered agreement. The union would refuse to install non-union millwork; the producers would employ only union members, offering them increased employment at better wages; and the installing contractors would receive discounts for using locally-produced millwork. As such, the arrangement was to prove similar in all essentials to the *Allen Bradley* case, which followed nearly two decades later.

The Attorney General brought an action charging the participants with "combining and conspiring" to restrain interstate trade and commerce, in violation of antitrust. The defendants were found guilty in a jury trial, but obtained reversal in the appellate court on failure of proof. The Supreme Court then reversed the circuit court, holding that the evidence fully supported the charge.

Here matters differed rather sharply from the other cases, since the issue clearly was intentional restraint of trade on behalf of product price, not as an indirect effect of a labor controversy, but as part and parcel of the union's primary goal. It gained a wage advantage by agreeing to shelter the Chicago producers' market. By joining that agreement, the union waived any conceivable immunity conferred by the Clayton Act. So much the court made plain: such agreements contravene antitrust, even if the union could claim that its real goal were betterment of the wages and working conditions of its members. But in drawing the line at collusive market-rigging agreements with employers, the court still left unsettled some vital questions. What about trade restraints having indirect price effects occasioned by routine and non-collusory activities within conventional collective bargaining? Were organizational strikes, even in self-defense, outlawed? Were production strikes for wages and other conditions of employment outside the pale if their impacts were massive? In sum, how broad were the prohibitions intended by the antitrust laws?

Although it is dangerous to look for rigorous logic in the history of the law, there is a thread of consistency running through the decisions of the Supreme Court during this lengthy period. Trade unionism was still very much a minority movement in industrial life, commanding in the minds of most of the justices neither much sympathy nor understanding of its purposes and its methods. On the one hand, the court acknowledged the legality of the union as an institution, including those national bodies that had long since begun to concert their local activities in industry-wide programs. On the other, the court's sympathies were undoubtedly allied to the consumer-oriented and competitive spirit of the Sherman Act. From this point of view, it looked askance at the monopolizing efforts of industry-wide unions, in particular attempts through boycotts and sympathetic strikes to drive competing non-union goods off the market. A "legitimate" labor dispute, notwithstanding the broad scope of Section 20, was one limited to an employer and his own employees. Beyond this, fraternity had to yield to liberty. Boycotts and sympathetic strikes improperly widened what Brandeis had called "the allowable area of economic conflict," because they introduced outsiders who had no lawful interest at stake. Where used, they converted a labor dispute into an illegal restraint of trade, depriving the union of statutory protection. So far as industry-wide unionism was concerned, it could legally exist, but under this construction of the law its freedom of action was narrowly circumscribed.

THE TRIUMPH OF THE DOCTRINE OF LICIT MONOPOLY IN LABOR MARKETS, 1932-1941

The Norris-LaGuardia Act

Between 1932 and 1941, the legal status of unionism and collective bargaining in the United States underwent a sea-change. On the union side, restraint by the judiciary gave way to liberation by statute, in the Norris-LaGuardia and Wagner Acts, passed in 1932 and 1935. Then in 1940 and 1941 the Supreme Court, perhaps following Mr. Dooley, turned liberator itself, largely freeing the unions from the incubus of the antitrust laws by major decisions in the *Apex* and *Hutcheson* cases. These events marked the abandonment of the antitrust approach to the labor market in favor of the doctrine of licit monopoly.[15]

There is a difference between the underlying theories of the Norris-LaGuardia and the Wagner Acts, and it is this. Norris-LaGuardia, as Gregory points out, was premised upon the doctrines of *laissez faire* and self-help. By restricting the use of federal injunctions, it opened the way to free resort to the classic weapons of trade unionism, at both the local and the industry-wide levels. However, union progress was still left to voluntary initiative and market power, while apart from the injunction employers continued to enjoy access to conventional means of resistance, with the government a rather indifferent neutral at the outset. The Wagner law represented the next step. Section 7(a) of the National Industrial Recovery Act of 1933 had proclaimed the desirability of collective bargaining, but included no means of enforcement. Wagner completed the evolution: the particular form of monopoly implied and necessitated by collective bargaining became a desirable public purpose, which it is the duty of the government not merely to protect but actively to promote. To this end, it imposed a collection of stern restraints and duties upon employers, providing also means to determine employee wishes concerning union representation of their bargainable interests.

By comparison, the basic purpose of Norris-LaGuardia was to

restrict and carefully to regulate the use of the federal injunction in labor disputes. In passing the measure, Congress was responding to judicial frustration of the almost unrestrained freedoms seemingly granted the unions in Section 20 of the Clayton Act. The new law did not, of course, entirely end the restrictions implicit in antitrust, for it did not declare legal the array of union weapons contained in Section 4. It merely made them non-enjoinable. Further, both criminal and damage suits remained possible.

Section 2 of the new law served as its informing major premise. It declared public policy to be that because the individual employee cannot bargain effectively in his own behalf, he must have full freedom of association to organize and to bargain collectively. Here was the real beginning of what was to become the labor policy of the New Deal. Following this major premise with rigorous logic, Section 3 made yellow-dog contracts unenforceable, while Section 4 declared a whole panoply of employee activities in labor disputes immune from the injunction: striking, joining a union, payment of strike benefits, picketing and persuading, publicizing, and related devices for self-help.[16]

But what is a "labor dispute"? To the judicial theory that it was limited by law to an employer and his employees alone, Congress gave short shrift, in Section 13, which is the companion clause to the equally vital Section 4. Giving precise content to Brandeis' conception of "the allowable area of economic conflict," Congress declared a "labor dispute" to include *any* controversy over the terms or conditions of employment, "whether or not the disputants stand in the proximate relation of employer and employee" [13(c)]. In 13(a) the parties at interest in such disputes are declared to embrace "persons who are engaged in the same industry, trade, craft, or occupation; or have direct or indirect interests therein"; or who are employee or employer members of the same or an affiliated organization. The dispute, moreover, might embrace a variety of employees and employers, and of unions and employer associations.

By adopting this broad conception of a lawful labor dispute, Congress rendered immune from injunction the use of "strangers" in the prosecution of the issue, particularly on the union side, so long as they could be shown to have a tangible economic interest in the outcome. By implication, at least, the exemption covered organizational and sympathetic strikes, primary and secondary boycotts, stranger picketing, and related formerly judicially-circumscribed techniques of self-help and self-defense. By opening up the field, the law gave expression to a notion akin to a syndicalist or cartel version of affected economic interests—still well short of class conflict, but nonetheless a realistic version of the doctrine of bargaining struggle in American unionism. Having cleared the field of conflict from enjoinder by the federal courts, Congress introduced a peculiar version of *laissez faire* for the labor market. However, it was organizational *laissez faire*, not the atomistic competitive individualism of classical economics. Because it was organizational, it rested upon a form of preclusive monopoly, the very foundation of free collective bargaining. And for the same reason, the social-economic system implied for the labor market, and now in the process of formation, lacked the precise balancing and equilibrating mechanism inherent to traditional competition. Examination of the relevant provisions of the Wagner Act will make this more apparent.

The Wagner Act

Between the Norris-LaGuardia and the Wagner Acts there is a direct line of continuity. In both, public policy was committed in favor of collective over individual bargaining. Norris-LaGuardia approached the purpose in a quite limited way, merely restraining the federal judiciary in its use of the injunction in labor disputes. Wagner added decisive statutory restraints directly against employers, imposed the duty to bargain collectively where the majority had chosen a union to represent it, and provided an administrative body to deal with charges of unfair employer labor practices and to conduct representation proceedings. Wagner, and not Norris-LaGuardia, amounted to direct federal intervention into labor-management relations, to serve the same end for public policy as the one proclaimed by the earlier statute. Yet the intervention was far from total. The terms and conditions of employment still remained for private negotiation, between the parties where collective representation prevails, or between the employer and his individual employees if the latter choose not to bargain collectively. Thus the Wagner law abandoned strict non-intervention, but in preserving both the freedom and the privacy of negotiations, it left intact the principle of *laissez faire* for the determination of the terms and conditions of employment.

So far as the labor market is concerned, the Wagner Act was anticompetitive in both intent and effect because it encouraged collective bargaining. Without entering into the metaphysics of what it is that the union attempts to maximize by monopoloid behavior—surely a futile exercise at best—the patent fact is that it does act as a monopolist. It replaces individual with collective negotiations, and enforces the terms so arranged; call it price-fixing by a workers' cartel of indeterminate membership and one will be not far from the truth. Now how did the Wagner Act strengthen the monopolization of the labor market?

Foremost, through Section 9, and by the non-discrimination clause in Section 8(a)(3), the law established the principle of exclusive representation. According to 9(a), the union representatives chosen by the voting majority in the bargaining unit ". . . shall be the exclusive representatives of all employees . . . in respect to rates of pay, wages, hours of employment, or other conditions of employment." That did it, for it put the National Labor Relations Board in the role of granting official patents of monopoly through its certification procedure. Section 8(a)(5) made it the duty of the employer to bargain collectively with the union so certified, under penalty of enforcement proceedings in the courts where necessary.

This raises the critical problem of how contracts of employment between the employer and the employee are related to the collective agreement, an issue considered by the Supreme Court in the *Case* case.[17] Case had introduced the practice of making separate annual contracts with each employee. When the union won a representation election in 1941, Case claimed that these personal contracts were a bar to collective bargaining. The Board thought not, ordered the firm to bargain collectively, and was upheld in Supreme Court.

In the court's view, expressed by Justice Jackson, a collective agreement is not a contract for employment, but more like a freight-rate schedule: it does not establish but it does govern individual transactions. The employer still hires and employs each man separately, but "the terms of the employment have already been traded out." He now becomes a third-party beneficiary of the collective agreement. The employer may not offer, nor the employee accept, lesser terms. Both might settle for more than the collective minima, although this tactic is suspect. In Jackson's words,

> . . . the majority rules, and if it collectivizes the employment bargain, individual advantages or favors will generally in practice go in as a contribution to the collective result.

One more point about the Wagner Act has relevance to antitrust—what it said, and did not say, about bargaining units and representation. Section 9(b) gave the Board power to designate the unit "appropriate" to collective bargaining, allowing it latitude to choose among plant, company, and craft units, or subdivisions of these. The administrative authority so conferred had much to do with the rapid growth of industrial unionism in the later thirties. But the main point is a different one: the law contained no bar either to industry-wide unions or to employer-representation associations.

So long as a given national union could win representation elections or gain voluntary recognition, it could enlarge the scope of its bargaining power to encompass an entire industry. There was precedent for such expansion in the long history of national unions, and it found early expression in the printing, building, and railroad industries. It also has its inherent logic: for labor monopoly to be fully effective, the union must extend its range of organizational control in the labor market to match the competitive span of the product market—in other words, it must gain indirect control of the product market as well. In any case, the law permitted the rapid advance of industry-wide unionism in a host of new fields. Further, employers in the same trade or industry were also left free to organize themselves for collective representation, so long as they stayed within the law—an equally logical tactic for meeting common pressure. Thus the act also permitted the rise of industry-wide bargaining.[18] Both the industry-wide union and the multiple-employer association were eventually to become targets for those who were to propose later the re-application of the antitrust laws to the labor field.

Omission from the act of any prohibitions against comprehensive organization by unions and employers for purposes of collective bargaining illustrates well the dual standard under antitrust. There is no doubt that the exclusion was intentional, in deference to the already long-established institution of national unionism. Acting as a kind of cartel, the national union can expand to embrace most, if not all, of the employers serving a common product market.[19] But while the market occupancy ratio of such a union could reach even 100 percent of the relevant labor market, and extend into others besides—with obvious implications for costs and prices in the allied product market—no business enterprise could attempt or achieve similar dominance in its product market without running afoul of antitrust. Nor could any group of business competitors, through trust, cartel, or organized collusion, escape a similar fate. This is the heart, if not the whole, of the problem of labor monopoly today.

Judicial Emancipation of Organized Labor from Antitrust: The Apex *and* Hutcheson *Cases.*

Although Norris-LaGuardia made the federal labor injunction largely a nullity, both criminal and damage suits under antitrust remained a real threat where, on the *Coronado* precedent, a union called an organizational strike or resorted to a boycott to end competition from non-union products. With the *Apex* and *Hutcheson* decisions in 1940 and 1941, the court virtually removed the Sherman Act from the union scene, save in cases of outright collusion with employers to fix commodity prices.[20]

On May 4, 1937, the Hosiery Workers struck Apex, turning it into a sit-down strike two days later. Organized violence and damage were committed. During the almost seven weeks' occupation of the plant, the employer was forceably prevented from shipping his product. He sued under the Sherman Act, and the issue before the Supreme Court was whether the strikers had committed an illegal restraint of trade. The majority thought that they had not, while conceding the tortious and criminal character of their acts.

According to Justice Stone, the Sherman law was not conceived as a measure for policing interstate shipments. Its purpose, or so he thought, was to prevent suppression of commercial competition.

The intent of the Apex union was not such a restraint, but to organize the firm, of which the blockade of shipments, while probably a violation of local law, was a necessary consequence. There was no effect upon hosiery prices, nor was such intended. Indeed, union activities may restrict the competitive freedom of employers in the product market, but this does not make them illegal. A successful product-market wide union inevitably reduces competition from non-union goods, but this is essential and "has not been considered . . . the kind of curtailment of price competition prohibited by the Sherman Act."[21]

If one thinks that the Sherman Act should not be employed to establish labor policy through judicial interpretations of lawful means and lawful purposes, then the *Apex* decision was a great step forward. Yet, as Cox points out, it left some troublesome questions: (1) could the Teamsters lawfully encourage retail employees not to handle the products of a supplier with whom the union has a dispute? (2) Is the question of intent still decisive where a union makes preclusive agreements requiring that machinery may only be installed by contractors also having agreements with it? (3) If product price is adversely affected by the union's acts, do the latter become illegal trade restraints?[22]

The *Hutcheson* case involved a jurisdictional dispute between the carpenters and the machinists over construction work at the Anheuser-Busch brewery in St. Louis. Despite a prior agreement to arbitrate, President Hutcheson and three other officials called a strike against the company and its contractor, also promulgating a boycott against Budweiser beer. The government then obtained an indictment under the Sherman Act, charging a criminal combination and conspiracy in restraint of trade.

Speaking for the majority, Justice Frankfurter began by asking whether the acts complained of were prohibited by the "three interlacing statutes"—Sherman, Clayton, and Norris-LaGuardia. Nothing in Section 20 precluded a jurisdictional strike, or picketing in its behalf, or a boycott in its support. All three were protected acts in self-defense, lawful under Clayton. The fact that outsiders shared in the conduct—a decisive point in the *Duplex* case—did not remove this protection. Under Norris-LaGuardia, a legitimate labor dispute was confined no longer to those who "stand in the proximate relation of employer and employee." Admittedly, Norris-LaGuardia was directed at injunctions, not criminal proceedings, but to contend that *Duplex* still survives for the latter "is to say that that which on the equity side of the court is allowable conduct may in a criminal proceeding become the road to prison." The statute was the legislature's answer to judicial doctrine in the *Duplex* and *Bedford* cases, hence the means of effectuating its original purpose in enacting Section 20.

There is a certain disingenuousness about this opinion that was not lost on Justice Roberts, who submitted a scathing dissent. As with *Apex*, however, the virtue, or lack of it, of the *Hutcheson* decision depends upon one's view of the use of the antitrust laws to regulate the labor-market activities of unions. What this verdict did was to make them immune from the doctrine of illegal trade restraints. Consistent with the very premise of the dual standard, the law regarding the coercive weapons of unionism was now completely divorced from the restrictions of the Sherman Act.

Later History of the Doctrine of Licit Labor Monopoly

In his rather involved majority opinion in the *Apex* case, Justice Stone confessed that "to some extent not defined" unions remain subject to the Sherman law. But to what extent? Very little beyond the prohibition of union-employer collusion in the product market, which survived with the *Brims* decision.

This question came up again in the *Allen Bradley* case, decided by the Supreme Court in 1945.[23] This was a flagrant instance of a protected local market for the manufacture and sale of electrical equipment in New York City. Local 3 of the Electrical Workers had negotiated a series of closed-shop agreements binding contractors to buy equipment only from local producers also having agreements with the local. All three groups joined to put pressure on recalcitrant producers and contractors, as part of their larger design for market and price control. Wages, employment, and benefits rose for the union members, while prices and profits also soared. The question presented was whether the union violated antitrust by participating in this scheme.

In his well-argued majority opinion, Justice Black faced up at the outset to the main issue. There was no doubt that the employers had violated antitrust: the real question was whether the union had, or whether its participation had thrown a cloak of immunity around what the employer did. The court was confronted with "two declared congressional policies, which it is our responsibility to try to reconcile." One was the statutory purpose of preserving an economy of competitive private enterprise; the other, of preserving the right to organize for collective bargaining.

Apart from its collusory aspect, what Local 3 did here was protected conduct under Section 20. Did this protection clothe with legality the larger combination with the employers? Black thought not. Congress had never authorized union collusion with non-labor groups. Local 3's preclusive agreements, binding the contractors not to buy equipment from firms not employing its members, "standing alone would not have violated the Sherman Act." But they were tainted by being part of the larger design, to aid the employers to monopolize the product market. "Our holding means that the same labor union activities may or may not be in violation of the Sherman Act, dependent upon whether the union acts alone or in combination with business groups." "A business monopoly is no less such because a union participates, and such participation is a violation of the Act."

The majority finding means that the union could negotiate separate but parallel labor agreements requiring exclusion of unsheltered products, yet stay within the statute while still effecting market control. The restriction itself is lawful, pursued by the union alone. Uniform agreements are equally licit. But could an association of employers negotiate a uniform agreement containing the restriction, and yet qualify for immunity? The answer is not clear, because, as Cox suggests, under the dual standard "unions are free to impose the very same market restraints that are criminal for employers."[24]

Events from 1932 present a record of attrition so far as the applicability of antitrust to labor matters is concerned, until little more than a shell remained by 1947. The Taft-Hartley Act in part was an attempt to fill the void by legislation. With Section 8(b)(4), Congress tried somewhat unsuccessfully to outlaw the secondary boycott, a provision further strengthened in the Labor-Management Reporting and Disclosure Act of 1959. It also made an abortive effort in 8(b)(6) to get at make-work practices. Further, it outlawed the jurisdictional strike, and introduced federal control over national-emergency disputes. But Congress left untouched both the industry-wide union and employer-association bargaining although unsuccessful efforts were undertaken to make them illegal. In the main, therefore, the dual standard survives today in full force and effect.

Proposals to Renew Application of Antitrust to Regulation of the Labor Market

Since the end of World War II, many proposals have arisen for revitalizing antitrust as a means for remaking national labor policy. Some of these hardly go beyond incantation, and amount to little more than an indiscriminate attack on a whole range of admittedly difficult problems—corruption, coercion, big unionism, national strikes, and even collective bargaining itself. What this line of thinking involves is far more than a return to antitrust. In reality, it intends a complete reconstruction of national labor policy, a subject beyond the scope of this paper.

The more carefully framed proposals to resurrect antitrust either aim to correct specific abuses, such as make-work rules, or to reduce the economic impacts of collective bargaining. Some of them would have the courts again distinguish the licit from the illicit without precise statutory guidance—an act of supreme folly in view of past experience. Yet some of the problems with which they purport to deal are serious. They give every indication of becoming even more acute in the sixties, where the now-permanent combination of cold war and intense foreign competition has made uninterrupted and more efficient production a national imperative.

These proposals would renew antitrust to cope with four major problems: national-emergency strikes, make-work policies, direct efforts to control the product market, and the effects of collective bargaining upon wages.

Regarding the first, the argument runs that the dual standard now allows national unions to do what no group of producers could do on their own: close down almost an entire industry by use of concentrated organizational power. This, it is said, is restraint of trade in its most extreme form. It should no longer be permitted.

So stated, the argument is really mostly about industry-wide unionism, and will be discussed later under that head. However, the short answer is that strikes are essential to collective bargaining, while collective bargaining continues to be national policy. The Taft-Hartley law already recognizes that some stoppages may unreasonably impose upon third parties; hence it contains a special procedure for national emergencies. In certain respects, it has proved defective. Correction lies either in legislation to improve the technique of intervention, or possibly to provide return to strict non-intervention, although the latter obviously would be unacceptable to those who demand strike control. Either way, antitrust supplies no solution. What it would do is to resurrect the old judicial concept that obstruction of production and transit is a restraint of trade, which would outlaw many strikes unqualifiedly. Then, if this were tempered by a test of intent to control the product market, the obsolete dicta in the second *Coronado* decision would stand revived. Again the courts would make labor policy, undoubtedly in the narrow and haphazard fashion of those earlier days.

The second area—make-work policies—covers a host of complex and vexing problems. Here the short answer is that the issues are too technical for the courts to handle with informed discretion, while to call this group of policies attempted trade restraints would not only go far off the mark but would threaten the whole bargaining system.

The problems in this field range widely: refusal to work with new materials, prefabricated products, tools, and machines; manning requirements, regulation of equipment speeds, and output controls; job and work jurisdictions, and full-crew regulations. Not all such devices are intended to "make work"—often their rationale is safety or reasonable working speeds, arrived at by bargaining. But odious cases of make-work are not hard to find, usually in craft-ridden industries such as construction, railroads, and entertainment. They may arise because the union has created unemployment by monopolistic wage-fixing, or because the industry is in attrition and the union resorts to crude methods of job protection. However, work rules are not inevitably a trade restraint, even under a broad conception of the term. A manning rule, for example, does not qualify, even if costly enough to affect product price. By contrast, a refusal of carpenters to work on pre-glazed sash is a deliberate trade restraint, denying such producers access to a market.[25]

Work rules lie at the heart of the collective agreement. Their origins are diverse and their nature complex. Good and bad alike, they express equities established by bargaining, as part of the web of rules by which the parties govern themselves. Wise men do not lightly tear this fabric apart. Thus to make work rules subject to antitrust would be far too sweeping. It would assign to the courts the impossible technical burden of segregating licit from illicit strikes and supportive union activities, in a field in which the judiciary is notoriously inexpert. Neither jurists nor lawmakers are competent to prescribe in detail the appropriate contents of a collective agreement. The whole approach rests upon a major premise that is *simpliste:* that all work rules are suspect and most of them economically and morally wrong; that collective bargaining should restrain the employer only in the area of wages and hours; that in all else his demands are proper, and the verdict of a court the last word.

It would seem more prudent to consider less risky alternatives. One of these would be a carefully drafted statute to get at concerted refusals to work with new materials, products, tools, or machines, all of which are union tactics to control product markets. However, even this interdiction might be easy for a union to evade, simply by translating the issue into one involving wages appropriate to a change in job content. Another line of attack, suggested by Gomberg, is to establish a technically qualified equity court to undertake "valuation proceedings" for hampering work rules, handing down awards under which the employer could "buy out" a particular rule for a decreed sum to be paid the union —an approach akin to eminent domain. In itself, this is a major departure, free neither of difficulties nor of objections. Short of it, there is the current proposal to give voluntary methods another chance, through extended mediation and bargaining, using "adopted" neutrals and study committees, on the premise that conventional bargaining can still yield constructive results in this difficult field if its procedures and resources are strengthened.

The third area of renewed antitrust embraces direct efforts by unions, through strikes and collective agreements, to control the product market. In part, the *Allen Bradley* decision dealt with this problem, by outlawing collusive agreements between the union and *groups* of employers in which control of market price was the larger explicit design. However, the majority opinion in that case suggested both that the union might still negotiate *separate* agreements lawfully excluding outside products for the benefit of its members and a preferred group of employers, and that, since the purpose was improved wages and conditions, such a demand could still give rise to a valid "labor dispute" within the meaning of Norris-LaGuardia. Beyond this, the construction trades are replete with devices to restrict the market to certain contractors, to fix bid prices, and to limit market access.[26]

Here, at least, there is a measure of agreement that the consumer interest is predominant, that antitrust can be applied consistently under the dual standard. As Cox suggests, the task is to guide the courts with precision, by an explicit statutory declaration carefully separating protected union activity from efforts to rig the product market. Agreements with employers to fix prices, limit production, or close off access to a market would become illegal, and strikes, boycotts, and other concerted acts to compel such agreements would also be illicit. However, Cox would exempt exclusion of an employer from the market incidental to disputes over representation or wages and working conditions, even if "strangers" participate. In its sole proposal affecting labor policy, the Attorney General's National Committee recommended a similar approach, but with a more comprehensive definition of proscribed activities and without the exemption noted.[27]

The fourth target for revived antitrust is reduction of the monopoly power of unions in the labor market itself. What must be abolished are multi-product or multi-industry unions such as the Teamsters, and along with them industry-wide unions as well. To the extent that its spread is economically motivated, the multi-industry union attempts to end competition *among* industries, such as railroads, water shipping, and trucking. The industry-wide union would end competition *among* firms in the same industry—a lesser type of indirect control over the product market.

Both must go, it is argued, because the only tenable economic case for labor monopoly is at the local level, to correct employer monopsony. Multi-industry and industry-wide unionism yield extra monopoly gains by reducing indirect competition among substitutes—through the elimination of non-union products and the establishment of uniform wages and conditions. The consequences have been adverse to the economy in three ways: major distortions in relative wages and reduced national income; sustained inflationary pressures from wage costs; and damaging large-scale strikes. Growth, full employment, and price stability have thus become incompatible ends for policy. The remedy is to break the monopoly power of multi-employer unions, by limiting labor organizations to the plant or company level, by prohibiting collusion among them, and by outlawing employer-bargaining associations.[28]

There is rather a radically utopian quality in this limitist approach. To conserve a competitive system it would undertake a major reconstruction of unionism, bargaining institutions, and the entire body of labor law, breaking decisively with the past. Not since *Commonwealth* vs. *Hunt* have unionism as such, and national unions in particular, been seriously threatened by the courts. To be sure, in the *Loewe, Duplex,* and *Bedford* decisions, the justices were groping toward a concept of legitimacy founded upon local unionism, but those verdicts went against the boycott rather than industry-wide unionism itself.

Considered on its own terms, localized or "enterprise" unionism poses serious questions and difficulties. One is that the stabilizing role of the national union would be destroyed. Usually the locals produce the hot-heads and put forward the most extreme demands, while the national office exerts restraint because it must take a wider view of the employment effects of the wage bargain.

Closely allied is the question whether rival enterprise unions in the same industry would reduce or increase wage pressure. In cases where sellers are few, wage and price leadership by the strongest firm seems likely to continue. An aggressive local union could use the claim of "ability to pay" with moral fervor and with no less force than now. Armed with the standards won in such a settlement, the other local bodies would still have both incentive and opportunity to follow along without overt collusion, while the employers could no longer unite against them. Furthermore, it is difficult to see why the threat of added unemployment would be any more effective than it is now among workers in weaker concerns, or why such firms would be better able or more willing to stand out than they do now against industry-wide unionism. In consequence, enterprise unionism in concentrated industries offers no assurance of improved wage behavior, and some prospect of worse. To better the results and to provide even-handed justice to the workers involved, it would be necessary to break up the firms as well.

For highly atomistic industries, equally difficult problems emerge. In very small firms, local unions could hardly survive, or if they could they would lack the financial resources and technical skills required for effective bargaining and contract administration. Beyond this, the proposal would make incomplete organization of an industry a powerful threat against any effective bargaining. In addition, the hard-won standards of unions in the casual trades would necessarily disintegrate. Indeed, the built-in weakness of local unionism in atomistic industries would have precluded most, if not all, of the undeniable achievements of centrally-directed national unions in the areas of private social security, work rules, and industrial jurisprudence. Finally, atomization would probably serve the objective of more flexible, market-responsive wages in highly diffuse industries, but it is doubtful that interfirm differentials or internal wage structures would be cured of monopsonistic —in contrast to monopolistic—distortions.

To sum up, the difficulties with the limitist approach derive not from its sound technical critique of multi-employer unionism, nor from its proper concern about the adverse economic consequences of present collective bargaining, but with the cure itself. While the statistical evidence for wage distortion is not yet conclusive, there is little doubt that unions in industries such as steel, construction, railroads, and coal have pushed wages far beyond competitive levels. The grounds are even stronger for attributing part of the creeping inflation of recent years to union-imposed cost pressures and the price policies they invoke.[29]

However, the cure may prove worse than the disease. Politically, the attempt to achieve enterprise unionism would unleash a costly and divisive struggle, for men do not lightly yield up institutions they have dedicated a century in building. Nor is this all. Dissolution of national unions seems certain to destroy the present balance of political power. At the same time, it implies new and comprehensive areas for government intervention—in "divestiture proceedings" against national unions and in enforcement of non-collusory behavior. This would be an odd kind of limitism indeed, for it would merely substitute one kind of concentrated power for another—public for private. And because it would greatly weaken, if not destroy, collective bargaining, it would divert the functions performed by bargaining to government instead, promising even further expansion of political intervention into the labor-management field. The situation is not yet so desperate that it requires so Draconian a measure.

CONCLUSION

Whatever may have been the intent of the framers of the Sherman law, during the first forty years of its life it served as a back door through which the judiciary entered into the making of national labor policy, even to the extent of largely rejecting the dual standard affirmed by Congress in the Clayton Act. In the notable line of decisions beginning with *Loewe* vs. *Lawlor,* the court crystallized two principles. One was that if strikes, boycotts, and/or violence obstructed the production and transit of goods destined for interstate markets, then these activities were tantamount to the kind of trade restraint exerted through the monopolizing efforts of commercial producers and distributors. The other was that the only legitimate parties to a labor dispute were a particular employer and his own employees. The main consequence of these judicial doctrines was that they hampered seriously the activities of national unions.

Between 1932 and 1941, official policy shifted radically to acceptance and encouragement of an industry-wide or syndicalist conception of licit union interests and activities. Except for outright collusion with employers in the product market, national unions were now released from the crippling doctrines of trade restraint and of the limited labor dispute. This was accomplished in two steps. Through the Norris-LaGuardia and Wagner Acts, Congress committed the nation to a policy to promote and effectuate collective bargaining. By the manner in which it did so, Congress opened the way to the great organizing campaigns of the later thirties, aiding rather than obstructing the advance of national unionism in both its industry-wide and multi-industry forms. The Supreme Court completed this evolution with the *Apex* and *Hutcheson* decisions. All that now remained of antitrust in the labor field were proscribed collusion of the *Allen Bradley* type and restrictions upon unions of non-employees.

These developments meant full acceptance, at last of the dual standard of licit labor monopoly. There were real benefits in the outcome, in two respects. It promoted the spread of collective bargaining, and it divorced national policy in the labor-management field from entanglement with actions to protect or restore commercial competition among business firms. Behind this separation lay recognition that the consumers' welfare optimum, while highly important, is not the only relevant guide to national policy. Workers as workers have a welfare interest of their own, one that inheres in the employer-employee relationship and that in certain ways clashes with the welfare of consumers.

Workers' welfare is an awkward concept to define, and it probably is not susceptible of the logic of maximization. However, one point is clear: It is an interest that will not, and cannot, be denied in modern industrial society. The only question is how it is to be served—by repression and ensuing sabotage, by dictatorial decree, by paternalism, by detailed statutory regulation, or by the decentralized system of private and accommodative rule-making called collective bargaining. For the labor-management field, the American version of freedom finds expression through bargaining institutions. This, in turn, is the informing major premise for the dual standard that now is the foundation of national labor policy.

Our experiment with relatively unhampered national unionism in the labor market has yielded some undeniable benefits and some unquestionable costs. The benefits require no elaboration. Among the costs are some upward push on wages and prices, some distortion of wage structure, some wage-induced unemployment, some great strikes, and some sobering revelations of corruption and abuses of power involving certain union leaders. It was proper that unions again would come under critical scrutiny, and inevitable that they would be blamed beyond fair warrant for the economic difficulties of recent times. Public criticism is a vital ingredient of a free society, for it is the one reliable means to well-conceived reforms.

Granting the problems, what promise does a return to antitrust actually hold? The answer is: relatively little for the problems at hand. What renewed antitrust really means is a return to judicial appraisal of the means and ends of union policy. Unless the courts are carefully circumscribed by statute, the outcome could only be chaos and uncertainty. If they are confined by measures to deal with specific abuses such as make-work or exclusion from the product market, antitrust could yield some modest benefits. But this approach would not cure the problems of corruption, of great strikes, or of the arrogant use of power. If antitrust were applied as the limitists propose, it would not only bring in the courts again with a vengeance, but would require government intervention so extensive that the whole bargaining system would be disrupted, if not destroyed. The price is too high for the quite speculative benefits such a change would bring. Labor-management relations today are not that desperate, nor are they lacking potential for constructive development on a voluntaristic basis. Legislative reforms are also needed. To be sound, they must derive from careful study and well-drafted statutes. To this end, antitrust has little to contribute but confusion.

NOTES

1. Louis B. Schwartz, *Free Enterprise and Economic Organization: Legal and Related Materials*, 2nd ed., Brooklyn: Foundation Press, 1959, p. 3.

2. The supporting arguments are various, partly inconsistent, and diverse in quality of reasoning: (1) the economic impacts of unionism are negligible; (2) unions can achieve a more "just" distribution of income, in favor of all wage-earners at the expense not of consumers but of property-owners; (3) unions have no intent to injure consumers; (4) unions do injure consumers, but workers have separate interests as workers, and the consumers' welfare optimum should not be the exclusive standard for policy or appraisal; (5) unions overcome the bargaining handicaps of the isolated worker; (6) unions provide countervailing power against the ubiquitous monopsony advantages of employers. All but one of these contentions are discussed by Donald Dewey, *Monopoly in Economics and Law*, Chicago: Rand McNally, 1959, pp. 265-269. The most thoroughgoing economic analysis of these and related arguments is in Fritz Machlup, *The Political Economy of Monopoly: Business, Labor and Government Policies*, Baltimore: The Johns Hopkins Press, 1952, pp. 339-417.

3. *United States* vs. *Debs*, U.S. Circuit Court, N.D., Illinois, 1894, 64 F. 724.

4. In reviewing the case, the Supreme Court chose to by-pass its antitrust aspect entirely, upholding the Circuit Court on the doctrine of sovereign powers. *In re* Debs, 158 U.S. 564 (1895).

5. *Loewe* vs. *Lawlor*, 208 U.S. 274 (1908); *Lawlor* vs. *Loewe*, 235 U.S. 522 (1915).

6. Dewey, *op. cit.*, p. 272.

7. Charles O. Gregory, *Labor and the Law*, 2nd rev. ed., New York: W. W. Norton & Company, Inc., 1958, pp. 207-208.

8. *Duplex Printing Press Co.* vs. *Deering*, 254 U.S. 443 (1921).

9. Gregory, *op. cit.*, pp. 211-222.

10. *Dowd* vs. *United Mine Workers*, 235 Fed. 1 (1916): *United Mine Workers* vs. *Coronado Coal Co.*, 258 Fed. 829 (1919); *United Mine Workers* vs. *Coronado Coal Co.*, 259 U.S. 344, 347 (1922); *Coronado Coal Co.* vs. *United Mine Workers of America*, 268 U.S. 295, 309 (1925).

11. *United Mine Workers* vs. *Coronado Coal Co.*, 259 U.S. 344, 347 (1922).

12. Dewey, *op. cit.*, p. 278.

13. *Bedford Cut Stone Co.* vs. *Journeymen Stone Cutters' Association*, 274 U.S. 37 (1927).

14. *United States* vs. *Brims*, 272 U.S. 549 (1926).

15. The word "monopoly" is used throughout in its descriptive sense, to refer to exclusive control of supply by sellers in order to fix price—in this case combinations of workmen in unions to control wages. That is all.

16. Section 4(a) by implication allows the secondary boycott in its strict form, but there is no language to suggest that the consumer boycott also now became immune. Gregory, *op. cit.*, pp. 194-195.

17. *J. I. Case Co.* vs. *National Labor Relations Board*, 321 U.S. 332 (1944).

18. Industry-wide, or employer-association, bargaining may be local, regional, or national, usually according to the geographic reach of product competition. Although it may accompany product-market wide unionism, the two are not identical, although they are often confused.

19. This, of course, was true long before the Wagner law, so long as the means used were compatible with a narrow judicial view of antitrust. As they did with Section 20 in 1914, the lawmakers took the national union for granted as a natural institutional development under a regime of organizational *laissez faire*.

20. *Apex Hosiery Co.* vs. *Leader*, 310 U.S. 469 (1940); *United States* vs. *Hutcheson*, 312 U.S. 219 (1941).

21. Justice Stone was indulging in fiction here, for the *Loewe*, *Duplex*, *Coronado* and *Bedford* decisions all belie the claim. As Gregory suggests, Stone was trying to salvage consistency with the past while facing up to the times. Gregory, *op. cit.*, p. 265.

22. Archibald Cox, "Labor and the antitrust laws—a preliminary analysis," *University of Pennsylvania Law Review*, 104:2 (November 1953), pp. 263-264.

23. *Allen Bradley Co.* vs. *Local Union No. 3, International Brotherhood of Electrical Workers*, 325 U.S. 797 (1945).

24. Cox, *op. cit.*, p. 271.

25. For illustrative cases, see *National Labor Relations Board* vs. *United Brotherhood of Carpenters and Joiners of America*, 184 F. 2d 60 (10th Cir. 1950); *Joliet Contractors Association* vs. *National Labor Relations Board*, 202 F. 2nd 606 (7th Cir. 1953); *certiorari denied* 346 U.S. 824 (1953). The

Joliet decision suggests that concerted refusal may be legal before work has begun, and that individuals may refuse at any time.

26. Cox, *op. cit.*, pp. 266-267.

27. *Ibid.*, pp. 283-284; *Report of the Attorney General's National Committee to Study the Antitrust Laws*, Washington: Government Printing Office, 1955, pp. 304-305.

28. See Machlup, *op. cit.*, pp. 429-432; Cox, *op. cit.*, pp. 275-279; and H. Gregg Lewis, "The labor-monopoly problem: A positive program," *Journal of Political Economy*, LIX:4 (August 1951), pp. 277-287.

29. Robert Ozanne, "Impact of unions on wage levels and income distribution," *Quarterly Journal of Economics*, LXXIII:2 (May 1959), pp. 177-196; W. Fellner, M. Gilbert, B. Hansen, R. Kahn, F. Lutz, and P. de Wolff, *The Problem of Rising Prices*, a study for the OEEC (1961); and Frank C. Pierson, "The economic influence of big unions," *Annals of the American Academy of Political and Social Science*, vol. 333 (January 1961), pp. 96-107.

7

LEGAL REGULATION OF

INTERNAL UNION AFFAIRS

JOSEPH R. GRODIN

Neyhart & Grodin, Attorneys at Law, San Francisco
Associate Professor of Law, Hastings Law School

Within the past few years legal regulation of internal union affairs has emerged from a state of relative unimportance to a position of pre-eminence in the labor law field. Stimulated by Senate Committee disclosures and by the Labor Management Reporting and Disclosure Act,[1] attention has shifted substantially from traditional labor-management problems to the relationships between union and worker. So rapid has been this change, and so fraught with controversy, that it is often difficult to determine precisely where we are or where we are going. In this short space, we cannot hope to sketch in all the features of the contemporary landscape;[2] our primary aim is to provide a perspective from which the scene can be viewed.

The perspective we have chosen is both geographical and historical. Geographically, it takes into account the experiences of Great Britain as well as the United States—experiences sufficiently similar, because of a shared common law and democratic background, to be meaningfully compared, yet sufficiently diverse to provide insight by contrast. Historically, it considers the development of the law relating to internal union affairs, in an effort to understand the forces at work in this constantly changing field. For in this area, perhaps more than most, it is apparent that the law is a dynamic force, responsive to changes in social conditions and attitude.

Using this combined perspective, we propose to examine what may conveniently be viewed for purposes of analysis as three stages of development in the law: stage one, in which unions were regarded as close to criminal conspiracies, outside the law with respect to either protection or regulation; stage two, in which unions were viewed in the same class with social clubs and fraternal groups—lawful yet relatively autonomous; and stage three, in which the law tends to treat unions as if they were public utilities or governmental entities, subject to rather extensive legal control over their internal operations. On the basis of this analysis, British law is for the most part still in the second stage, while the third provides the best explanation of contemporary American law and its direction.[3]

STAGE ONE: THE UNION AS AN ILLEGAL ASSOCIATION

A century ago, in England, unions were still close to being outlaw organizations. While the theory that they were criminal conspiracies was on the wane,[4] their actions were subject to the (then) extremely restrictive notions of civil conspiracy;[5] and their internal trade rules were regarded as unlawful because in "restraint of trade."[6]

One consequence of this situation was that British courts would deny enforcement, not only to rules which they regarded as unlawful, but to all union rules, on the theory that they were all "tainted" with illegality.[7] On that ground, among others, unions were said to be unable to obtain effective relief against members who violated trade or financial rules, and union members were unable to obtain any relief against rules violations which resulted in improper discipline, wrongful denial of benefits, and the like.[8] Courts were unwilling to help either unions or their members with respect to a relationship they deemed contrary to public policy. Unions were, in a literal sense, outside the law.

British unions had an ambivalent attitude toward this state of affairs. They disliked what we would now refer to as the "public image" which resulted from restraint of trade doctrine,[9] and they objected to various of its legal consequences;[10] but they welcomed the autonomy which resulted from judicial abstention. They had no need to sue their members for enforcement of financial obligations, and they had no desire to have members sue them before judges who were not likely to be sympathetic with labor's cause.[11]

This ambivalence was enshrined in the Trade Union Act of 1871, which was largely the result of trade union pressure.[12] Sections 2 and 3 of the Act provide that the purposes of a trade union shall not "by reason merely that they are in restraint of trade" be deemed unlawful so as to render any member liable to criminal prosecution, or to render void or voidable any agreement or trust; but Section 4 provides that nothing in the Act should be interpreted to enable a court to entertain any legal proceedings instituted with the object of "directly enforcing or recovering damages" for the breach of certain agreements, including trade rules, agreements for the payment of dues or fines, and agreements to provide benefits or payments to members. Thus, such agreements were relegated to the effect of the common law, which meant, everyone assumed at the time, that they would not be enforced. As one trade union counselor put it:[13]

> Section 4 prevents any interference on the part of courts of justice with the internal organization and working of unions. If it were not for this section, any member might sue the union, and every union would be constantly harassed by lawsuits.

As a prediction what the courts would do, this statement about the effects of Section 4 proved to be quite erroneous, but that is getting ahead of our story.

In the United States, this first stage was never so marked as in Britain—perhaps because by the time American courts were faced with suits involving intra-union disputes they had already rejected the notions of *per se* illegality which lay behind the British doctrine.[14] Nevertheless, many American courts did regard as unlawful attempts by unions to "monopolize" the labor market by closed shop conditions, and this attitude, in some cases, gave rise to theories akin to those established in Britain. For example, a Missouri court in 1902 denied relief to a wrongfully expelled member of a musicians union on the basis of a union rule (not directly involved in the case) which provided that members should not work with non-members.[15] The court said:

Such a confederation and combination is a trust pure and simple.
. . . The plaintiff is in the attitude of asking the court to keep him
where the law says he has no right to be and to retain him in a
position where he may support and maintain an illegal association,
where he may continue to support and keep up a monopoly of the
services of musicians. Courts have never dealt with monopolies,
except to restrain or destroy them, and we decline to depart from
this wholesome rule in this case.

The following year a New Jersey court followed suit: [16]

To compel, by injunction or otherwise, the continuance of association or membership in these voluntary trade unions, either local
or general, would, in my judgment, result in enforcing the performance of their restrictive regulations, and it would, therefore,
be an unjustifiable interference with the freedom of contract and
of trade.

Direct expressions of this view are rare; but other courts did,
during this early period, display great reluctance to assist union
members in suits against their unions; and it is reasonable to assume that to some extent similar attitudes played a part in their
rulings.

STAGE TWO: THE UNION AS A SOCIAL CLUB OR FRATERNAL ORGANIZATION

As unions grew in size, strength, and influence, and as they became committed to peaceful, organizational pursuit of their goals,
they became more respectable in the eyes of the community. This
respectability was enhanced, particularly in Britain, by a growing
tolerance of pressure groups generally and by acceptance of the
principle of freedom of association. These changes led to gradual
relaxation of the negative attitude which the law displayed toward
internal union affairs during the first stage, and to application of
principles of intervention which courts had developed for other
unincorporated, non-profit associations.

Since the first stage in the United States was expressly evidenced
only by scattered decisions, the transition in this country was barely
noticeable. In Missouri, the early decision refusing to intervene because of trade union illegality was simply ignored in later cases,
and the New Jersey decision was first distinguished[17] and later
overruled.[18] In Britain, however, where the principle of non-

interference was supposedly codified in Section 4 of the 1871 Trade Union Act, the transition presents one of the most fascinating examples of the effects of social change upon statutory interpretation.[19]

The first decisions under the 1871 Act followed the spirit of Section 4 in refusing to order reinstatement of wrongfully expelled union members (on the ground that such relief would constitute direct enforcement of a benefit rule),[20] and in denying jurisdiction over a suit to restrain application of union funds in violation of a union rule.[21] But gradually courts adopted a "narrow" interpretation of the words "directly enforcing" as they appear in Section 4, and held that section was no bar in either fund misapplication[22] or expulsion[23] cases, even where the funds were allegedly misapplied in breach of a benefit rule or the member expelled for violation of a trade rule. In one expulsion case[24] the House of Lords ordered reinstatement of a member disciplined for violation of an ambiguous trade rule on the ground that:

> To construe a rule is not directly to enforce any agreement between the members, and *I am unable to see any reason why the words of the statute should be so extended as to exclude a trade union itself or any of its members from having obscure words construed by a wholly independent tribunal* (emphasis added).

For a time, British courts attacked the assumption behind the 1871 Act that intra-union agreements were unenforceable at common law, and held that in the case of unions which were found to be established "primarily" for benefit purposes rather than trade purposes, even rules providing for benefits could be directly enforced without reliance upon the Act, and therefore without regard to Section 4.[25] But in 1912 the House of Lords held that at least where a union's rules provide for penalties for violation of trade regulations such rules must be regarded in restraint of trade at common law.[26] Since that decision, and perhaps in part as a result of it, there have been few unions whose rules do not "qualify" for application of the Section 4 test.[27] As a practical matter, then, all that probably remains of the strictures of Section 4, so far as suits by members are concerned, is that a British court will not order a union to pay benefits allegedly due under a union's rules, and even in that case it is possible that the court will grant a declaration that the money is owing, or an injunction against use of the money for any other purpose.[28] Needless to say, the resulting situation is a far cry from the expectations of those who supported the 1871 Act.

This retreat from total abstention did not, however, signal a massive judicial onslaught into internal union affairs in either country. Courts applied to unions principles derived from the law relating to other associations, such as social clubs, religious groups, and fraternal societies; and those principles had their limitations. Members would be entitled to "due process of law" (or, as the British call it, "natural justice") in the event they were disciplined,[29] at least unless the union's rules provided otherwise.[30] A union's rules, like those of other associations would be regarded as in the nature of a contract among members, or between each member and the group, and would be enforced by the courts.[31] A member could be disciplined, for example, only on the grounds,[32] by the procedures,[33] and with the sanctions[34] provided for in the union's constitution and by-laws. But unions could, within rather wide limits, if any, make whatever rules they liked. Like a private club, they were free to place restrictions upon admission to membership,[35] and to legislate with respect to membership conduct and union government without significant legal restraint. In America, before a member could sue, he would usually be required to exhaust intra-union remedies, often without regard to the degree of hardship he might suffer in the interim or the likelihood of effective relief.[36] In some cases, courts refused to interfere because no "property rights" were involved.[37] And in England, an expelled member, even if he were successful in getting a court to agree that his expulsion was wrongful, could not recover damages because it was said that, as a party to the intra-union agreement, he was partially responsible for authorizing the wrongful act.[38]

Chafee, in a classic article on this subject,[39] has colorfully characterized some of the judicial attitudes which lay (usually well concealed) behind these doctrines of cautious intervention, There was the "Living Tree" policy, which favored autonomy for private groups whose roots might be destroyed by unwarranted judicial intervention; the "Dismal Swamp" policy, according to which courts felt themselves on unfirm ground in dealing with the frequently esoteric affairs of secret societies and religious groups; and the "Hot Potato" policy, which recognized the political problems inherent in regulating powerful private organizations.

In addition, courts displayed the attitude that most interests in an association were primarily "social" in nature and, like other intangible, non-pecuniary interests, were neither worthy nor capable of equitable protection. This attitude found doctrinal expression in the requirement of "property" rights as a condition to equitable relief. Said Sir George Jessel in a trade union expulsion case,

> A dozen people may agree to meet and play whist in each others houses for a certain period and if eleven of them refuse to associate with the twelfth any longer, I am not aware that there is any jurisdiction in any court of justice in this country to interfere.

To carry out Chafee's theme, this decision might be said to imply two additional plant-metaphors: a "Worthless Weed" policy with respect to the value of the interests at stake, and a "Shrinking Violet" policy with respect to the efficacy of the law.

It is consistent with these latter attitudes that when it came to handling of union funds, courts were quite willing to intervene, and rather extensively. Here the analogy was to trust and corporation law. A member was recognized as having a "property right" in his union's assets and, like a shareholder or trust beneficiary, could bring suit to enjoin misapplication of such assets for purposes not authorized by the union's rules.[41] In addition, it was quite clear that a union officer had much the same fiduciary responsibility as a trustee or corporate director to use his position for the best interests of the group,[42] and American courts would require union officers to account for any funds allegedly misapplied.[43] Exhaustion of internal remedies, normally required by American courts, was excused.[44]

There was one point on which British law was in the lead, and that was the principle of disclosure. The Trade Union Act of 1871, in the course of assimilating unions to other non-profit associations, applied to them the same administrative principles as had been created for fraternal benefit societies. By registering with the Registrar of Friendly Societies, unions could obtain certain modest advantages;[45] but as a condition of registration they were (and still are) required to file with the Registrar annual financial statements, and copies of their rules and amendments to rules specifying the purposes for which union funds could be used. The financial statement is required to be in a form and with the particulars required by the Registrar, and must indicate the rule authorizing each expenditure. Copies of the statement must be made available to members upon request. In addition, every registered union must render periodic accounts to its trustees or members at a union meeting; and the accounts must be audited by some "fit and proper" person or persons selected by the trustees. Finally, each member must be allowed to inspect the union's books upon request.

Thus, British law provided the pattern for the reporting and disclosure requirements of the Taft-Hartley Act, which likewise conditioned benefits (use of the NLRB) upon the filing of reports. The LMRDA goes somewhat beyond that pattern by requiring disclosure irrespective of benefits, by establishing certain substantive "safeguards" (for example, limits on loans to officers and members; bonding of officers), and by granting to the Secretary of Labor enforcement and investigative powers which he did not have under Taft-Hartley, and which the Registrar lacks under the Trade Union Act of 1871.

Stage Three: The Union as Public Utility or Government

The two adjectives used most frequently by courts in describing non-profit associations were "voluntary" and "private"; and in a way these words epitomized the assumptions which underlay judicial policy. "Voluntarism" was the keystone of *laissez-faire* philosophy. By voluntary agreements individuals would make laws for themselves; this was the driving force behind the trend of the common law from status to contract, the legal vehicle for social and economic mobility. Further, what a group of individuals, freely associating together, decided to do among themselves was their own "private" affair, with which the law was not particularly concerned, except perhaps to enforce their agreements, and even then subject to the methods of deciding disputes which they provided for themselves.

It has been the collision between these concepts of the nineteenth century and the social and economic reality of the twentieth which has given impetus to changes in the law relating to internal union affairs. Ours is an age of institutionalized power in a highly inter-dependent society. Individuals must work through and deal with organizations—business, political, and professional—in order to be effective and to fulfill their wants. Frequently the individual has no significant choice among organizations, either because a par-ticular organization is the only one of its kind or because a number of similar organizations have standardized their practices. The negotiated agreement assumed by common law to be the backbone of contract doctrine has given way, in terms of relative practical importance, to the "contract of adhesion"—the standard form agree-ment which an individual either accepts or rejects but does not have real opportunity to bargain over.[46] There is little that is "voluntary" in such a situation; and, if the impact of the relation-ships upon the public generally is to be considered, little that is "private." Such "contracts" have become the legal vehicle for the imposition of new forms of status.

The constitution and bylaws of a union, if they are to be called a contract at all, constitute such a contract of adhesion, though of a special variety akin to Rousseau's *contract social*. There is typi-cally only one union that a worker may join in order to have a voice in the determination of his working conditions; and fre-quently he must join, as a condition of retaining his employment. Upon joining, he takes the union's rules, and its internal political structure, as he finds them. His ability to effect change is then dependent upon the degree to which he can exert effective power within his union. To say under such circumstances that he has "voluntarily" agreed to all the provisions of the union's rules is often not very helpful, even as a metaphor; and, in view of the wide and powerful effect of the modern union upon the lives of the worker and the public at large, to say that its internal affairs remain a wholly "private" matter is neither realistic as a descrip-tion of fact nor necessarily wise as a matter of policy.

The courts in both Britain and the United States, and the legis-latures here as well, have reacted to these changes by imposing obligations upon the union-worker relationship independent of consensual agreement. This reaction parallels that of the law in other fields,[47] and is accelerated in both countries by a political atmosphere which imposes greater responsibility upon government for the welfare of its citizens—which recognizes, in other words, less of a distinction between what is "public" and what is "private." In Britain, the reaction has taken the form of a "liberalized" application of the 1871 Act;[48] judicial pronouncements to the effect that there may be limits to the intra-union "contract";[49] and a House of Lords decision overturning the rule which prevented a wrongfully expelled member from suing for damages.[50] In this country, the reaction has been expressed by judicial use of fact-finding and interpretation of union rules in the light of the courts' notions of public policy;[51] invalidation, where necessary, of union rules which conflict with that policy;[52] a relaxation of the requirement of exhaustion of remedies;[53] a greater willingness to protect rights in participation;[54] and, of course, the LMRDA.

We are primarily concerned here, however, with the pattern which intervention has taken rather than with the techniques by which it is accomplished. Subject to the limitations of any legal generalization, the pattern and direction of control in this country is best described through analogy of a union to a public utility or government. In Britain, however, where the changes have been less rapid and extensive, these analogies have limited descriptive utility. Courts still, with some exceptions, treat unions in the same category as the club and fraternal society, though the situation is changing.

A number of factors probably contribute to this difference. British courts are frequently slower to react to changing social conditions, for one; and the British public may be less likely to rely upon the law for solutions of its problems. Then, too, Britain has been relatively free of (or at least of publicity about) the type of scandal which has plagued the American labor movement in recent years. The factor we choose to emphasize, however, because of the light it throws on the picture we are describing, is the difference in general legal situation between unions in the two countries.

The force of the public utility analogy in this country derives primarily from the union's "monopoly" position as statutory bargaining representative, and its contractual control over the job situation. Stressing the latter factor, the California Supreme Court said in *James* vs. *Marinship Corp.*:[55]

Where a union has, as in this case, attained a monopoly of the supply of labor by means of closed shop agreements and other forms of collective labor action, such a union occupies a quasi public position similar to that of a public service business and it has certain corresponding obligations. It may no longer claim the same freedom from legal restraint enjoyed by golf clubs or fraternal associations. Its asserted right to choose its own members does not merely relate to social relations; it affects the fundamental right to work for a living.

In the *James* case the court utilized the public utility analogy to hold that a union which maintains job control through closed shop agreements may not deprive persons of employment by arbitrarily excluding them from membership, or (what the court held to be equivalent) by forcing them to accept second-class, voteless membership because they are Negroes. That would be comparable to a public utility arbitrarily denying service to a class of consumers. Beyond that limitation, the analogy is helpful in analyzing cases which hold that unions may not discriminate arbitrarily (i.e., for reasons irrelevant to their statutory function) in the services to be rendered (i.e., in the terms and application of the collective bargaining agreement);[56] and those cases which suggest that a union has an affirmative legal obligation to render services which are reasonably adequate.[57] Most of these cases, however, can be as easily, if not more easily, explained on the basis of the governmental analogy, as we shall discuss presently.

The governmental analogy is similarly dependent in substantial degree upon the union's legal status. In part it derives from the similarity of a union's internal structure to that of a government, and from its internal rules to legislation; but in part, also, it derives from the government-like powers the union exercises in the collective bargaining sphere, frequently pursuant to authority and support from the state itself. An agency of the government decides what unit of employees is "appropriate" for bargaining; and, if doubt exists as to what labor organization, if any, has been designated by a majority of such employees it holds an election and certifies the results. The victorious union then becomes their exclusive bargaining representative, and may compel the employer to negotiate with it, free from interference or discrimination. The collective bargaining agreement which results (perhaps analogous to a treaty) has binding legal effect, and no "private" agreements can detract from its terms. The agreement may, and frequently does, condition employment upon membership, or at least upon payment of "taxes." Such state participation in union authority suggests the possibility that union action is governmental action for constitutional purposes;[58] but we are concerned here primarily with the application of constitutional principles by analogy.

In Britain unions have seldom asked of the law more than to be let alone, and this the law has done with minor exceptions. No law requires a British employer to bargain with any union,[59] nor to refrain from discrimination against employees because of their union activities.[60] Collective bargaining agreements are probably unenforcible in the courts, or at least they have never been enforced.[61] In any event, an employer seems to be legally free to make separate agreements with individual employees, even if they conflict with the provisions of the collective agreement.[62] Quite frequently there are a number of unions representing employees of a single employer, and their representation may overlap work classifications without regular pattern.[63] Some unions oppose "compulsory unionism" as a matter of principle, and where union membership is made a condition of employment it is more often by tacit understanding than by formal agreement. While British unions may exert as much *de facto* power as their American counterparts, they do so for the most part on their own, and without the benefit (or the hindrance) of the law.[64]

Thus, British unions still retain, so far as legal form is concerned, many characteristics of the "voluntary," "private" associations which formed the basis for the second-stage doctrines; and to that extent the public utility and governmental analogies are less applicable. Moreover, the implications of the governmental analogy are not, conceptually, the same in Britain. Britain has no written constitution, no doctrine of judicial review, and no federal system. Consequently, the notion that a union is like a government does not, in Britain, lead to the conclusion that it is subject to constitutional restrictions but rather, in accordance with the doctrine of parliamentary supremacy, that it should be free to legislate as it sees fit. Only if the union were analogized to an administrative agency would regulation follow conceptually, and on that basis judicial review would be quite limited.

Even in this country, of course, the governmental analogy is subject to qualifications. There are some areas of intervention (such as legal control over union funds) which it cannot explain as well as other analogies; and as a normative theory it falls short insofar as there are differences between a union and a government which ought to be reflected in differences in policy. In some respects, for example, a union may be more like an army than like a government—or at least more like a government frequently at war. Its functions (depending upon the union) are often narrowly defined and it may periodically be engaged in industrial warfare which might warrant strong internal controls.[65] Even when it is not at war, the union does not easily lend itself to the multi-party system characteristic of the modern democratic state, though some union governments are cast in the form.[66] Goals are frequently so well accepted, and achievement so easily measured (in terms of collective bargaining gains) that there may be insufficient differences (or interest) in policy to sustain continuing rival factions. In this respect, the union is like most large-scale organizations which, upon becoming moderately successful, tend to become encrusted with what Michels has termed the "iron law of oligarchy" —an intrenchment of leadership and policy resulting from a combination of membership apathy and operational complexity.[67]

In addition, the kinds of policies which restrained courts from interfering in the second stage are not to be wholly ignored. While the union cannot claim to be a fragile seedling at this point, the "Living Tree" policy has considerable merit; the law should not interfere in such a way as to hamper the union's effectiveness unduly or to weaken its responsibility for conducting its own affairs in a proper manner. A union's internal affairs may well be a "Dismal Swamp" to judges or legislators unfamiliar with (and sometimes hostile to) the labor movement; and unwarranted intervention can be harmful. Moreover, the limits to the effectiveness of law must still be taken into account. It may be that the problem of membership apathy will render the legal guarantee of constitutional principles relatively meaningless in some unions.

Despite these qualifications, the governmental analogy corresponds closely to the pattern of intervention which has taken place, and to the policy assumptions which seem to underlie that pattern. It implies majority rule: that adequate procedures exist for the expression of the majority will, and that all employees subject to the union's rule should be allowed to participate in its affairs. It also implies minority rights: the right to be free from arbitrary discrimination; the right to fair procedure in disciplinary cases; the right to express and effectuate dissenting views; and the right to carry on activities outside the union's sphere of "sovereignty" without undue limitation. In each of these areas, however, it implies a corresponding obligation to the union as an institution. We shall explore these generalizations in the following pages.

Majority Rule: A Republican Form of Government

The governmental analogy implies, in the context of our society, a republican form of government, that is to say, a government ruled by persons fairly elected by, and responsible to, in some institutional fashion, the will of the majority. For the most part this criterion can be, and has been, satisfied by enforcement of union rules at common law.[68] Probably every union in both Britain and the U.S. provides in its constitution and bylaws for periodic election of officers; and, while one American court has held that it has no "jurisdiction" to order an election because no "civil or property rights" were involved,[69] most courts have directed that elections be held where it is shown that the incumbent officers are attempting to avoid or delay an election beyond the time specified in the union's rules.[70] Similarly, union rules typically provide for the manner in which elections are to be conducted and those rules, also, have been enforced at common law by courts of both countries, at least where impropriety raises a substantial doubt as to the wishes of the majority.[71] On this score American courts have gone somewhat further than the British by appointing receivers to conduct the election and count the ballots.[72]

The LMRDA goes beyond the common law of either country both by providing an administrative remedy (through the Secretary of Labor) for the enforcement of union election rules, and by prescribing government-like standards for the frequency and the conduct of union elections to which union rules and practices are required to conform. Officers must be elected by secret ballot (or, in the case of national unions and intermediate bodies, by delegates elected by secret ballot); reasonable opportunity for nomination must be afforded; fifteen days' notice of the election must be given; votes of each local union must be counted separately; candidates must have an opportunity to distribute campaign literature on a non-discriminatory basis and to inspect membership lists prior to the election; and other safeguards must be provided. The Act also provides for removal of officers by the membership "for good cause shown and after notice and hearing," unless the union's rules contain other provisions for removal which comply with standards promulgated by the Secretary of Labor. While these standards in most cases do not require substantial revision of existing practices, they nevertheless constitute an important departure from the principle that unions are free to establish their own rules.

The governmental analogy does not necessarily imply membership control beyond the election and recall of officers and delegates; direct democracy is as impracticable for the modern union as for the modern state.[73] Nevertheless, both British and American unions have traditionally modified the representative principle by providing for limited membership control at the local meeting level, and by use of the initiative or referendum on certain matters. As in the case of elections of officers, courts of both countries will intervene to prevent or remedy substantial violation of such rules.[74] In addition, there are now statutes in both countries which require that specified issues be put to membership vote, though the issues specified are quite different and unrelated. In Britain, statutes prescribe special procedures for adoption of political rules (creating a fund for political purposes)[75] and for amalgamation of one union with another;[76] and in both cases secret ballot vote of the membership is required. In this country the LMRDA requires membership vote for increase of dues or initiation fees, or for imposition of assessments, at the local union level. At the intermediate or national levels, however, the same actions can be undertaken by delegates who themselves were selected by secret ballot; and to that extent the principle of government by representation is preserved.

The Right to Participate

A corollary to the principle of representative government is the right to participate—to vote, nominate, and hold office subject to reasonable and non-discriminatory qualifications. To some extent this right, like others, is protected by enforcing union rules on the subject—something both British and American courts will do at common law and which may now be done through the Secretary of Labor under the LMRDA. There are procedural difficulties in both common law and statutory remedies, but they need not concern us here.[77] The serious substantive question is what kind of qualifications a union may impose upon the right to participate. The traditional common law approach is to say any qualifications it likes, and that is probably the answer a British court would give if faced with the problem today.[78] In this country, however, the situation is quite different.

Here a distinction must be made between a person who is already a member of a labor organization and one who would like to be. As among members, courts of some states held at common law, on the basis of the public utility or governmental analogies, that a union may not arbitrarily discriminate with respect to the right to participate, at least where membership is made compulsory by a union security agreement. It was held, for example, that a union could not deny the franchise to a permanent category of "junior" members,[79] nor (under closed shop conditions) to Negroes[80] or self-employed persons.[81] This principle is now extended and codified in Section 101(a)(1) of the LMRDA which provides, without regard to job control, that every member of a labor organization shall have "equal rights and privileges" to nominate, vote, and attend and participate in union meetings "subject to reasonable rules and regulations in such organization's constitution and by-laws." Similarly, under Section 401(e) every member in good standing must be eligible to hold union office, subject again to "reasonable qualifications uniformly imposed" and to certain statutory disqualifications for membership in the Communist Party or for conviction of specified crimes. What is a "reasonable" qualification on the right to participate under these sections will presumably be determined by the same sort of standard used in constitutional law: whether the restriction is reasonably related to a proper legislative (i.e., union) purpose.

The LMRDA protects only the participation rights of members, however. Both the Act and the common law place certain restrictions on the right of a union to discipline members; but so far as the Act is concerned, a member who has been validly expelled or suspended loses all rights to participate, and a union is free to exclude workers from membership (and therefore from participation) on whatever basis it sees fit.[82]

In this respect the LMDRA is consistent with prevailing common law in both Britain and the United States;[83] and, except for Fair Employment Practices Acts which prohibit discrimination on grounds of race, color, religion, creed, or nationality, there is no statutory law expressly to the contrary.[84] There is, however, authority for a different result. The California Supreme Court in the *Marinship* case recognized participation rights only insofar as membership was made a condition of employment, and directed the union *either* to admit the Negroes to full membership rights *or* to cease interference with their employment; but a more recent decision of the same court, upon a finding of arbitrary exclusion, upheld a writ directing the union to admit the plaintiff to membership without allowing that alternative.[85] The Supreme Court of Kansas, in a 1946 decision,[86] went even further to hold that where a union is certified as bargaining representative, it is "acting as an agency created and functioning under provisions of federal law," and that exclusion of persons on grounds of race deprived them of rights guaranteed directly under the federal constitution. A federal circuit court of appeals, however, has held to the contrary,[87] and the Supreme Court has denied *certiorari* "in view of the abstract context in which questions sought to be raised are presented by this record."[88] On the basis of recent decisions in the civil rights area, it is possible that the Supreme Court would hold action by a certified union to be governmental action for constitutional purposes, though such a holding is not necessary (and perhaps not desirable) in order to reach the conclusion that a certified union should not discriminate in its admission policies on grounds of race.

Fair Disciplinary Procedure: Due Process of Law

Both British and American courts required at common law that unions, in disciplining members, observe the provisions of their own constitutions and by-laws, with respect to procedure,[89] as with respect to the grounds for discipline and[90] the sanction.[91] The principle difference has been that British courts have tended to insist on strict, technical compliance[92] whereas American courts have allowed greater leeway, holding that minor variances may be permissible where they do not result in unfairness,[93] and that a member may under some circumstances waive or be estopped by his conduct from insisting that union rules be followed.[94]

In addition, courts of both countries have long insisted that union disciplinary procedure adhere to what British courts called "natural justice" and American courts "due process of law." The requirement seems first to have been applied in the case of private clubs.[95] At one time, consistent with their "voluntary-private" philosophy, British courts explained the requirement as something "implied" from the organization's own rules, indicating that unions could, if they desired, dispense with it by appropriate provisions in their constitution or by-laws.[96] More recently, however, some British judges have expressed the opinion that a union rule purporting to dispense with "natural justice" would be invalid as contrary to public policy,[97] and that is clearly the position of American courts.[98] Thus, the requirement is not contractual but imposed upon the parties because of their relationship to one another; and it derives, quite clearly, from the governmental analogy. The due process principle has now been substantially codified in Section 101(a)(5) of the LMRDA:

> No member of any labor organization may be fined, suspended, expelled, or otherwise disciplined except for non-payment of dues by such organization or by any officer thereof unless such member has been (A) served with written specific charges; (B) given a reasonable time to prepare his defense; (C) afforded a full and fair hearing.

Though agreed on general principles, British and American courts do not appear to agree entirely on what constitutes a "fair hearing" in union cases. In the United States, most of the procedural safeguards of a court trial must be provided. While members probably need not be permitted representation by counsel,[99] unless required by union rule,[100] they must be granted the right to be confronted by contrary evidence,[101] to cross-examine adverse witnesses,[102] and to present evidence on their own behalf, including the testimony of witnesses.[103] Though legal rules as to the admissibility of evidence need not be strictly followed,[104] their gross violation may amount to denial of due process.[105]

It is not clear to what extent these rules are applicable in Britain. The decisions state that an accused member must be granted an adequate opportunity of defending himself,[106] and this probably includes the opportunity to be present at an oral hearing and produce evidence.[107] One English court, however, stressing the "very wide differences between the principles applicable to courts of justice and those applicable to domestic tribunals," has indicated that in the latter (including the trade union) not only is the tribunal free to depart from rules of evidence, but it need not allow cross-examination.[108] And in another case a court held that the principles of natural justice were not violated when an accused was denied the opportunity to see a report used in evidence against him, nor when he was prevented from having his wife testify in his behalf.[109] It is doubtful whether that decision would stand in this country.

By far the most crucial question in union disciplinary matters, however, is how far the law should go in insisting upon impartial tribunals. The governmental analogy would suggest that the same rules of disqualification for bias or interest be applied as in the case of courts or administrative agencies, but in most unions that would require substantial change in organizational structure. Except for the United Auto Workers and the Upholsterers, which have established independent appellate tribunals composed of neutral persons outside the union, most unions maintain little or no separation of powers. At the local level, members are typically tried by the union's executive board, with right of appeal to the president and/or executive board of the national union, and ultimately to the convention. Where the "crime" is political in nature, or has political overtones, objectivity under such circumstances is difficult.[110] Unless courts are willing to invalidate a union's entire disciplinary procedure they must, in many cases, confine themselves to a narrow application of the rules of bias and good faith.

That is, for the most part, the position of British courts. While they may be prepared to disqualify an individual on a tribunal who has a personal interest in the case,[111] or who demonstrates bad faith,[112] it can fairly be implied from their decisions that British courts will not disqualify an entire tribunal, constituted in accordance with the union's rules, even where the members of the tribunal were the victims of the conduct for which the accused member is to be tried,[113] or where they had, prior to the trial, declared their opposition to the accused.[114]

American courts have at times expressed a similar view,[115] but some have taken a more restrictive position. Where, for example, a member was disciplined for alleging that a union election had been conducted in a fraudulent and dishonest fashion, and his trial board was composed entirely of persons who held office as a result of the challenged election, a New York court ruled the trial board "disqualified by a direct interest in the subject matter of the controversy," even though there was no other body qualified under the union's rules to try the plaintiff.[116] In a more recent case the same court, holding a union's executive board incompetent to try charges of defamation against its members, said:[117]

> The fact that there were no members of the board who could qualify as disinterested judges is irrelevant. If there was a problem as to how to provide an impartial appellate tribunal for these cases the burden of its solution was (the union's).

Free Speech and Assembly

It does not appear that British courts have granted any protection to the interest of a member in expressing his opposition to union officers or policies.[118] In one case a member was disciplined for complaining to the national office about misconduct on the part of local officials,[119] and in another for distributing election speeches and circulars critical of incumbent officers,[120] and in both cases the discipline was upheld, as being in conformity with the union's rules.

American courts, on the other hand, have given substantial protection to the right of opposition at common law. For many years this protection was indirectly and implicitly exercised through interpretation of union discipline rules, findings of fact, and on the basis of procedural defects.[121] In recent years, however, judicial policy in favor of the right to criticize union officers or policies in good faith, and to form opposition political groups, has reached the level of direct expression, the courts relying upon the governmental analogy for their views. "Viewing the important role of labor unions in this era," said one court, striking down discipline for criticism of officers, "courts may well determine in a particular case that protection of their democratic processes is essential to the maintenance of our democratic government."[122] Said another court, protecting members who formed an opposition group: "In America we have a two-party system—Republican and Democrat— and our country prospers and freedom is protected. Is not such a system desirable for Local 88?"[123]

Conversely, American courts have permitted unions to discipline members for the sort of opposition which would not be constitutionally protected within the state, though the lines of demarcation are not clear. Discipline for deliberately false and defamatory statements about union officers, for example, has generally been upheld.[124] Similarly, courts have sustained discipline against a member who unnecessarily carries on his campaign against union officers and policies in public,[125] or who incites members to support a rival organization.[126] These are the sorts of limitations on speech probably implied by Section 101(a)(2) of the LMRDA, which declares the right of union members to free speech and assembly, but which provides that:

> nothing herein shall be construed to impair the right of a labor organization to adopt and enforce reasonable rules as to the responsibility of every member toward the organization as an institution and to his refraining from conduct that would interfere with its performance of its legal or contractual obligation.

Limits on Union Sovereignty

If a union is like a government, it must operate within a pluralistic, federalist system: it is a government within a government. Its "sovereignty" extends only to matters which affect it as an organization; moreover, it cannot command the total allegiance of its members, to the unreasonable exclusion of their obligations and interests as citizens of the state. Thus, for example, if the trade policy behind union discipline conflicts with the law of the state, as where a union seeks to discipline a member for non-participation in a strike which is unlawful, American courts have held at common law that the union policy must give way.[127] Similarly, American courts have held that a union member may not be disciplined for bringing suit against his union,[128] at least where he has exhausted available internal remedies;[129] for consulting an attorney with respect to such a suit;[130] for testifying in a suit against the declared interests of the union;[131] for signing a petition to the state legislature in opposition to a law which his union supported;[132] for testifying before a legislative committee contrary to his union's desires;[133] or for failing to obey his union's instructions to vote, as a member of a municipal Board of Plumbing Examiners, for a particular person as plumbing inspector.[134] These rules are now substantially codified in Section 101(a)(4) of the LMRDA, which provides, in effect, that unions may not limit the right of members to institute action, testify, or petition legislature, except to require exhaustion of reasonable internal hearing procedures, for a period not to exceed four months.

On the other hand, it appears that courts make a distinction between a member's conduct as a citizen (with which unions may not interfere) and his conduct as a member (with which they may interfere, so long as they do not require an illegal act). For example, it has been held that a union may discipline a member who circulated letters advocating a Republican candidate for President and signed his name as a past-president of the union;[135] or who, writing as a union officer, urged congressmen to defeat union shop legislation which the union supported.[136] It is not clear to what extent, if any, these precedents are affected by Sec. 101(a)(4).

The line between union sovereignty and citizenship rights is nowhere more difficult to draw than in the area of union political expenditures. In Britain the problem is dealt with by a compromise. Overruling the *Osborne* case,[137] in which the House of Lords held any political expenditure to be *ultra vires* for a union, the Trade Union Act of 1913 permits a union to spend money for political purposes if authorized to do so by its own rules—which, on this point, must be adopted by secret ballot among the membership. Political funds must be kept separate from the union's general funds, however, and any member who does not wish to contribute to the political fund must be allowed to "contract out" of the obligation to do so, without loss of any union privilege or benefit. Members aggrieved by breach of such rules may obtain relief through the Registrar of Friendly Societies.

In this country the Taft-Hartley Act imposes an Osborne-type prohibition on union contributions in connection with federal elections;[138] but except for that statutory prohibition the case law has, until recently, supported the right of a union to make, and to enforce assessments toward, political expenditures despite minority opposition.[139] The rationale, according to the California Supreme Court in the *De Mille* case,[140] was that a member's conduct *qua* member was separable from his conduct as a citizen of the state. Recently, however, the United States Supreme Court has modified the *De Mille* rule, at least so far as railway unions operating under union shop agreements are concerned.[141] With respect to such unions the court has ruled that dissident members may not be compelled to contribute to political causes, or at least to support political candidates. The union is free to make political expenditures, however, the dissident member being limited to the right to object and recover that portion of his total dues attributable to the questioned activity. The result is strikingly close to the compromise of the 1913 Act.

The requirement of exhaustion of internal remedies constitutes another compromise between the union's sovereignty and its members' rights as citizens. While some courts have attempted to explain it on contract theory,[142] that explanation fails to take account of the fact that exhaustion is required even in the absence of express language on the subject in the union's rules,[143] and that exceptions to the requirement are applied regardless of the existence of such language.[144] The doctrine is more easily explained by the governmental analogy. As in the case of the rule requiring exhaustion of administrative remedies, its function is partly to protect courts against unnecessary litigation and partly to encourage the union to formulate its own policy and be responsible for the conduct of its own affairs.

At one time the exhaustion requirement was rather harsh, and took little note of exceptions.[145] Perhaps during that period it served much the same function as Section 4 of the British Trade Union Act of 1871. Later, like Section 4, it became superimposed with so many exceptions that, in some states, it became nearly meaningless.[146] Some courts, for example, held that exhaustion was excused, not only where the union's appeal procedure was likely to be futile or unduly burdensome, but in any case where the union tribunal lacked "jurisdiction"—which meant, in effect, whenever there was some defect which would justify intervention in the first place.[147] More recently, however, apparently in response to the greater degree of intervention imposed by common law and statute, there are signs of resuscitation of the exhaustion requirement and a recognition of its proper function.[148]

It is possibly due to Section 4 of the 1871 Act that Britain never developed the doctrine of exhaustion of remedies.[149] Recently the Privy Council did apply the doctrine to the extent of enforcing an express bylaws provision requiring appeal before suit, but in doing so it relied primarily upon the "contractual" nature of the requirement.[150] This, as we have seen, is consistent with the classical British view of the union as an essentially private, voluntary organization.

Protection against Discrimination: Equal Protection of the Laws

We have been concerned thus far with what might be called the "procedural" aspects of the union-worker relationship—the union's internal political structure and its operation. There are, however, legal limitations on the "substantive" aspects of the relationship—the collective bargaining process—which are also derived from the governmental analogy. In *Steele vs. Louisville & Nashville R.R.*[151] the Supreme Court, holding that a union certified under the Railway Labor Act could not properly make an agreement with an employer which would arbitrarily deprive non-member Negroes of seniority, said:

> We think that the Railway Labor Act imposes upon the statutory representative of a craft at least as exacting a duty to protect equally the interests of the members of the craft as the Constitution imposes upon a legislature to give equal protection to the interests of those for whom it legislates.

The Steele doctrine of equal representation is applicable to unions acting under Taft-Hartley as well as under the Railway Labor Act;[152] it extends not only to the negotiation of a collective agreement but to its administration as well;[153] it applies to discrimination among classes of members as well as against non-members;[154] and it is not limited to discrimination on account of race but extends to any discrimination deemed to be arbitrary.[155]

In most non-racial stituations, however, courts have been extremely reluctant to intervene unless the basis for discrimination is clearly unreasonable.[156]

The Steele doctrine points to an uncharted area. Apart from discrimination, would a collective bargaining provision that is clearly unreasonable violate an obligation of the union akin to substantive due process? Does a union (like a public utility) have an affirmative legal obligation to render reasonable service?[157] It is too early to attempt answers, but the fact that such questions can reasonably be asked is evidence of the distance the union and the law have travelled together since unions were outlaw organizations.

NOTES

1. 73 Stat. 519, Pub. Law 86-257, hereinafter referred to as LMRDA.

2. For discussion of common law, see Summers, "Legal Limitations on Union Discipline," 64 Harv. L. Rev. 1049 (1951); "Union Powers and Workers Rights," 49 *Mich. L. Rev.* 805 (1951); "Judicial Settlement of Internal Union Disputes," 7 *Buff. L. Rev.* 405 (1958). For discussion of LMRDA, see Aaron, the Labor Management Reporting and Disclosure Act of 1959, 73 *Harv. L. Rev.* 85 (1960).

3. For more detailed discussion of this general thesis see the author's *Union Government and the Law: British and American Experiences Compared* (1961).

4. See Hedges & Winterbottom, *Legal History of Trade Unionism*, Ch. IV.

5. *Ibid.*

6. *Hornby* vs. *Close* (1867) L.R. 2 Q.B. 153; *Farrar* vs. *Close* (1869) L.R. 4 Q.B. 602.

7. *Hilton* vs. *Eckersley* (1855) 6 E & B 45; cf. *Hornby* vs. *Close, Farrar* vs. *Close, supra.*

8. See Erle, Memorandum on the Law Relating to Trade Unions (1869), and cases cited *supra*, notes 6 and 7.

9. Webb, *History of Trade Unionism* (1920) pp. 255-257.

10. E. g., inability to take advantage of the Friendly Societies Act, 1855. See Hedges & Winterbottom, *op. cit.*, p. 55.

11. Webb, *op. cit.*, pp. 270-271.

12. *Ibid.*, pp. 274-279.

13. Article in *Beehive*, reprinted in T.U.C. Parliamentary Committee Publication, 1871-75.

14. E.g., *Commonwealth* vs. *Hunt*, 4 Metc. III (1842); see Teller, *Labor Disputes and Collective Bargaining* (1940) Vol. I., Sec. 60.

15. *Froelich* vs. *Musicians Mutual Beneficial Association*, 93 Mo. App. 383 (1902).

16. *O'Brien* vs. *Musical Mutual Protective Union*, 64 N.J. Eq. 525, 54 Atl. 150 (1903).

17. *Brennan* vs. *United Hatters*, 73 N.J.L. 729, 65 Atl. 165 (1906).

18. *Harris* vs. *Geier*, 112 N.J. Eq. 99, 164 Atl. 50 (1932).

19. For more complete discussion see Kahn-Freund, "The Illegality of a Trade Union," 7 *Mod. L. Rev.* 192 (1944).

20. E.g., *Rigby* vs. *Connol* (1880) 14 Ch. D. 482.

21. *Duke* vs. *Littleboy* (1880) 49 L.J. Ch. 802.

22. E.g., *Yorkshire Miners* vs. *Howden* 1905 A.C. 256.

23. E.g., *Amalgamated Society of Carpenters and Joiners* vs. *Braithwaite* (1922) 2 A.C. 440.

24. *Ibid.*

25. E.g., *Swaine* vs. *Wilson* (1890) 24 Q.B.D. 252; *Gozney* vs. *Bristol Trades Union* (1909) 1 K.B. 901.

26. *Russell* vs. *Amalgamated Society of Carpenters and Joiners, supra.*

27. See Kahn-Freund, *op. cit.*, note 19, at p. 203.

28. Cf. *Sansom* vs. *London & Provincial Union* (1920) 36 T.L.R. 666.

29. See *infra, pp.* 199-200.

30. *Infra,* note 96.

31. See *Bonsor* vs. *Musicians Union* (1956) A.C. 104 (1955); *Gonzales* vs. *International Association of Machinists,* 356 U.S. 617 (1958).

32. E.g., *Amalgamated Society of Engineers* vs. *Braithwaite* (1922) A.C. 440; *Polin* vs. *Kaplan,* 257 N.Y. 277, 177 N.E. 833 (1931).

33. E. g., *Bonsor* vs. *Musicians Union supra; Cason* vs. *Glass Blowers Association,* 37 Cal. 2d 134, 231 P. 2d 61 (1951).

34. E. g., *Burn* vs. *National Amalgamated Labourers Union* (1920) 2 Ch. 364; *Dachoylous* vs. *Ernst,* 20 Misc. 377, 118 N.Y.S. 2d 455 (1952).

35. See *infra, pp.* 197-8.

36. E. g., *Greenwood* vs. *Building Trades Council,* 71 Cal. App. 159, 233 Pac. 223 (1925).

37. E.g., *Rigby* vs. *Connol, supra,* (expulsion case); *Blek* vs. *Kirkman,* 148 Misc. 522, 266 N.Y.S. 91 (1933) (suspension case).

38. *Kelly* vs. *National Society of Operative Printers Assistants* (1915) 31 T.L.R. 632, followed in *Bonsor* vs. *Musicians Union* (1954) Ch. 479, rev'd (1956) A.C. 104.

39. "Internal Affairs of Associations Not for Profit," 43 *Harv. L. Rev.* 993 (1930).

40. *Rigby* vs. *Connol, supra,* note 20.

41. E.g., *Yorkshire Miners* vs. *Howden* (1905) A.C. 256; *Roberts* vs. *Kennedy,* 12 Del. Ch. 133, 16 Atl. 255 (1922).

42. E.g., *Dusing* vs. *Nuzzo,* 29 N.Y.S. 2d 882 (1941); *Tate* vs. *Williamson* (1866) L.R. 2 Ch. App. 55.

43. E.g., *Duke* vs. *Franklin,* 177 Ore. 297, 162 P. 2d 141 (1945).

44. E.g., *De Monbrun* vs. *Sheet Metal Workers,* 140 Cal. App. 2d 456, 298 P. 2d 981 (1956).

45. E.g., a limited income tax privilege; some facility in dealing with property as an entity; summary remedies against misappropriation of union assets. See discussion in Kahn-Freund, "Trade Union Democracy and the Law," 22 *Ohio St. L.J.* 4 (1961).

46. See Kessler, "Contracts of Adhesion," 43 *Col. L. Rev.* 629 (1943).

47. See Friedmann, *Law and Social Change* (1956).

48. *Supra,* pp. 186-7.

49. E.g., Lord Denning in *Bonsor* vs. *Musicians Union* (1954) Ch. 479, 485.

50. *Ibid.,* note 31.

51. E.g., *Crossen* vs. *Duffy*, 90 Ohio App. 252, 103 N.E. 2d 769 (1951).
52. E.g., *Bricklayers Union* vs. *Bowen*, 183 N.Y.S. 885, aff'd without op., 198 App. Div. 967, 189 N.Y.S. 938 (1920).
53. *Infra*, pp. 204-5.
54. E.g., *Dusing*, vs. *Nuzzo*, 177 Misc. 35, 29 NYS 2d 882 (1941).
55. 25 Cal. 2d 71, 155 P. 2d 329 (1945).
56. *Infra*, pp. 205-6.
57. *Infra*, p. 206.
58. *Infra*, p. 198.
59. An exception exists in the case of public corporations administering nationalized industries. E.g., Transport Act, 1947, Sec. 195.
60. The Fair Wages Resolution of the House of Commons, 1946 (427 Hansard 628) provides, however, that government contracts shall not be granted to employers who do not permit their employees to join a union.
61. See discussion in Kahn-Freund, "Legal Framework," in Flanders & Clegg, (ed.), *Industrial Relations in Great Britain* (1954) at pp. 56-58, and note, 22 *Mod. L. Rev.* 408 (1959). The collective agreement may acquire indirect legislative effect through application of minimum wage orders under the Wages Councils Acts of 1945; or under the Fair Wages Resolution of the House of Commons, *supra* (which requires employers holding government contracts to observe prevailing rates); or by order of the Industrial Court under the Terms and Conditions of Employment Act, 1959.
62. Cf. *Hulland* vs. *Saunders* (1945) K.B. 78.
63. See Bell, "Trade Unions," in Flanders & Clegg (ed.), *op. cit.*, Note 61.
64. See Roberts, *Trade Union Government and Administration in Great Britain*, (1957) pp. 42 ff. For qualifications to this proposition; see the review of the author's book, *op. cit. Supra.*, by Cyril Grunfeld in 30 *Geo. Wash. L. Rev.* 390 (1961).
65. See Allen, *Power in trade Unions* (1954).
66. See the study of the Typographical Union in Lipset, Trow, and Coleman, *Union Democracy* (1956).
67. Michels, *Political Parties* (1919).
68. See Summers, "Judicial Settlement of Internal Union Disputes," 7 *Buff. L. Rev.* 405 (1958).
69. *State* ex. rel. *Givens* vs. *Superior Court*, 65 Ind. App. 471, 117 N.E. 2d 553 (1954).
70. E.g., *Bianco* vs. *Eisen*, 75 N.Y.S. 2d 882 (1941).
71. E.g., *Siblia* vs. *Western Electric Employees Ass'n*, 142 N.J. Eq. 77, 59 A. 2d 251 (1948).
72. *Ibid.*
73. See Webb, *Industrial Democracy* (2nd Ed. 1920).
74. E.g., *Brodie* vs. *Bevan* (1921) 38 T.L.R. 172; *Waldman* vs. *Ladisky*, 101 N.Y.S. 2d 87 (1950).
75. Trade Union Act, 1913, Sec. 4.
76. Trade Union (Amalgamation) Act, 1917 (7 & 8 Geo.5, c.24).
77. See the author's work, *op. cit.* in note 3.
78. Cf. *Innes* vs. *Wylie* (1844) 1 Car. & K. 257.
79. *Cameron* vs. *International Alliance of Theatrical and Stage Employees*, 118 N.J. Eq. 11, 176 Atl. 692 (1935).
80. *James* vs. *Marinship Corp.*, *supra*, note 55.
81. *Bautista* vs. *Jones*, 25 Cal. 2d 746, 155 P. 2d 343 (1944).

82. LMRDA, Sec. 3(o).
83. E.g., *Mayer,* vs. *Journeymen Stonecutters Ass'n.,* 47 N.J. Eq. 519, 20 A. 2d 492 (1890).
84. See Aaron & Komaroff, "Statutory Regulation of Internal Union Affairs," 44 *Ill. L. Rev.* 425, 631 (1949).
85. *Thorman* vs. *International Alliance of Theatrical & Stage Employees,* 49 Cal. 2d 629, 320 P. 2d 494 (1957).
86. *Betts* vs. *Easley,* 161 Kan. 459, 169 P. 2d 831 (1946).
87. 262 F. 2d 359 (6th Cir. 1958). To the same effect, see *Ross* vs. *Ebert,* 275 Wis. 523, 82 N.W. 2d 315 (1957).
88. 355 U.S. 893 (1959).
89. E.g., *Bonsor* vs. *Musicians Union, supra,* note 31; *Cason* vs. *Glass Blowers Association, supra,* note 33.
90. E.g., *Amalgamated Society of Engineers* vs. *Braithwaite, supra,* note 32; *Polin* vs. *Kaplan,* 257 N.Y., 277, 177 N.E. 833 (1931).
91. E.g., *Burn* vs. *National Amalgamated Labourers Unions, supra,* note 34; *Dachoylous* vs. *Ernst, supra,* note 34.
92. E.g., *Andrews* vs. *Mitchell* (1905) A.C. 78 (friendly society case).
93. E.g., *Davis* vs. *International Alliance of Theatrical & Stage Employees,* 60 Cal. App. 2d 713, 141 P. 2d 486 (1943).
94. E.g., *Bush* vs. *International Alliance of Theatrical & Stage Employees,* 55 Cal. App. 2d 357, 130 P. 2d 788 (1942); cf. *Hopson* vs. *National Union of Marine Cooks & Stewards,* 116 Cal. App. 2d 320, 253 P. 2d 733 (1953).
95. *Innes* vs. *Wylie,* (1844) 1 Car. & K. 257.
96. *Maclean* vs. *Workers Union* (1929) 1 Ch 602.
97. E.g., Denning, L. J., in *Bonsor* vs. *Musicians Union, supra,* note 31.
98. E.g., *Bricklayers Union* vs. *Bowen, supra,* note 52.
99. *Local No. 2* vs. *Reinlib,* 133 N.J. Eq. 572, 33 A. 2d 710 (1943).
100. *Savard* vs. *Industrial Trades Union,* 72 A. 2d 660 (R.I. Sup. Ct. 1950).
101. E.g., *Cason* vs. *Glass Bottle Blowers Assoc., supra,* note 33.
102. *Ibid.*
103. E.g., *Lo Bianco* vs. *Cushing,* 117 N.J. Eq. 593, 117 Atl. 102, aff'd per curiam 119 N.J. Eq. 377, 182 Atl. 874 (1935).
104. E.g., *Bush* vs. *International Alliance of Theatrical & Stage Employees, supra,* note 94.
105. E.g., *Harmon* vs. *Mathews,* 27 N.Y.S. 2d 656 (Sup. Ct. 1941) (conviction overturned where based only on affidavit of accuser).
106. E.g., *Fisher* vs. *Keane* (1879) 11 Ch. D. 353.
107. Cf. *General Medical Council* vs. *Spackman* (1943) 2 All E.R. at p. 340.
108. *Maclean* vs. *Workers Union, supra,* note 96.
109. *Byrne* vs. *Kinematograph Renters Society Ltd.* (1958) 2 All E.R. 579.
110. See Summers, "Disciplinary Procedures of Unions," 4 *Ind. & Lab Rel. Rev.* 483 (1950).
111. *Allison* vs. *General Council of Medical Education* (1894) 1 Q.B. 751.
112. *Tantussi* vs. *Molli* (1885) 2 T.L.R. 731.
113. *Maclean* vs. *Workers Union, supra,* note 96.
114. *White* vs. *Kuzych* (1951) 2 All E.R. 435.
115. E.g., *Hall* vs. *Morrin,* 293 S.W. 2d 435 (Mo. App. 1927).
116. *Cohen* vs. *Rosenberg,* 262 App. Div. 274, 27 N.Y.S. 2d 834 (1942).

117. *Madden* vs. *Atkins,* 162 N.Y.S. 2d 576, 4 App. Div. 2d 1 (1957), aff'd with mod., on other grounds, 4 N.Y. 2d 283, 151 N.E. 2d 73 (1958).

118. Persons who object to payment of political contributions are protected by statute against discipline on that ground, Trade Union Act, 1913, Sec. 3(3).

119. *Wolstenholme* vs. *Amalgamated Musicians Union* (1920) 2 Ch. 388.

120. *Maclean* vs. *Workers Union, supra,* note 96.

121. See Summers, "The Political Liberties of Labor Union Members," 33 *Tex. L. Rev.* 603 (1955).

122. *Crossen* vs. *Duffy,* 90 Ohio App. 252, 103 N.E. 2d 769 (1951).

123. *Madden* vs. *Atkins,* 4 N.Y. 2d 283, 151 N.E. 2d 73 (1958).

124. E.g., *Taxicab Drivers* vs. *Pittman,* 322 P. 2d 252 (Okla. Sup. Ct. 1957).

125. E.g., *Elfer* vs. *Marine Engineers Beneficial Association,* 179 La. 383, 154 So. 32 (1934).

126. E.g., *Local No. 2* vs. *Reinlib, supra,* note 99; but cf. *Leo* vs. *Local Union No. 612,* 26 Wash. 2d 498, 174 P. 2d 523 (1946). See discussion in Wollett & Lampman, "The Law of Union Factionalism," 4 *Stan. L. Rev.* 177 (1951).

127. E.g., *Nissen* vs. *International Brotherhood of Teamsters,* 229 Iowa 1028, 295 N.W. 858 (1941).

128. E.g., *Polin* vs. *Kaplan, supra,* note 90.

129. Cf. *Burke* vs. *Monumental Div. No. 52,* 273 Fed. 707 (D.C. Md. 1919), aff'd 298 Fed. 1019 (4th Civ. 1924).

130. *Lo Bianco* vs. *Cushing,* 115 N.J. Eq. 558, 171 Atl. 778 (1938).

131. *Angrisani* vs. *Stearn,* 167 Misc. 731, 3 N.Y.S. 2d 701, aff'd 255 App. Div. 975, 8 N.Y.S. 2d 997 (1938).

132. *Spayd* vs. *Ringing Rock Lodge,* 270 Pa. 67, 113 Atl. 70 (1921).

133. *Abdon* vs. *Wallace,* 65 Ind. App. 604, 165 N.E. 68 (1929).

134. *Schneider* vs. *Local Union No. 60,* 116 La. 270, 40 So. 700 (1905).

135. *Pfoh* vs. *Whitney,* 43 Ohio A. 417, 62 N.E. 2d 744 (1945).

136. *Harrison* vs. *Railway & Steamship Clerks,* 271 S.W. 2d 852 (Ky. Sup. Ct. 1954. Cf. *Mitchell* vs. *International Association of Machinists,* 196 Adv. Cal. App. 903, 16 Cal. Rep. 813 (1961) (holding union may not discipline members for publicly advocating, as individuals, a right-to-work law).

137. *Osborne* vs. *Amalgamated Society of Railway Servants* (1910) A.C. 87.

138. 29 U.S.C.A. Sec. 304. Cf. *United States* vs. *Congress of Industrial Organizations,* 335 U.S. 106 (1948).

139. *De Mille* vs. *American Federation of Radio Artists,* 31 Cal. 2d 139, 187 P. 2d 769 (1947). See also *Knox* vs. *Local 900 U.A.W.,* 36 C.C.H. Labor Cases Par. 65, 752 (Mich. Cir. Ct. 1959).

140. *Ibid.*

141. *International Association of Machinists* vs. *Street,* 367 U.S. 740. (1961).

142. E.g., *Malloy* vs. *Carroll,* 272 Mass 524, 172 N.E. 790 (1930).

143. E.g., *Porth* vs. *Local Union No. 201,* 171 Kan. 177, 231 P. 2d 252 (1951).

144. E.g., *Cameron* vs. *Durkin,* 321 Mass. 590, 74 N.E. 2d 671 (1947).

145. E.g., *Greenwood* vs. *Building Trades Council,* 71 Cal. App. 159, 233 Pac. 223 (1925).

146. See Comment, "Exhaustion of Remedies in Private, Voluntary Associations," 65 *Yale L.J.* 369 (1956).

147. E.g., *Leo* vs. *Local Union No. 612, supra,* note 126.
148. E.g., *Holderby* vs. *International Union of Operating Engineers,* 45 Cal. 2d 843, 291 P. 2d 763 (1955); *Detroy* vs. *American Guild of Variety Artists,* 286 F. 2d 75 (2nd Cir. 1961).
149. Cf. *McKernan* vs. *United Operative Masons Association* (1873) 1 S.C. (4th) 453 (exhaustion argument made but ignored, court dismissing suit on basis of Section 4).
150. *White* vs. *Kuzych, supra,* note 114.
151. 323 U.S. 192 (1944).
152. E.g., *Syres* vs. *Local 23, Oil Workers International Union,* 350 U.S. 892 (1956), reversing per curiam 223 F. 2d 739 (5th Cir. 1955).
153. E.g., *Conley* vs. *Gibson,* 355 U.S. 41 (1957).
154. E.g., *Hargrove* vs. *Brotherhood of Locomotive Engineers,* 116 F. Supp. 3 (D.C.D.C. 1953).
155. Cf. *Ford Motor Co.* vs. *Huffman,* 345 U.S. 330 (1953).
156. E.g., *Goodin* vs. *Clinchfield R.R.,* 229 F. 2d 588 (6th Cir. 1956).
157. Cf., *Glover* vs. *Brotherhood of Railway and Steamship Clerks,* 108 S.E. 2d 79 (N.C. Sup. Ct. 1959).

8

UNITED STATES AND CANADIAN
EXPERIENCE: A COMPARISON

HARRY D. WOODS

Professor of Industrial Relations, McGill University

INTRODUCTION

United States labor relations policy has attracted the attention of
American and foreign scholars for many years. Canada is less for-
tunate in this regard. A powerful influence delaying study of labor
relations in Canada has been the similarities, both real and super-
ficial, between the Canadian and United States industrial relations
systems. Seventy-two percent of organized labor in Canada belongs
to international unions, most of which are affiliated with the AFL-
CIO. These internationals operate under United States constitutions, their head offices are all in the United States; while there is
sometimes a Canadian director and in some cases a vice-president
from Canada, Canadian delegates attend union conventions in the
United States. Union constitutions, by-laws, and general policies
covering both countries originated in the United States. The structure of government of the unions, the systems of dues payment,
the general goals in collective bargaining, the form of union agreements, and the general conception of the role of unionism in Canada bears the label "made in U.S.A.," at least so far as the internationals are concerned.[1] And even the national unions in Canada
which are not affiliated with the United States internationals are
profoundly influenced by them and tend to reflect a continental
pattern.

On the employer side also United States influence is strong. The subsidiary character of many Canadian industries is reflected in the national identification of attaching the word Canada or Canadian. Thus, we have Canadian General Electric, Ford of Canada, Canadian International Paper Company and so on. Perhaps even more than with the unions, management direction of these Canadian subsidiaries comes from the United States, either as authority or in the form of technical assistance. There is also a vast influence from trade papers, professional journals, managerial training in the United States and Canadian branches of United States-oriented study and technical bodies such as the American Management Association, the National Office Management Association and many others.

Canada has accepted either through indigenous experience or by imitation the principles of freedom of association, of compulsory collective bargaining, and freedom to negotiate labor agreements without the imposition of contractual obligations by some agency of government.[2] The labor relations board technique operates in both countries. Terminal collective agreements are negotiated in Canada[3] as in the United States. Canadian collective agreements, in many cases, could only be identified as Canadian by scrutinizing the place name of the company or the congress affiliation of the union; the substantive clauses cover similar issues and use much the same language as do U.S. agreements.[4] The work stoppage, either strike or lockout, is generally available as the ultimate weapon in the hands of the parties.

These similarities in the two countries have discouraged independent research in Canadian problems partly because it has been assumed in Canada that answers are available in the literature of the United States.[5] Researchers in Canada have tended to seek out the unique[6] in the Canadian experience and very rarely to do more than add to the general accumulation of American publication. There does not exist a single comprehensive study of Canadian labor economics and labor relations such as is so commonly available in the United States.[7] Yet the magnitude of the differences between the two countries is sufficient to justify the hope that comparisons will produce fruitful insights which would be less clear if one country only is examined.

CONTROL OF PUBLIC POLICY

The first major difference between Canada and the United States is to be found in the constitutional allocation of powers between the respective federal and secondary levels of government.[8] It is correct to say that the United States constitution, as interpreted by the courts, has assigned the major role in labor relations to the Federal Government, whereas in Canada the reverse is true; the Dominion Government has a decidedly limited, though particularly troublesome,[9] jurisdiction while the provincial governments retain authority in the major industrial sector where the vast majority of labor relations issues are to be found. Under the circumstances it is to be expected that United States public policy would display a unity not present in the divided jurisdiction prevailing in Canada. Nevertheless, while differing policies are found among the provinces, yet until recently, with a few notable exceptions, there existed considerable uniformity of labor relations public policy and administrative agencies across the country.

The major Canadian legislative steps, which established the present structure, were taken either before certain important court interpretations of constitutional jurisdiction were rendered and while the assumption of primary Dominion authority still existed, or during emergency periods such as the Second World War when normal constitutional provisions were temporarily replaced by special Dominion emergency powers. In both of these circumstances the country did in fact operate under the assumption or the reality of a concentration of power in the hands of the Dominion Government, and a national system seemed to be emerging. But ultimately constitutional interpretation and the end of the Second World War terminated the emergency powers of the Dominion Government and established the basis of some balkanization of Canadian labor relations policy.

The basic document of the Canadian constitution is the British North America Act passed by the British Parliament in 1867 as the principle legislative instrument bringing into existence the federation of four original Canadian provinces to form the Dominion of Canada. It is this Act which establishes the respective jurisdictions of the Dominion and Provincial Governments. The powers of the Canadian (Dominion) parliament are described in Section 91, and of the provincial legislatures in Section 92. In the enumeration of these powers there is no mention of labor relations as such. Jurisdiction in labor matters has been determined by court interpretation of these sections, particularly head 13 of Section 92 which assigns to the provincial legislatures the exclusive power to make laws in relation to matters involving property and civil rights in the province concerned. As early as 1925 the Judicial Committee[10] of the Privy Council in Britain declared a Dominion Act[11] dealing with industrial disputes and their settlement to be *ultra vires* the Canadian Parliament, on the grounds that it dealt with property and civil rights in the provinces. The Act had been passed in 1907 and provided for compulsory three-member conciliation boards and a suspension of strikes or lockouts while the board was investigating the dispute, attempting mediation, and preparing a report containing proposals designed to resolve the dispute. It was compulsory with regard to mines, transportation and communication agencies, and public service utilities. There was also a section[12] which provided that a conciliation board would be set up in any business or trade if the parties to a dispute mutually requested such a board. "Thus all industries in Canada in which there was an element of wide public interest were compulsorily covered, and all the rest voluntarily covered."[13] In the years from 1907 when it was passed until 1924 when the Act was challenged successfully, 619 applications for boards were received, of which approximately one-fifth involved disputes not falling clearly within the direct scope of the Act.[14] During this period provincial legislation dealing with labor relations was negligible. Only the Quebec Trade Disputes Act of 1901 dealt at all effectively with the subject.[15] The Dominion Act was, however, providing machinery for the settlement of labor disputes on a national basis until the Privy Council ruling of 1925.

In this celebrated case[16] a trend toward a national labor relations policy was arrested. But it had been a near thing. Canadian courts upheld the validity of the Act, only two of the twelve Canadian justices, who, in one court or another over the years considered the legislation, holding with the later final decision of the Privy Council.[17] As Scott points out,[18] the language used in the Canadian judgments is very similar to that used by Chief Justice Hughes in the crucial Jones and Laughlin case which established the legality of the Wagner Act in 1937. Ironically the Privy Council rejected the notion that the Canadian Act was valid as coming within the Dominion authority to regulate trade and commerce,[19] the very basis of the United States Supreme Court's ruling which guaranteed the ascendancy of the Federal Government in labor relations.

Following this reversal the Dominion Parliament amended the Industrial Disputes Investigation Act so as to limit its compulsory application to industrial disputes in industries clearly within the legislative authority of the Dominion as interpreted in the Snider case.[20] Parliament also tried to salvage something of what had been lost by including a permissive clause[21] by which disputes coming within the exclusive legislative jurisdiction of a province could be processed by the machinery of the revised Industrial Disputes Investigation Act if the province concerned made it subject to the provisions of the Dominion Act. Within a few years all of the then existing nine provinces except Prince Edward Island enacted legislation bringing the Act into force in their respective jurisdictions. It would appear that there existed in the country at that time a strong sentiment in support of a national system.

Thus, the permissive clause of the Act and the voluntary action of the provinces appeared to have restored the national system. However, in 1950 the Supreme Court of Canada ruled that neither the Parliament of Canada nor the provincial legislatures can delegate one to the other any of the legislative authority respectively conferred upon them by the British North America Act.

This ruling effectively blocked the attempt to protect a national system of industrial relations through delegation of power by the provinces to the Dominion.[22] But it came after the unifying influence of the period of the Second World War when, for all practical purposes, the Dominion Government assumed enlarged control of the labor relations function, and developed a national system. This was not done in defiance of the constitutional interpretation; the ruling was based on the emergency powers of wartime and the War Measures Act which had been passed in 1914 and which automatically became operative when again Canada went to war in 1939. The Government merely used these powers to extend the scope of the Industrial Disputes Investigation Act. In other words, the I.D.I. Act, while inflexible in peacetime and limited in coverage to the areas permitted by the 1925 interpretation, became flexible and was expanded under constitutional authority operative only in wartime.[23]

The national system was never completely unified under the Dominion Government. The wartime labor relations regulations enacted by the Government were applied to three groups of industries: (1) those that normally in peacetime fell within Dominion jurisdiction; (2) those that were declared by the Government to be "essential to the efficient prosecution of the War";[24] and (3) those that by virtue of certain provincial enactments were brought within the scope of the regulations.[25] Left out were industries in the remaining provinces which would not be included in the "essential" group. Insofar as a national policy developed, it did so because of the emergency powers which the Dominion could exert during the war, and because most of the provinces were prepared to cooperate, even beyond the level required by the Dominion. Indeed, at the end of the Second World War when the provinces resumed their normal jurisdiction over labor relations, there was for a short period a strong trend toward adopting in peacetime the policies which had been uniformly applied to the whole country in wartime. Several provinces passed their own labor relations acts prior to the termination of hostilities; and in the years immediately following, while there were differences among the provinces at the start, there was an attempt to maintain the principles and practices of the war experience under the divided jurisdiction. In 1948 the Dominion passed its own Industrial Relations and Disputes Investigation Act which, unlike its predecessor, the I.D.I. Act, contained no permissive clause by which a province could extend its coverage to industries within the province and not normally under Dominion jurisdiction. Since that time, with control of the bulk of labor relations in the hands of the provinces, the trend has been toward local experiment, and provincial policies have tended to evolve in different and even conflicting directions.

This decentralized character of Canadian labor relations authority needs to be kept in mind when comparing policy in the United States and Canada. There is not one system in Canada, there are as many as there are political jurisdictions, and they are constitutionally independent.

AREAS OF CONTROL OF LABOR RELATIONS

Labor relations policy based primarily on the principle of free collective bargaining presupposes a structure of industrial relations which presents opportunities for public control at a number of crucial points. In Canadian and United States experience the evolution of public industrial relations policy is largely the history of the identification of the major points of contact or areas of dispute, and the gradual development of either agencies of assistance or instruments of compulsion designed to reduce or eliminate the effect of conflict as well as to guarantee the freedom to exercise certain recognized rights. Differences in policy over time, or as between jurisdictions within and between the two countries, reflect different definitions of rights and varying appreciations of the most effective ways of achieving socially determined goals. In both countries public policy has, with exceptions, left to the direct parties of interest the determination of the terms and conditions of employment and has preserved the work stoppage as the ultimate right of the parties to influence the negotiations. The major conflict areas include disputes over the freedom of employees to associate, the negotiation of agreements governing employment relations, and the operation of managerial discretion in carrying out administration as it affects employees covered by these agreements.

The conflicting parties are not limited to the simple dichotomy of union and management. Included in the conflict pairs must also be the employee and the union, the employee and the employer, the union and other unions, a union or group of unions, employer or group of employers, and even employer and employer. Organized power in industrial relations, however, is exercised by employers, unions, and the state. The evolution of public policy represents the changing pattern of power relations among these three "actors."[26] And the conflict over policy is to a considerable extent a matter of protecting an established power position by one of these actors against a threat from one or both of the others to alter the relative positions.

Both Canada and the United States have adopted compulsory collective bargaining as public policy although the United States has done so with a greater element of assurance than has Canada. There is nothing comparable in Canadian law to the United States statement of principle "sound and stable industrial peace and the advancement of the general welfare, health and safety of the Nation and the best interests of employers and employees can most satisfactorily be secured by the settlement of issues between employers and employees through the processes of conference and collective bargaining between employers and the representatives of their employees. . . ."[27] Canadian legislators are inclined to avoid statements of policy in preambles or other sections of legislative enactments. Even the modest suggestion of the Select Committee of the Ontario Legislature[28] to include as a preamble to the Ontario Act: "Whereas it is in the public interest that industrial peace be achieved and maintained in the Province of Ontario" was rejected when the Ontario law was amended in 1960. Generally the full title in Canadian law conveys some suggestion about workers' welfare,[29] or equitable relations,[30] or workers' rights to organize,[31] or no indication of purpose at all,[32] and then plunges directly into definitions followed by the full body of the legislation. There is an implication that collective bargaining is public policy, but it is not stated explicitly anywhere in Canadian law, as it is in the United States. And it will be seen that this is more than a difference in draftsmanship. In general terms it can be said the Canadian policy is not as favorable to the promotion of collective bargaining relationships, and interferes very much more in the actual bargaining process, but has fallen far short of the United States effort to control and influence the internal organization of the parties, particularly the unions.

JURISDICTIONAL SCOPE OF THE LEGAL FRAMEWORK

Labor relations legislation in both countries limits the application of the general positive policy[33] in a number of ways. Some groups are excluded from the coverage of the acts and left to operate without collective bargaining, or to win it without the protection of unfair labor practice provisions, compulsory recognition, and compulsory bargaining. In other words, these groups retain whatever rights they had before the legislation but receive no protection from it. While this does not necessarily impose a direct control on who shall be admitted to membership in unions, it discourages the inclusion in the unions of persons occupying jobs excluded from the coverage of the law. Canadian and United States labor relations acts exclude several groups in common. In the

United States the coverage of the Labor Management Relations Act is largely determined by the definitions of employer and employee. In Canada most jurisdictions establish the coverage of the Acts through the definition of employee; there is less use of the definition of employer, and one province[34] defines the coverage of the Act with only a negative reference to employee. The Taft-Hartley Act excludes from the category of employer the United States, any state or political subdivision thereof, and wholly owned government corporations. This is not fully repeated in Canada. One province, for example, New Brunswick,[35] excludes from the definition of employer: "Her Majesty or any person, board, or commission acting for or on behalf or as an agent of Her Majesty."[36] Saskatchewan, on the other hand, declares that the term employer "includes Her Majesty in the right of Saskatchewan." This means that in the latter province civil servants and employees of government agencies may join unions, become certified as bargaining agents, and negotiate collective agreements with the government as employer. In fact such practices have become the normal machinery of industrial relations in the Saskatchewan government services. The strike, which is also retained by public service employees in Saskatchewan, has been used very sparingly. In the Dominion service and some other provinces, civil servants have been considered to be not covered by the labor relations acts even though not excluded by statute.[37] Whatever elements of collective bargaining are available to these public servants are so by leave of the government which employs them.

The rights of Canadian municipal employees are even more confused than are those of employees of higher levels of government. Municipalities are creations of the province in which they are located. Consequently they operate under whatever legislation the respective provinces enact.[38] Their rights and privileges may be covered in the applicable labor relations act, or they may be provided for in the specific laws dealing with civic government. Frankel and Pratt[39] identify three Canadian approaches as revealed in legislative policy of the provinces regarding municipal labor relations:

1. Provinces which make no fundamental distinction between general municipal employees (i.e., excluding police and firefighters) and the employees of any private employer.

2. Provinces which allow the municipal authority to contract in or out of the general labor relations law.
3. Provinces which have special enactments covering all categories of municipal employees.

British Columbia, Alberta, Saskatchewan, Manitoba and Nova Scotia are mentioned as coming within the first class, Ontario and New Brunswick fall in the second, and Quebec in the third.

Canadian legislation generally excludes, as does United States legislation, domestic servants and farm labor. In addition, certain classes of professional employees such as lawyers, architects, engineers, medical doctors, dentists and others are excluded in Canada either by the definition of employee or by a specific clause limiting the coverage of the Act. United States federal law does not go this far. The definition of "professional employee"[40] is broad enough to include the professions rendered completely outside the coverage of Canadian laws, and these professional employees are to be included in a unit of non-professionals only if they vote as a group to be so included.[41] Thus engineers, for example, in the United States can bargain under the Act, unless excluded as managers, whereas in Canada they have no benefit from the labor relations laws if employed in their profession.

The laws of both countries exclude supervisors, and United States law provides a long list of functions which determine who is a supervisor.[42] Canadian laws are usually couched in more general terms and leave to the respective labor relations boards the task of refined definition. The Dominion Act[43] says:

(i) "employee" means a person employed to do skilled or unskilled manual, clerical or technical work, but does not include

(1) a manager or superintendent, or any other person who, in the opinion of the Board, exercises management functions or is employed in a confidential capacity relating to labour relations. . . .

In Canadian experience the determination by the boards of who is a manager has not been too difficult, but the decision as to who is employed in a confidential capacity in matters relating to labor relations has been very difficult, especially in office worker units.[44]

DIRECT CONTROL OF INTERNAL UNION AFFAIRS

The United States labor relations law has gone much farther than Canadian in attempting to impose direct control of internal union affairs. The passage of the Labor-Management Reporting and Disclosures Act of 1959 opened a wide gulf between Canadian and United States public policy. There are certain circumstances which make the problems with which the United States was contending less important for Canada. Whether rightly or wrongly Canadians generally appear to believe that the worst abuses of union power revealed by the United States Senate Select Committee on Improper Activities in the Labor or Management Field have not occurred in Canada, or if they have occurred, it has been to a limited extent. Secondly, the fact that in Canada an employer is not compelled to recognize the trade union claiming to represent the majority until it is certified, and that in most jurisdictions the union can only apply for certification if it can establish that it has a majority of the employees in the unit as members of the union, and that if a vote is taken the union must have the support of at least 50 per cent of the eligible voters rather than of the votes cast, makes certification much more difficult than in the United States where there is an obligation on the employer to recognize the union with majority support, where a union membership percentage is not required, and where the union is not required to gain a majority of the bargaining unit. Add to this the fact that in Canada the unions are prohibited by law from engaging in organizational or jurisdictional strikes, and it becomes fairly clear that a union wishing to gain recognition must first build up a membership of at least fifty per cent of the employees in the bargaining unit. A union has to have a much more solid foundation of worker support in Canada than in the United States.

Another factor is that so many Canadian unions are branches of "internationals" which are really American. Consequently, while formally United States law does not apply in Canada, in a *de facto* indirect sense it does in some situations. Insofar as provisions of the United States legislation on, for example corrupt practices, find their way into international union constitutions, they will apply in Canada as well. International union policies tend to reflect the requirements of United States federal law, and thereby to infiltrate the provisions of such law into Canadian practice.

Yet there are some provisions of the reporting and disclosures type in Canada. There is in Ontario a provision[45] requiring a union on request of a member to furnish without charge a copy of the audited financial statement at the end of the fiscal year with power given to the Labour Relations Board to order compliance. The recent Ontario revision also authorizes the government to make regulations for the filing with the Department of Insurance of audited financial statements of the affairs of pension or welfare funds. Alberta[46] requires the filing of the union's constitution, by-laws, the slate of officers, changes in officership, and any amendment to the constitution, rules or by-laws. In this regard it goes much further than any other Canadian jurisdiction. But even so it falls far short of the United States Labor-Management Reporting and Disclosure Act of 1959 with its requirements for information on identification, dues and fees, operating rules, financial reports, and dealings with employers, and with its requirement for individual filing by officers and employees of labor organizations. Important in this respect also is the different attitude displayed toward the use of the information to be filed. In the United States the information is clearly intended to be public[47] and is to be made available to all union members who also are to be free to inspect books and records and accounts for purposes of verification. The Alberta Act[48] states that the information collected shall not be open to public inspection.

Canadian legislators have not taken the positive steps to control trusteeships as has the Federal authority in Table III of the Labor-Management Reporting and Disclosure Act of 1959. But here particularly it is to be expected that the influence of United States legislation will be felt in Canada through amendments of international union constitutions. There is of course the protection of the common law for interested parties,[49] but no public policy as such in Canada. The same is true with regard to union elections and public control over union finances. The United States in the 1959 amendments embarked on a far-reaching experiment of public control of the internal affairs of unions. It remains to be seen if Canadian legislators will also embark on this same stream of union constitution writing by statute.

Public Policy and the Negotiating Process

Perhaps the greatest difference between Canadian and United States policies and practices occurs in the area of bargaining dispute settlement. Aside from the National Emergency Provisions[50]

United States policy is reflected in the statement: "That it is the policy of the United States that settlement of issues between employers and employees through collective bargaining may be advanced by making available full and adequate governmental facilities for conciliation, mediation, and voluntary arbitration to aid and encourage employers and the representatives of their employees to reach and maintain agreements . . . and to make all reasonable efforts to settle their differences by bargaining or by such methods as may be provided for in any applicable agreement for the settlement of disputes."[51] This preamble to the setting up of the Federal Mediation and Conciliation Service clearly imposes the responsibility for making decisions on the parties of direct interest, and recognizes the service as a catalyzing agency. The Service is required to "assist parties to labor disputes . . . to settle such disputes through conciliation and mediation."[52] The parties are required "to exert every reasonable effort to make and maintain agreements."[53]

Apart from this mild element of compulsion to accept mediation there is little direction of negotiation in United States policy. On renegotiation of an agreement the party desiring change must give 60 days' notice prior to the termination of the existing agreement, or where no termination date exists, to the date on which the notifying party wishes to terminate the agreement or modify it.[54] Within 30 days of such notification the Federal Service must be advised also. The Service is thus put in the position that it has a period of at least 30 days to effect an agreement before the restraint on the strike or lockout is removed by time.[55] But since this 60 days could all be included within the life of the agreement, and since the vast majority of agreements includes no-strike and no-lockout clauses, the statutory requirement would normally not delay the possibility of resort to work stoppage.

Canadian policy, balkanized into watertight jurisdictional compartments, ranges from little compulsion to much more extreme interference and restraint than in the Federal jurisdiction in the United States. The least restraint is imposed by Saskatchewan. In that province the Minister is authorized[56] to establish conciliation boards to "investigate, conciliate and report upon any dispute . . . affecting any terms and conditions of employment . . . or relating to the interpretation of any agreement. . . ." It is an unfair labor practice for an employer[57] to lockout, or for an employee or any person acting on behalf of a labor organization[58] to instigate a strike "while a matter is pending before a board of conciliation appointed under the provisions of this Act." This means that either party requesting a conciliation board, if the Minister of Labour acquiesces, could impose a period of restraint on the use of the work stoppage. It also means that the Minister could take the initiative and set up a conciliation board, thereby imposing the same restraint even when no one applied for such a board. It should be noted that Saskatchewan legislation makes no provision for either compulsory conciliation by a conciliation officer or for conciliation officers[59] themselves.

The more usual situation in Canada is represented by the provisions in Dominion policy. Briefly this forbids the taking of a strike vote, or the strike itself, until a union which is entitled to give notice to require an employer to commence collective bargaining has done so, until a conciliation officer has been requested, has failed to achieve an agreement, has reported his failure, has recommended the setting up of a conciliation board, the board has functioned and reported to the Minister, and seven days have elapsed from the date of the receipt of the report by the Minister. Only then may a strike vote be taken or a strike or lockout commenced. There is some ministerial discretion to short circuit some of the steps; but aside from this, the alternative open to the parties of interest is to settle. If there is an impasse they must work their way through the various stages of compulsory conciliation before they can use the work stoppage as a tactical weapon.[60]

The origin of this policy in Canadian legislation was the Industrial Disputes Investigation Act of 1907 which was the piece of legislation later declared *ultra vires* the Dominion Parliament.[61] The original act provided for a compulsory conciliation board with power to investigate, conciliate, and report. It was this law which first introduced into Canada the principle of compulsory delay on the strike and lockout. Through the process of history the principle of compulsory delay has become almost universal in Canada and is found in the Dominion and in practically all the provincial Acts. The widening of compulsory conciliation to include the officer stage came later during the Second World War,[62] and also has become a standard procedure in most Canadian jurisdictions.

It is now customary to refer to the two-stage system of compulsory conciliation in Canada. But this could be misleading because compulsory intervention in some jurisdictions has gone beyond two stages, and in others the earlier two-stage structure has shown signs of crumbling, or at least of being weakened, either by statutory changes or by the use of administrative discretion. The increase in intervention requires attention first.

The object of Canadian compulsory intervention has always been to reduce or eliminate strikes and lockouts.[63] Two streams of experience have been merged into current Canadian labor relations policy. On the one hand, all Canadian jurisdictions during the late years of the Second World War or shortly thereafter adopted the Wagner Act principle of compulsory recognition through certification if necessary, which carried with it compulsory negotiation. On the other hand was the earlier Canadian device of the compulsory conciliation board to which was later attached the compulsory conciliation officer. There is no doubt that to some extent compulsory conciliation boards, prior to the introduction of certification, were used partly to solve the problem of recognition as well as to deal with disputes about substantive issues.[64] But after the introduction of the labor relations board function the problem of recognition could be solved by certification. Indeed, in some jurisdictions the belief in this notion has carried legislation to its logical conclusion and jurisdictional or recognition strikes have been prohibited by law.[65] In any case it is clear that the continuing purpose of compulsory conciliation is to resolve negotiation issues. In one or two jurisdictions experiments have been undertaken involving the increase in the number of interventionist steps prior to releasing the parties from restraint on the strike or lockout. The principal steps of this character are the supervised vote on the recommendations of the conciliation board and the supervised strike vote. The provinces which have experimented with either or both of these instruments are British Columbia and Alberta.

British Columbia law contains the usual Canadian provision that parties negotiating a new agreement or rebargaining an existing agreement shall, before resorting to strike or lockout, be required to accept the services of a conciliation officer.[66] The conciliation officer is required within a statutory time limit of ten days, or longer by agreement of the parties or the authority of the Minister, to report to the Minister setting out: [67]

(a) the matters upon which the parties have agreed;
(b) the matters upon which the parties cannot agree, and his recommendations with respect thereto; and
(c) where the parties cannot agree, his recommendations as to the advisability of appointing or not appointing a conciliation board.

From this point the British Columbia system differs markedly from the general pattern for intervention in Canada. The conciliation officer may,[68] having decided against the wisdom of setting up a conciliation board, substitute his own recommendations in lieu of board recommendations. If the Minister approves this action the recommendations are sent to the parties, either of whom is now free to request a government supervised vote[69] on the question as to whether there shall be a strike or not.[70] The right to request a strike vote is somewhat academic since the Act prohibits strikes or lockouts until after secret ballots have been taken among the employees regarding a strike,[71] or among the employers, if more than one, on the question of lockout.[72] What these sections amount to is that they require secret votes which either party can require to be government supervised. It is to be noted that this is not strictly a vote on the conciliation officer report and recommendations; it is on whether or not the necessary majority in the unit is prepared to authorize the calling of a strike; and it is the unit appropriate for collective bargaining, not the union membership, which is the voting constituency.

Should the conciliation officer decide in favor of the setting up of a board of conciliation, the Minister may do so. In that case the report of the conciliation board becomes the instrument which activates the right of either party to request a supervised vote. But regardless of which report is involved, the strike vote means that the issue of strike or no strike is to be settled by the unit of workers, not the union or the union executive. The unions are subjected to a binding compulsory referendum among members of the unit.[73]

There is still further restraint on the use of the strike in the province. The strike authority acquired by the executive through the supervised strike vote is a wasting instrument; it must be used within three months following the date of the vote or not at all.[74]

The most recent amendment to the British Columbia Act,[75] introduced in 1961, provides that the Minister may conduct a vote of the employees affected who are on strike or are locked out if an offer of settlement is made by the employer. Similarly if the offer comes from the union the Minister may conduct a vote among the employers if there are more than one involved. This legislation is too recent to be appraised in practice, but the logic of the power relations in collective bargaining would suggest that it can surely be expected to delay genuine negotiation even more than has compulsory conciliation. It will be almost a certainty that the vote would be conducted if an offer is made, and men on strike would be strongly motivated toward acceptance. Employers would surely conceive it to be in their interest to take advantage of this probability by refraining from negotiation. Anything that reduces the possibility of the strike continuing strengthens the relative position of the employer.

The Alberta situation differs somewhat from British Columbia, although it does include impediments to the use of direct action by the parties beyond those found in the Dominion and eastern legislation. Whereas in British Columbia there is only one vote required following the report of the conciliation board before the parties are confronted with the right to strike, in Alberta two such votes are required. These are the vote on the "award" of the conciliation board, which is not specifically required in British Columbia, and the strike vote which is.

The Alberta Act provides that: "The employees directly affected by the award may accept or reject the award by a majority vote of the employees voting by secret ballot on such a date as may be appointed by the Minister."[76] "The Board of Industrial Relations[77] may supervise the taking of a vote. . . ."[78] "Where the award of the conciliation board has been accepted by the employees and the employer . . . the award is binding on the parties and they shall give effect to it and include the terms of the award in a collective agreement."[79] This is the Alberta system of voting on conciliation board awards. It is not a strike vote. The ballot contains the following question: "In the matter of collective bargaining with your employer are you in favour of accepting the award of the conciliation board?"[80] If the parties fail to agree by this process to accept the award of the conciliation board they have still the hurdle of the strike vote to jump before they can reach the strike. ". . . no employee shall go on strike until a vote has taken place under the supervision of the Board . . . and a majority of the employees entitled to vote have voted in favour of the strike." Any strike is illegal if the union has not complied with the provisions for compulsory conciliation, the award vote and the strike vote.[81] A trade union or an employees' organization that authorizes, calls or consents to an illegal strike is guilty of an offense and liable to a fine not exceeding one dollar for each person for each day that the person participated in the illegal strike.[82] There is also provision that the employer shall check off from the wages the money required to pay the fine, or divert the dues check-off to this purpose where a dues check-off to the union is part of the agreement.[83]

The Alberta system may be summarized as one in which the parties, the union and the employer, are free to negotiate a collective agreement, but without the catalytic influence of the threat of a work stoppage until they have availed themselves of an industrial relations officer, followed by a conciliation board, the workers have voted to reject the award, have voted for a strike, and the union has decided to exercise this delayed right. At several points settlement may take place. It may do so in direct bargaining, or before the conciliation officer or while the conciliation board is functioning. In all these circumstances agreement may be reached by action of the employer and the union officers, and a binding contract written. Failure of such an agreement to emerge leads to the first vote which transfers the decision making role from the union officers to the employees. Ultimately the question of the strike is also allocated by law to the employees rather than to the union executive.

Alberta legislation represents the most extreme policy of intervention in Canada designed to reduce the resort to the strike, or at least to place obstacles in the way of its use. British Columbia is close to Alberta. Saskatchewan is on the other end of the scale with almost no provision for compulsory delay on the strike and with reliance on voluntary conciliation in negotiation disputes. The Dominion and other provinces fall somewhere in between these extremes. Yet even in these jurisdictions there are some minor experiments and at least one major one which suggest an evolutionary direction contrary to that of Alberta where the trend has been running strongly toward increased intervention and restraint.

British Columbia[84] and Ontario[85] have introduced voluntary devices by which the parties to a negotiation may mutually short circuit the required machinery with their own instrument. In British Columbia the parties may at any time prior to the appointment of a conciliation board agree to refer the dispute to a mediation committee which may replace the conciliation officer and the conciliation board otherwise required. The mediation committee functions as a conciliation board but differs from it in two respects. Its composition and membership is entirely in the hands of the parties, and the government does not pay the Chairman's fees and expenses. The Ontario system substitutes a single mediator jointly chosen by the parties for both the conciliation officer and the conciliation board, and clothes the mediator with all the powers of the board. In British Columbia it would be the mediation committee report which would open the door to the strike vote. In Ontario the mediator's report opens the way to a strike. These have not been used to any great extent. The British Columbia provision has been available in the law since 1950 and the Ontario since 1960.

Perhaps the most drastic change in public intervention in negotiation disputes has taken place in Quebec, which, along with Ontario, contains a very significant portion of Canadian industrialism. Prior to the 1961 Amendment[86] to the law, Quebec also required a compulsory conciliation officer followed by a compulsory board.[87] The new provision sets strict time limits to the operation of the conciliation board, and makes a most important modification by taking from the board the power to recommend or "award." The board is required to report within forty-five days, declaring merely if agreement has been reached or if there is still disagreement. The board may make an award only if the parties agree in advance to abide by its decision. This change has been introduced so recently that there is no accumulated experience on which to judge the results.

While there are other features of Canadian conciliation devices which would be covered in detail in a more exhaustive study, the basic features have been outlined here, along with certain experiments now under way. It is difficult to appraise the value of the procedures. Certainly no aspect of Canadian labor relations policy has been subjected to as much controversy in recent decades as has this one.[88] Support and opposition do not conform to a labor-management division. Large powerful unions, particularly where they are principally made up of large locals, are inclined to oppose compulsory conciliation, whereas small local unions usually support this device. Some management personnel strongly condemn the system, but it is unquestionably true that it was employer pressure which extended intervention in British Columbia to the compulsory supervised strike vote, and in Alberta to this and the supervised vote on the board report. It is a reasonably safe generalization that the weaker party in the labor relations equation favors intervention and the stronger opposes it. But this generalization is an over-simplification.

A fundamental weakness in the Canadian system is that it overlooks the positive role of the work stoppage as a catalyst in negotiations. There is no conclusive evidence that the whole complicated paraphernalia of Canadian compulsory conciliation has in fact reduced the total number, or the intensity, or the duration of strikes. Comparisons are difficult either within the country or as between Canada and other countries. Alberta, which has the most extensive intervention system, has very few strikes, a fact which officials of the Alberta government attribute to the legal restraints, and to the excellence of their conciliation efforts. The Saskatchewan record is equally impressive, although Saskatchewan imposes no compulsory conciliation. But these provinces are relatively unindustrialized in comparison with Ontario, Quebec and British Columbia where the strike record appears to be little different from roughly comparable sections of the United States where compulsory conciliation is not applied. The studies of Cunningham and Phillips cast considerable doubt on compulsory conciliation, and of Anton on strike votes; and these are the only empirical studies available.[89]

Most Canadian jurisdictions have no counterpart to the emergency dispute provisions of the Taft-Hartley law.[90] One obvious reason for this is that all disputes in Canada[91] are subject to compulsory conciliation, and therefore to a board which, unlike the U.S. emergency board of inquiry, has power to recommend. Since

Canadian unions are prohibited from striking until after the conciliation board has reported, the dispute can reach the level of an emergency only after the conclusion of the intervention. Nevertheless, intervention in emergency disputes, or indeed in many which would not qualify as emergencies under Taft-Hartley definitions, does not stop at the formally provided conciliation officer and board. Several other devices are available.

First, conciliation officers may in some jurisdictions[92] engage in post-conciliation board intervention, although at this stage the parties are not compelled by law to accept the service. In other jurisdictions this is very rare and is not encouraged.[93] Where such post-conciliation board informal conciliation takes place, it usually is performed by higher-level officials of the service, and at times deputy ministers as well as ministers, and on rare occasions, the provincial premier may intervene.

Secondly there is the use of the more formal industrial inquiry commission. The Dominion and some of the provincial laws contain provisions for the setting up of industrial inquiry commissions empowered, among other things, to make inquiry into industrial dispute problems with the object of providing conditions calculated to assist in the settlement of disputes. These commissions have been used in stubborn strike situations, especially where the authorities believe the extra publicity associated with this rare action will bring public pressure to bear on the parties.

Another technique used very infrequently in Canada is simply to bring a dispute to an end by legislation. There are two classic illustrations in relatively recent experience. The first of these was the nation-wide strike of 1950 when 125,000 railway employees in the non-operating unions struck practically the entire railway system of Canada. The formal steps of compulsory conciliation, including the officer and board stages, had been complied with, and following this an Industrial Inquiry Commissioner was appointed. Failure of the commissioner to achieve a settlement led to the passage of an act of parliament.[94] The law ordered the railway companies to start up rail service within forty-eight hours, required the employees on strike to return to work, established provisional terms and conditions of work, instructed the parties to renew negotiations and provided for delayed compulsory arbitration if agreement was not reached. Ultimately the delayed arbitration was used.

It will be observed that in the railway dispute the Dominion government acted to stop a strike by imposing compulsory arbitration. A much more drastic action to stop a strike was taken by the Newfoundland legislature when it used the device of a special act[95] to revoke the certification of two locals of the International Woodworkers of America which had been on strike, after having complied with the requirements of compulsory conciliation. The Act also voided any existing agreement between the decertified unions and employers, and required the unions to seek permission from the government before they could apply for recertification. In this case the legislature assumed the role of the labor relations board. The stated reason for this drastic action was the extent of violence associated with the strike.

PUBLIC DETERMINATION OF THE CONTENTS OF COLLECTIVE AGREEMENTS

A second area of industrial relationships where policy differs strongly as between the United States and Canada concerns the content of collective agreements. Only those involving considerable contrast will be discussed. There is in Canadian law[96] a series of requirements regarding the compulsory settlement of disputes during the term of a collective agreement, as well as the prohibition of the strike or lockout. The Dominion Act[97] states that collective agreement entered into by a certified bargaining agent is binding upon the bargaining agent, the employees in the unit, and the employer. It also requires[98] that every collective agreement shall contain a provision for final settlement "without stoppage of work, by arbitration or otherwise, of all differences between the parties . . . concerning its meaning or violation." Furthermore the labor relations board is authorized on application of either party to an agreement to write in an arbitral clause when the parties have failed to do so. The parties are required to comply with the provision for settlement. Finally, strikes and lockouts are prohibited during the life of a collective agreement except on issues arising under reopening provisions included in the agreement.[99] This pattern is followed by some of the provinces, but others follow the Ontario modification which requires a clause prohibiting strikes and lockouts without exception "so long as the agreement continues to operate."[100]

The Ontario Act does not provide for any alternative to arbitration. The words of the Dominion Act "or otherwise" do not appear in the Ontario law. Moreover, the Ontario Act contains a statutory arbitration clause which provides for a three-man board which is presumed to be in any agreement in which the parties have not included an arbitration clause.[101] The effect of this is that arbitration is available at all times from the signing of the agreement. The arbitral area is defined more clearly in the Ontario law. It covers ". . . all differences between the parties arising from the interpretation, application, administration, or alleged violation of the agreement, including any question as to whether a matter is arbitrable." Thus, the arbitrator is by statute given jurisdiction to determine the troublesome question of arbitrability.

This procedure establishes compulsory arbitration of rights disputes, and applies in one form or another in all of Canada except Saskatchewan.[102] Furthermore, Ontario has broken new ground by providing[103] that if an arbitration award is not implemented by the party required to do so by the award, the other party may, after fourteen days from the date of release of the decision or the date provided for compliance, file a copy in the Supreme Court of Ontario, "whereupon the decision shall be entered in the same way as a judgment or order of that court and is enforceable as such." The other jurisdictions have not yet adopted this support to the arbitration award. But the Canadian system in general clearly requires the insertion into agreements of a complete system of dispute settlement during the life of the agreement and, contrary to the United States, transfers the question of sanctions clearly to the courts. There is no place for the strike to enforce arbitration awards in Canada except in Saskatchewan.

Canadian law has gone farther than United States with regard to the termination dates of agreements. United States Federal policy permits agreements with terminal dates, and with no terminal dates, although it also provides rules for termination of both dated and non-dated agreements.[104] The general policy in Canada is that agreements are deemed to be in force for one year, are renewable for one year at a time, and can be mutually amended by the parties without limit.[105] This power to amend is limited in some respects. Thus the Dominion provides that revision is possible of a provision that ". . . under the agreement is subject to revision during the term thereof." But the Dominion Act prohibits the change of the terminal date. Ontario[106] does likewise but, except for this limitation regarding the life of the agreement, allows any other change mutually reached by the parties. This insistence that the parties leave terminal dates alone is related to the provision, in a number of jurisdictions, of the agreement as a bar to certification of a second union contesting the bargaining rights of the incumbent union.

APPRAISAL

Canada and the United States are engaged in an experiment involving the private settlement of industrial disputes in their respective economies. Constitutional interpretation of jurisdiction has emphasized the federal authority in the United States and the provincial authority in Canada. Canadian preoccupation in the first decade of the century with the opening of the western prairies, coupled with extreme dependence on coal as a source of heat, concentrated attention on industrial peace as a goal, and produced the basic pattern of Canadian industrial relations policy in the Industrial Disputes Investigation Act of 1907. United States preoccupation with mass production and its near collapse in the third decade, along with the rise of industrial unionism, led to the introduction of the principle of public recognition of rights to organize and to compulsory collective bargaining. The emergency of the Second World War induced Canada to borrow the United States invention of certification of bargaining units. But divided political jurisdiction in Canada after 1925 opened the way to provincial experimentation to a degree not available to the individual states. Basically Canadian policy represents a marriage of the old Canadian compulsory conciliation procedure with the later United States Wagner Act principle of compulsory bargaining.

There are thus two basic differences between Canada and the United States in the labor relations field. These are the different allocations of political authority, and the intermingling in Canada of two principal streams of experience in contrast to the single United States stream. These differences have influenced the development of policy in the two countries. There has been a more positive attitude toward collective bargaining in the United States than in Canada. Canadian policy regarding union membership, voting quotas, and the absence of a responsibility to bargain with uncertified unions has made recognition more difficult to attain in Canada. Canadian use of compulsory conciliation "award votes" in one jurisdiction and strike votes in two has detracted attention from bargaining and encouraged manipulation through the system. Finally, divided jurisdiction in Canada has encouraged experimenting, but has created serious problems regarding the size of bargaining units, and has slowed the rate of growth of industry-wide bargaining. Compulsory conciliation under a system of required strike postponement administered independently by provinces renders industry-wide bargaining beyond provincial boundaries difficult when desired by both parties, and impossible when opposed by either one.

The weakness of the United States approach is to be found in the growing volume and complexity of federal labor relations law designed to control the internal behavior of unions and the areas of bargaining, and the halting attempts to find a solution to emergency dispute situations. The principal weaknesses in the Canadian system are the overemphasis on industrial peace; the extension of a system, originally applied successfully to public interest dispute only, to cover all disputes; the consequent emasculation of collective bargaining; and the failure to solve the constitutional problem of reallocating jurisdiction from province to Dominion or vice versa as the realities of evolving Canadian industrialism dictate. Both countries suffer from a rising curve of reliance on law and litigation at the expense of private machinery privately designed and operated. In the process the casualty may be the power of independent action by unions and management.

NOTES

1. There are exceptions, especially outside the bargaining field. Canadian unionism is currently engaged in establishing a social democratic party somewhat on European lines and in disregard of U.S. union philosophy on political alliances.

2. This will be qualified later when we come to examine Canadian experience in compulsory conciliation and compulsory arbitration of certain disputes, and certain statutory inclusions in agreements.

3. In Canada termination dates are required by law.

4. In Quebec province many agreements are distinguished by being printed in both French and English.

5. Canadian universities rely very heavily for their teaching on U.S. publications dealing with labor economics and industrial relations.

6. See for example Ben M. Selekman, *Postponing Strikes*, New York: Russell Sage Foundation, 1927; H. A. Logan, *State Intervention and Assistance in*

Collective Bargaining, Toronto: University of Toronto Press, 1956; F. R. Anton, "Government Supervised Strike Votes," *C.C.H. Canadian Limited*, Toronto, 1961: A. Bromke, *The Labour Relations Board in Ontario*, Montreal: McGill University, Industrial Relations Centre, 1961.

7. Stuart Jamieson's *Industrial Relations in Canada*, Toronto: The Macmillan Company of Canada Ltd., 1957, comes closest to meeting this need, but is not more than a modest beginning of limited coverage.

8. To avoid confusion the Canadian federal government will be referred to as the Dominion Government and the U.S. as the Federal Government. The secondary levels are formally recognized as State and Provincial respectively in the United States and Canada.

9. Troublesome because a large segment of the Dominion jurisdiction concerns national public utilities such as railroads, airline and telecommunication which operate under publicly controlled rates.

10. At the time the Judicial Committee was the final Court of Appeal for Canadian cases. Later the Constitution was amended and the Supreme Court of Canada was made the final court of appeal.

11. The Industrial Disputes Investigation Act, 1907.

12. Section 63.

13. F. R. Scott, "Federal Jurisdiction over Labour Relations, A New Look," in *Unions and the Future*, Montreal: McGill University, Industrial Relations Centre, 1959, p. 38.

14. *Ibid.*

15. "Highlights in Labour Legislation in Canada," *Labour Gazette*, Vol. 50, 1950, pp. 1437-41.

16. *Toronto Electric Commissioners* vs. *Snider.*

17. F. R. Scott, *op. cit.*, p. 40.

18. *Ibid.*

19. B.N.A. Act, Section 91-2.

20. H. A. Logan, *op. cit.*, p. 5.

21. "I.D.I. Act 6-7, Edward VII, 2A(iv)," *Labour Gazette*, Vol. 50, 1950, p. 1429.

22. For a series of proposals designed to overcome this barrier to a national system see Scott, *op. cit.*, p. 47.

23. The coverage of the I.D.I. Act had been increased also for a two-year period during the First World War 1916-1918, and there was some increased activity under it. However, limited industrialism, the low level of union organization, as well as the placing of the turbulent coal industry under compulsory arbitration combined to keep industrial conflict to a minimum in this earlier period—see D. E. & Muriel Armstrong, "Third Party Intervention in the Alberta Coal Industry," in H. D. Woods (ed.), *Patterns of Industrial Dispute Settlement in Five Canadian Industries*, Montreal: McGill University, Industrial Relations Centre, 1958.

24. P.C. 1003, 1944. A list of 14 kinds of industry was established as within the scope of the regulations. This included mining and smelting, manufacture and assembly of aircraft, tanks, automobiles and trucks, oil production, synthetic rubber, chemicals, steel and so on.

25. Manitoba, British Columbia, New Brunswick, Nova Scotia, and Ontario enacted legislation making all industries in their respective jurisdictions subject to the national code.

26. J. Dunlop, *Industrial Relations Systems*, New York: Holt, 1958.

27. Labor Management Relations Act 1947 (Taft-Hartley Act), as amended

by Labor-Management Reporting and Disclosures Act of 1959 (Landrum-Griffin Act). Title 11, Sec. 201 (a).

28. Report of the Select Committee on Labour Relations of the Ontario Legislature, Toronto, July 10th, 1958, p. 40.

29. Alberta Labour Act.

30. Manitoba Labour Relations Act.

31. British Columbia Labour Relations Act.

32. Ontario Labour Relations Act.

33. By "general positive policy" is meant the policy of free collective bargaining in which rights of association are protected by law, compulsory bargaining is imposed, and freedom to use strikes or lockouts guaranteed.

34. Ontario.

35. Labour Relations Act, Sec. 1(1)(j).

36. The Government of New Brunswick may, however, declare any board or commission or government agency to be within the definition of employer.

37. For an informed view on collective bargaining by civil servants see F. P. Varcoe, Q.C., "Legal and Constitutional Aspects of Collective Bargaining in the Public Service," in *Collective Bargaining in the Public Service*, Canadian Labour Congress, 1960.

38. See S. J. Frankel and R. C. Pratt, *Municipal Labour Relations in Canada*, Montreal: McGill University, Industrial Relations Centre, 1958; also Antal Deutsch, *Provincial Legislation Governing Municipal Labour Relations*, Montreal: Canadian Federation of Mayors and Municipalities, 1960.

39. *Ibid.*, p. 17.

40. Labor-Management Relations Act, Sec. 2(12).

41. *Ibid.*, Sec. 9(b).

42. *Ibid.*, Sec. 2(11).

43. Industrial Relations and Disputes Investigation Act, Sec. 2(i).

44. Observations to the writer by board chairmen and members.

45. Ontario L.R.A., Sec. 63.

46. A.L. Act, Sec. 105.

47. L.M.R. & D. Act 1959, Sec. 201(c).

48. A.L. Act, Sec. 105(5).

49. A. C. Crysler, *Handbook on Canadian Labour Law*, Toronto: Carswell Company Limited, 1957.

50. L.M.R.A. 1947, Sec. 206.

51 *Ibid.*, Sec. 201(b).

52. *Ibid.*, Sec. 203(a).

53. *Ibid.*, Sec. 204 (a).

54. *Ibid.*, Sec. 8(d)(1).

55. Sec. 8(d)(4) requires that no strike or lockout shall be resorted to during the 60-day notice period.

56. Saskatchewan Trade Union Act, Sec. 18.

57. Sec. 8(1).

58. Sec. 8(2).

59. In fact much conciliation work is done by the Industrial Relations Officers of the Department.

60. The appropriate sections of the Dominion I.R.D.I. Act are Sections 21, 22, 23, 27.

61. For a full study of this Act see Ben M. Selekman, *op. cit.*

62. H. A. Logan, *op. cit.*, p. 26.

63. There has been some controversy as to whether the object of the

original Act was to promote collective bargaining which would make the Act the antecedent in principle of the Wagner Act in the United States, or whether the object was postponing strikes, providing a cooling-off period, and maintaining production. In this view the Act prevented hasty action by workers. For a suggestion in support of the notion that this Act was a step toward compulsory recognition and collective bargaining see H. D. Woods, "Canadian Collective Bargaining and Dispute Settlement Policy: An Appraisal," in *The Canadian Journal of Economics and Political Science*, Vol. XXI, No. 4, Nov., 1955.

64. H. D. Woods, *op. cit.*, p. 461.

65. Sec. 23 of the Dominion I.R.D.I. Act says that "No employee in a unit shall strike until a bargaining agent has become entitled on behalf of a unit of employees to require their employer by notice under this Act to commence collective bargaining. . . ." A union becomes entitled to bargain either through voluntary recognition or certification, hence the issue of non-recognition has been dealt with.

66. British Columbia L.R.A., Sec. 26, 45.

67. *Ibid.*, Sec. 28.

68. *Ibid.*, Sec. 29.

69. *Ibid.*, Sec. 52.

70. *Ibid.*, Sec. 50.

71. *Ibid.*, Sec. 50.

72. *Ibid.*, Sec. 51.

73. There is some belief in British Columbia that the compulsory supervised strike vote has not been the hardship to the unions it might appear to be. In this view strong unions welcome it because it always gives them an outward and respectable manifestation of support. Unions less sure of their position vis-à-vis the workers they represent usually can get a positive vote if they want one, not so much on the strike issue as on support of the executive. Certainly the impossibility of separating these quite different issues casts some doubt on the validity of such votes.

74. B.C. L.R. Act, Sec. 50.

75. *Ibid.*, Sec. 55.

76. Alberta Labour Act, Sec. 93(8).

77. Performs the functions of a labor relations board in other jurisdictions.

78. Alberta L.A., Sec. 93(10).

79. *Ibid.*, Sec. 93(11).

80. Quoted in F. R. Anton, *op. cit.*, p. 42.

81. Alberta L.A., Sec. 95.

82. *Ibid.*, Sec. 97.

83. *Ibid.*

84. British Columbia L.R.A., Sec. 43.

85. Ontario L.R.A., Secs. 14 and 30.

86. 10 Elizabeth II, 1961.

87. In Quebec terminology the boards are called "Councils of Arbitration," but since they are limited in function to that performed by conciliation boards in the rest of Canada, that term will be applied in this study.

88. W. B. Cunningham, *Compulsory Conciliation and Collective Bargaining*, Montreal: McGill University, Industrial Relations Centre, 1957; S. Jamieson, "Industrial Relations and Government Policy," *C.J.E.P.S.*, Feb. 1951; H. A. Logan, *op. cit.*, Kingston: Queens University, Department of Industrial Relations, "The Conciliation and Arbitration of Labour Disputes in Canada,"

Bulletin No. 13, 1949; W. G. Phillips, "Government Conciliation in Labour Disputes," *C.J.E.P.S.*, Nov. 1956; H. D. Woods, "Canadian Collective Bargaining and Dispute Settlement Policy: An Appraisal," *loc. cit.*; Montreal: McGill University, Industrial Relations Centre, 1955; and "Labour Relations Law and Policy in Ontario," *Canadian Public Administration*, Vol. 1, 1958, No. 2. The subject has also been debated in the financial press, business journals and trade union publications. It is also examined in briefs presented to government by trade union bodies, the Canadian Manufacturers' Association and others.

89. There are five industry studies in H. D. Woods (ed.) *Patterns of Industrial Dispute Settlement in Five Canadian Industries, loc. cit.* These studies while broader in scope than compulsory conciliation throw much light on the Canadian experience. The various labor departments publish results of conciliation service efforts but these reports cannot be taken as a reflection of the true situation. To give credit to a conciliation officer or board for the settlement of a dispute while the officer or board happen to be functioning is especially open to question when, as in Canada, the service of these agencies is compulsory before a strike is possible.

90. L.M.R. Act, Sec. 206. There has been a break in the Canadian pattern with the inclusion in the amendment to the Alberta Labour Act of Section 99 in 1960. This section establishes a category of emergency where "life or property would be in serious jeopardy" through the possibility or fact of a stoppage in a plant or system supplying water, heat, electricity, or gas, or in a hospital service. The government is authorized to proclaim it and the parties are forbidden to strike or lockout. The Minister of Labour is authorized to establish a procedure for settlement. No limit is set in the law as to what procedure may be used. He may do "all such things as may be necessary to settle the dispute."

91. With the exception of Saskatchewan, as already noted.

92. Alberta, for example.

93. In Manitoba the attitude of the service is that once the conciliation board has reported the parties have "exhausted conciliation."

94. An Act to provide for the Resumption of Operations of Railways and for the Settlement of the Existing Dispute with respect to the Terms and Conditions of Employment between Railway Companies and their Employees. For a full report see *Labour Gazette*, Vol. 50, p. 1638.

95. Trade Union (Emergency Provisions) Act, 1959.

96. Saskatchewan excepted.

97. I.R.D.I. Act, Sec. 18.

98. *Ibid.*, Sec. 19.

99. *Ibid.*, Sec. 22.

100. O.L.R. Act, Sec. 33.

101. *Ibid.*, Sec. 34(2).

102. Saskatchewan has provided in the Trade Union Act, Sec. 20, that the parties may by mutual consent ask the Labour Relations Board to act as an arbitration board. From time to time the board has acted, and in a few agreements the parties name the board in advance as the permanent arbitration body. Saskatchewan has thus begun to experiment with a kind of voluntary "labour court."

103. O.L.R. Act. Sec. 34(9).

104. L.M.R. Act, 1947, Sec. 8(d).

105. See for example A.L. Act. Sec. 73.

106. L.R. Act, Sec. 20(2).

INDEX